SYSTEM SIMULATION
WITH
DIGITAL COMPUTER

SYSTEM SIMULATION
WITH
DIGITAL COMPUTER

NARSINGH DEO
Professor of Electrical Engineering
and
Computer Science
Indian Institute of Technology, Kanpur

PRENTICE-HALL, INC., *Englewood Cliffs, New Jersey 07632*

Library of Congress Cataloging in Publication Data

Deo, Narsingh. (date)
    System simulation with digital computer.

    Includes bibliographies and index.
    1. Digital computer simulation. I. Title.
QA76.9.C65D46 1983   001.4'34'02854   82-48551
ISBN 0-13-881789-8

©1979 by **Prentice-Hall of India Private Limited,** *New Delhi*

This Prentice-Hall, Inc., edition published 1983.

Printed in the United States of America

10   9   8   7   6   5   4   3   2   1

0-13-881789-8

PRENTICE-HALL INTERNATIONAL, INC., *London*
PRENTICE-HALL OF AUSTRALIA PTY. LIMITED, *Sydney*
EDITORA PRENTICE-HALL DO BRASIL, LTDA., *Rio de Janeiro*
PRENTICE-HALL CANADA INC., *Toronto*
PRENTICE-HALL OF INDIA PRIVATE LIMITED, *New Delhi*
PRENTICE-HALL OF JAPAN, INC., *Tokyo*
PRENTICE-HALL OF SOUTHEAST ASIA PTE. LTD., *Singapore*
WHITEHALL BOOKS LIMITED, *Wellington, New Zealand*

To
Karen, Alok, and Sandhya

Preface

In the past two decades digital computer simulation has developed from infancy into a full-fledged discipline. This rapid growth of simulation is a direct consequence of the widespread availability and popularity of the digital computer itself. Even before the digital computer became available, complex dynamic systems were always with us which could not be analyzed by means of available mathematical tools. For the majority of such systems one was forced to find "intuitive" solutions. Now one need not accept an intuitive solution. We have a new tool in computer simulation, that allows us to mimic the behaviour of the real-life system, however complex, and get a measure of its performance.

To be able to use this powerful method of studying complex systems, a certain amount of experience is required. This experience has to be a well-balanced mixture in the areas of (i) modelling, (ii) computer programming, and (iii) statistics. No single volume, much less a small one like this, can hope to cover all three areas in depth. The purpose of this book is to get the reader started.

The book is meant for the students of engineering and business administration, as well as for practicing systems analysts, industrial engineers, and operations research workers. It is intended to give the reader enough grounding so that he can use simulation to solve simple (but mathematically intractable) problems.

It is assumed that the reader knows computer programming and has some knowledge of FORTRAN. FORTRAN was selected over other general purpose languages, such as, ALGOL, PL/I, or BASIC, for pragmatic reasons. It is by far the most universal computer language. The group of FORTRAN compilers readily available, WATFOR, WATFIV, FORTRAN H, provide faster compilation and better object code than do the compilers for other languages. Why not GPSS, SIMSCRIPT or any of the other simulation languages? There are several reasons: The most important being the author's firm conviction that the first course in simulation should be taught using a general-purpose language. A special-purpose language hides many of the essential ingredients of simulation (logic, data structures, statistical calculations, etc.), from the student. Such a student will feel lost when he finds himself in a computing centre without his particular simulation language or when he has to simulate a problem for which the special-purpose language he learned is not suited.

Perhaps 99 per cent of the students taking this first course in simulation will never be called upon to simulate models which are too complex to be conveniently simulated with FORTRAN. Some very large and complex systems have been and are being simulated in FORTRAN.

Although the emphasis in this book is on simulation of discrete, stochastic, dynamic systems, other, types of systems have also been discussed. Chapter 1 provides an introduction to computer simulation and its applications. Chapter 2 deals entirely with digital computer simulation of continuous systems. Chapter 3 lays the foundation for simulation of discrete stochastic systems. Chapters 4, 5, and 6 provide in-depth examples of simulations from three very important classes of problems; namely, queueing systems, stochastic networks, and inventory systems. Chapter 7 deals with a very important aspect of stochastic simulation—design of a simulation experiment, including the problem of statistical reliability in evaluating simulation experiments. Chapter 8 presents an overview of various special-purpose simulation languages. One of the purposes of this chapter is to provide guidance in selection of a simulation language for those who wish to acquire such a language for themselves, for their projects, or for their computing centres. Analog computer simulation has not been included in this book. Simulation in this book implies simulation with a digital computer.

Learning simulation does not consist of mastering a few theorems and applying them and their corollaries to solve different problems. There is no such thing as theory of simulation. By and large the technique of simulation can be learned only by doing, by solving a large variety of actual problems, and by watching how others solve them. This is why a great deal of emphasis in this book has been placed on examples. Exercises provided at the end of each chapter are an integral part of the text and must not be ignored. The section on *Remarks and references,* provided toward the end of each chapter, is intended to guide the reader through the literature for further study.

This book has been thoroughly classroom tested. In fact, it grew out of a simulation course given to advanced level undergraduate students and the first-year postgraduate students in electrical engineering and computer science at Indian Institute of Technology, Kanpur. The course was also taken by students from other engineering disciplines—civil engineering, mechanical engineering, metallurgical engineering, industrial and management engineering.

IIT Kanpur   Narsingh Deo

Acknowledgements

It is a pleasure to acknowledge the contribution made by Dr. M. S. Krishnamoorthy of IIT, Kanpur, in all stages of this project. Besides making numerous valuable suggestions and criticisms of the manuscript, he supervised the production of this book. Many helpful suggestions and encouragement from Professor V. Rajaraman are also appreciated. The students of EE 561 course of IIT, Kanpur, for the years 1975–77 have also contributed. In particular, the author wishes to thank Mr. S. C. Gupta and Mr. S. Agarwala, amongst those that took this course from him. Dr. A. S. Sethi also read portions of the manuscript and made helpful suggestions. The author would also like to acknowledge and thank Mr. H. K. Nathani and Mrs. Geraldine Crooker, secretaries at IIT, Kanpur, and Washington State University, Pullman, respectively, for their flawless typing.

I also wish to thank Indian Institute of Technology, Kanpur, for providing facilities to write this book. The Educational Development Centre at IIT, Kanpur, and its Head, Professor M. V. George, must also be thanked, for providing financial assistance in preparation of the manuscript.

Finally, the author would like to express his deep appreciation to his wife, Karen, for making a great deal of "visible" as well as "invisible" contribution to this book.

Contents

SYSTEM SIMULATION
WITH
DIGITAL COMPUTER

1

Introduction

Simulation is a powerful technique for solving a wide variety of problems. To simulate is to copy the behaviour of a system or phenomenon under study. Strictly speaking, we will be dealing with only *numerical sequential simulation;* numerical because there are other forms of simulation—for example, electrical analogue or physical simulation; and sequential because the calculations proceed in a time sequence. Some of the basic ideas in simulation can be best understood by performing actual simulations. Let us, therefore, consider the following two very simple examples and see how simulation is actually done.

1-1. Simulation of a pure pursuit problem—an example

A fighter aircraft sights an enemy bomber and flies directly toward it, in order to catch up with the bomber and destroy it. The bomber (the target) continues flying (along a specified curve) so the fighter (the pursuer) has to change its direction to keep pointed toward the target. We are interested in determining the attack course of the fighter and in knowing how long it would take for it to catch up with the bomber.

If the target flies along a straight line, the problem can be solved directly with analytic techniques. (The proof of such a closed-form expression which gives the course of the pursuer, when the target flies in a straight line, is left as an exercise for you. Problem 1-2.)

However, if the path of the target is curved, the problem is much more difficult and normally cannot be solved directly. We will use simulation to solve this problem, under the following simplifying conditions:

1. The target and the pursuer are flying in the same horizontal plane when the fighter first sights the bomber, and both stay in that plane. This makes the pursuit model two-dimensional.
2. The fighter's speed VF is constant (20 kms/minute).
3. The target's path (i.e., its position as a function of time) is specified.
4. After a fixed time span Δt (every minute, in this case) the fighter changes its direction in order to point itself toward the bomber.

Let us introduce a rectangular coordinate system coincident with the horizontal plane in which the two aircraft are flying. We choose the point due south of the fighter and due west of the target (at the beginning of the pursuit) as the origin of this coordinate system. Let the distances be given

1

in kilometers and the time in minutes.   We start measuring the time when the fighter first sights the bomber. (See Fig. 1-1.)

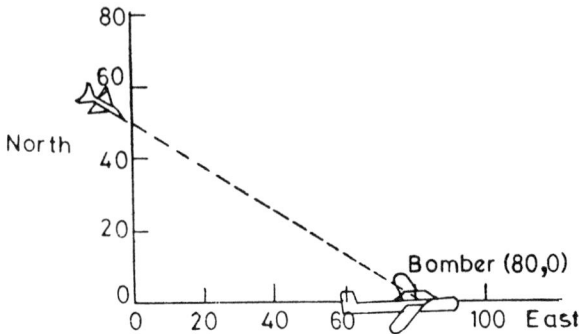

Fig. 1-1:   Positions of Pursuer and Target at Time Zero.

We will represent the path of the bomber (which is known to us in advance) by two arrays, the east coordinates and the north coordinates at specified moments (each minute).   We call these coordinates $XB(t)$ and $YB(t)$, respectively.   They are presented in the form of a table (in kilometers) below.

Time, t	0	1	2	3	4	5	6	7	8	9	10	11	12
$XB(t)$	80	90	99	108	116	125	133	141	151	160	169	179	180
$YB(t)$	0	−2	−5	−9	−15	−18	−23	−29	−28	−25	−21	−20	−17

Table 1-1.

Likewise, we will represent the path of the fighter plane by two arrays $XF(t)$ and $YF(t)$.   In this example, initially we are given

$$YF(0) = 50 \text{ kms}, \quad XF(0) = 0 \text{ kms}.$$

Our purpose is to compute the positions of the pursuer, namely, $XF(t)$, $YF(t)$ for $t = 1, 2, \ldots, 12$, or until the fighter catches up with the bomber.   We will assume that once the fighter is within 10 kms of the bomber, the fighter shoots down its target by firing a missile, and the pursuit is over.   In case the target is not caught up within 12 minutes, the pursuit is abandoned, and the target is considered escaped.   From the time $t = 0$ till the target is shot down, the attack course is determined as follows:

The fighter uses the following simple strategy: It looks at the target at instant t, aligns its velocity vector with the line of sight (i.e., points itself toward the target).   It continues to fly in that direction for one minute, till instant $(t + 1)$. At time $(t + 1)$ it looks at the target again and realigns itself.

The distance DIST (t) at a given time t between the target and the pursuer is given by

$$\text{DIST}\ (t) = \sqrt{(YB(t) - YF(t))^2 + (XB(t) - XF(t))^2}\qquad\ldots(1\text{-}1)$$

The angle θ of the line from the fighter to the target at a given time t is given by

$$\text{Sin}\ \theta = \frac{YB(t) - YF(t)}{\text{DIST}\ (t)}\qquad\ldots(1\text{-}2)$$

$$\text{Cos}\ \theta = \frac{XB(t) - XF(t)}{\text{DIST}\ (t)}\qquad\ldots(1\text{-}3)$$

Using this value of the position of the fighter at time $(t + 1)$ is determined by

$$XF(t + 1) = XF(t) + VF\ \text{Cos}\ \theta\qquad\ldots(1\text{-}4)$$

$$YF(t + 1) = YF\ (t) + VF\ \text{Sin}\ \theta\qquad\ldots(1\text{-}5)$$

With these new coordinates of the pursuer, its distance from the target is again computed using Eq. (1-1). If this distance is 10 kms. or less the pursuit is over, otherwise θ is recomputed, and the process continues.

A flowchart of the logic of this problem is given in Fig. 1-2 (page 4).

The following FORTRAN program (a format-free version) will implement the flowchart.

```
      DIMENSION XB (25), YB (25), XF (25), YF (25)
      INTEGER T, J
      READ, (XB (T), YB (T), T = 1,13)
      READ, XF (1), YF (1), VF
      T = 1
100   DIST = SQRT ((YB (T) − YF (T))** 2 + (XB (T) − XF (T))** 2)
      IF (DIST. LE. 10.0) GO TO 110
      IF (T.GT.12) GO TO 120
      XF (T + 1) = XF(T) + VF* (XB(T) − XF (T))/DIST
      YF (T + 1) = YF (T) + VF* (YB (T) − YF (T))/DIST
      T = T + 1
      GO TO 100
110   PRINT 990, T, DIST
990   FORMAT (10X, 10H CAUGHT AT, 13, 8H MTS AND, F10.3, 4H KMS)
      STOP
120   PRINT 1000
1000  FORMAT (10X, 16H TARGET ESCAPED)
      STOP
      END
```

(Note that since Fortran does not permit 0 as an index we had to set $T = 1$ to correspond to $t = 0$ in the flowchart.)

The output of this program for the specified data is as follows:

CAUGHT AT 10 MTS AND 2.969 KMS

This is an example of simulation. We had to resort to simulation be-

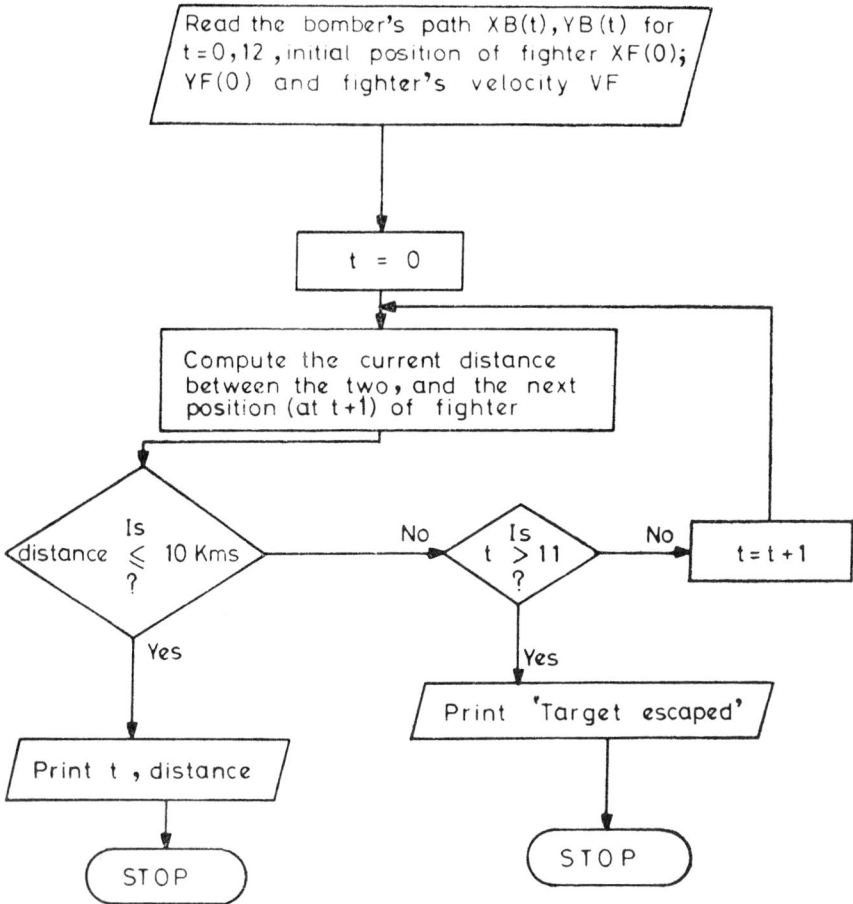

Fig. 1-2:   Flowchart of pursuit problem.

cause analytically we could not make a long-term prediction about the path that the fighter plane would take (given the initial position and path of the target). But by simulation we were able to make the computer go through the instant-to-instant predictions for as many instants as we wanted. This was possible only because we knew the basic process involved, namely, how the fighter plane behaves at any particular instant. Such knowledge of the basic process of the system under study is essential for all simulation experiments.

The simple strategy, of pursuer redirecting himself toward the target at fixed intervals of time, while the target goes on its predetermined path without making any effort to evade the pursuer, is called *pure pursuit*. Although in many situations, the strategy used by the pursuer is more sophisticated, this basic approach can be used for any pursuit problem as long as we know the path the pursued takes and the rule by which the pursuer redirects himself.

1-2. A system and its model

In any simulation experiment we have a system whose behaviour we are studying.   Loosely speaking, a *system* is a collection of distinct objects which interact with each other.   In the pure-pursuit example, the system consists of the two aircraft.   In order to study a system we generally gather some relevant information about it.   For most studies it is not necessary to consider all the details of the system.   For example, in the example in Sec. 1-1 we did not get the information about the sizes or weights of the aircraft. Such a collection of pertinent information about a system is called a *model* of the system.

The construction of an appropriate model of a system under study is a delicate and an all-important affair in simulation (as it is in analytic study). For example, we have assumed that the target takes no evasive action, nor does the pursuer use any predictive technique.   We assumed that the pursuer corrects its course only once a minute.   Thus we know the 'law' that governs the system. The same system may be described by different models.   Several variations of the pure-pursuit model are considered in problems at the end of this chapter.

Constructing appropriate mathematical models of complex, real-life systems is a vast and intricate subject in itself.   It requires a thorough knowledge of the system as well as of modelling techniques.   In this book, we will in most cases assume that a model has been arrived at and our concern is how to program the computer so that it behaves like the model as the time progresses.

For a given system there are a number of variables that describe what is known as the *state of the system* at any given time.   For example, the state of our system (of pure pursuit) is described by the positions of the two aircraft and their velocities.

For further understanding these and other concepts, let us simulate another very simple system, which is different in a fundamental sense from the pure-pursuit system.

1-3. Simulation of an inventory problem

Suppose you work in a retail store and it is your responsibility to keep replenishing a certain item (say, automobile tyres) in the store by ordering it from the wholesaler.   You want to adopt a simple policy for ordering new supplies:

'When my stock goes down to P items (called *reorder point*), I will order Q more items (called *reorder quantity*) from the wholesaler.'

If the demand on any day exceeds the amount of inventory on hand, the excess represents lost sale and loss of goodwill. On the other hand, over-stocking implies increased carrying cost (i.e., cost of storage, insurance, interest, deterioration, etc.). Ordering too frequently will result in excessive reorder cost. Assume the following conditions:

1. There is a 3-day lag between the order and arrival. The merchandise is ordered at the end of the day and is received at the beginning of the fourth day. That is, merchandise ordered on the evening of the ith day is received on the morning of the $(i + 3)$rd day.
2. For each unit of inventory the carrying cost for each night is Re. 0.75.
3. Each unit out of stock when ordered results into a loss of goodwill worth Rs. 2.00 per unit plus loss of Rs. 16.00 net income, that would have resulted in its sale, or a total loss of Rs. 18.00 per unit. Lost sales are lost forever; they cannot be backordered.
4. Placement of each order costs Rs. 75.00 regardless of the number of units ordered.
5. The demand in a day can be for any number of units between 0 and 99, each equiprobable.
6. There is never more than one replenishment order outstanding.
7. Initially we have 115 units on hand and no reorder outstanding.

With these conditions in force you have been asked to compare the following five replenishment policies and select the one that has the minimum total cost (i.e., reorder cost + carrying cost + lost sales cost).

	P (reorder point)	Q (reorder quantity)
Policy I	125	150
Policy II	125	250
Policy III	150	250
Policy IV	175	250
Policy V	175	300

(Since we are interested in simulation here and not in inventory theory, we will not investigate the reasonableness of the replenishment policy too critically. Ours is undoubtedly a very simplified model.)

The problem does not easily lend itself to an analytic solution; it is best therefore to solve it by simulation. Let us simulate the running of the store for about six months (180 days) under each of the five policies and then compare their costs.

A simulation model of this inventory system can be easily constructed by stepping time forward in the fixed increment of a day, starting with Day 1, and continuing up to Day 180. On a typical day, Day i, first we check to see if merchandise is due to arrive today. If yes, then the existing stock S is increased by Q (the quantity that was ordered).   If DEM is the demand for today, and $DEM \leqslant S$, our new stock at the end of today will be $(S - DEM)$ units.   If $DEM > S$, then our new stock will be zero.   In either case, we calculate the total cost resulting from today's transactions, and add it to the total cost C incurred till yesterday.   Then we determine if the inventory on hand plus units on order is greater than P, the reorder point.   If not, place

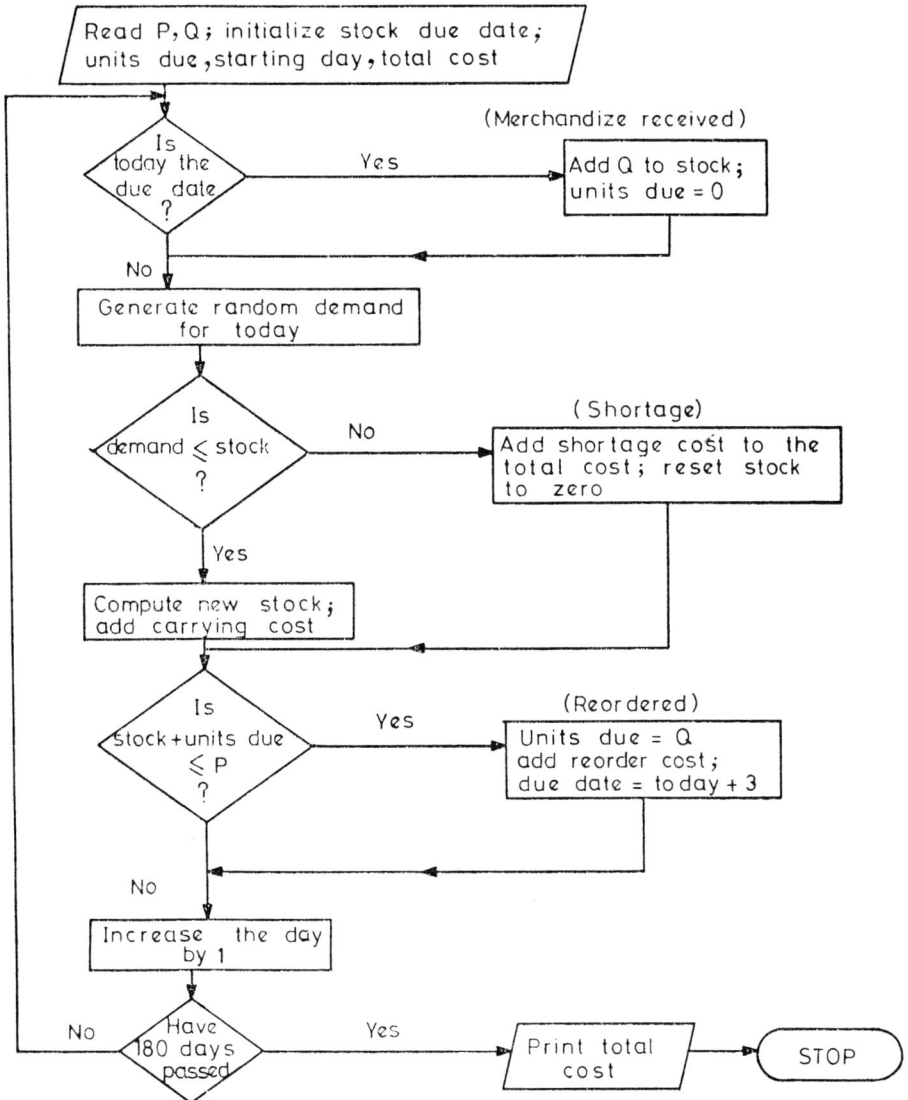

Fig. 1-3:   Cost of inventory policy (P, Q).

an order (to be delivered three days hence), by stating the amount ordered and the day it is due to be received.   We repeat this procedure for 180 days.

Initially we set day number $i = 1$, stock $S = 115$, number of units due $UD = 0$ (because there is no outstanding order), and the day they are due $DD = 0$.

The demand, DEM, for each day is not a fixed quantity but a random variable.   It could assume any integral value from 00 to 99 and each with equal probability.   We will use a special subroutine, which generates a 2-digit random integer, and will use the numbers thus produced as the daily demands.   (Random number generators will be discussed in Chapter 3.) A flowchart for simulating this problem is shown in Fig. 1-3 (page 7).

The following Fortran program (format free) implements the flowchart for evaluating the total cost for a given replenishment policy (P, Q) for 180 days.   Statement No. 110 in the program makes use of the subprogram $RNDY1 (DUM)$ which is a subprogram to generate a real pseudorandom number between zero and one.   The argument of this function can be any dummy number or variable.

Notice how condition 6, that there is no more than one reorder outstanding, has been taken care of.   In Statement 130, we add the number of units due (if any) UD to the current stock S to get the equivalent stock, ES.   It is this number which is compared to P before an order is placed.   Since $UD > P$ if we already have a replenishment order outstanding another order will not be placed.

This is an extremely simple model of an inventory-control system.   More realistic models will be dealt with in Chapter 6

```
      INTEGER P, Q, S, ES, UD, DD, DEM
      READ, P, Q
      C = 0.0
      S = 115
      I = 1
      UD = 0
      DD = 0
100   IF (DD .NE. I) GO TO 110
      S = S + Q
      UD = 0
110   DEM = RNDY1 (DUM)* 100.0
      IF (DEM .LE. S) GO TO 120
      C = C + (FLOAT (DEM) — FLOAT (S))*18.0
      S = 0
      GO TO 130
120   S = S — DEM
      C = C + FLOAT (S)*.75
130   ES = S + UD
      IF (ES .GT. P) GO TO 140
      UD = Q
      DD = I + 3
      C = C + 75.0
```

```
140   I= I + 1
      IF (I .LE. 180) GO TO 100
      PRINT, P, Q, C
      STOP
      END
```

The program yielded the following cost figures for the five inventory policies:

P	Q	Cost in Rs.
125	150	38679.75
125	250	31268.25
150	250	29699.25
175	250	26094.00
175	300	27773.25

Thus, Policy IV ($P = 175$, $Q = 250$) is the best amongst the five considered.

1-4.   The basic nature of simulation

There does not seem to be much that is common between the two problems and the methods of solving them.   The first problem (the pure pursuit) is basically continuous, in the sense that its state changes continuously with time; whereas the second problem is discrete, because the arrival and sale of merchandise occurs only in discrete steps.   The first problem is deterministic, while the second one is stochastic in nature.   Yet there are some common features and these are the features essential to simulation.

In both cases we started from a mathematical model of the system under study.   Some initial conditions (state at time zero) were assumed in both cases.   The change of state occurred in accordance with some equations (rules or laws).   Using these rules numerically we continued changing the state of the system as time moved forward.   This was done for as long a period as needed.   At the end of this period we collected the desired information about the system (which is the solution to the problem).   These calculations were programmed for a digital computer.   Thus the computer was made to simulate or mimic the real-life system as its variables changed.   Through this process we managed to get around the necessity of obtaining an analytic solution and therein lies the great advantage of simulation.

It should be noted that the simulation in both examples (pure pursuit as well as inventory control) could have been performed manually with pencil and paper.   In theory any system that can be simulated on a digital computer can also be simulated by hand.   In practice, however, simulation as an analytic tool is useful only when done on a computer.   This is because the practical problems that require simulation are complex and need a very large number of simple, repetitive calculations. In fact, simulation is one of the most important uses of the digital computer.

To simulate is to experiment: Simulation is basically an experimental technique. It is a fast and relatively inexpensive method of doing an 'experiment' on the computer. Consider, for example, the inventory-control problem. Instead of trying out in the actual store the five replenishment policies, each for a period of six months, and then selecting the best one, we conducted the experiment on the computer and obtained the results within a few minutes, at a very small cost (provided, of course, our model reflects reality). This is why computer simulation is often referred to as performing a *simulation experiment*.

No unified theory: There is no unifying theory of computer simulation. Learning simulation does not consist of learning a few fundamental theorems and then using them and their various corollaries to solve problems. There are no underlying principles guiding the formulation of simulation models. Each application of simulation is *ad hoc* to a great extent. In this sense simulation is an art, and one often hears the expression 'the art of simulation.'

1-5. When to simulate

All of us in our daily lives encounter problems, which although mathematical in nature, are too complex to lend themselves to exact mathematical analysis. The performance of such a system (say, weather or traffic jam) may be difficult to predict, either because the system itself is complex or the theory is not yet sufficiently developed. The difficulties in handling such problems (by means of classical mathematical tools) may also arise due to the effect of uncertainties, or due to dynamic interactions between decisions and subsequent events, or due to complex interdependencies among variables in the system, or due to some combination of these. Formerly (i.e., before the days of computer simulation), in such situations either an intuitive decision was made, or, if the stakes were too high to rely on intuition, elaborate laboratory experiments had to be conducted, which were usually expensive and time consuming. Simulation provides a third alternative which is cheap and fast, and thus fills the gap between exact analysis and physical intuition. Occasionally, simulation is also used even when an exact analytic solution is possible, but it is too expensive in terms of computation time.

Simulation in science and engineering research: Simulation has changed, in a very fundamental sense, the way in which research is conducted today. Earlier most experiments were carried out physically in the laboratories. Thousands and even millions were spent on physical models (e.g., wind tunnels, river basin models, network analyzers, aircraft flight simulators) and expensive experiments. Today a majority of these experiments are simulated on a computer. 'Computer experiments' besides being much faster, cheaper, and easier, frequently provide better insight into the system than laboratory experiments do. Not all laboratory experiments, of course, can be replaced with computer simulations. Typically, a few key experiments are performed in the laboratory after, say, 80–90 per cent of the experimenting has been done on the computer.

Simulation in soft sciences: Simulation can be expected to play even a more vital role in biology, sociology, economics, medicine, psychology, etc., where experimenting could be very expensive, dangerous, or even impossible. In these areas, the mathematical theories are even less developed than in physical sciences.   Moreover, in fields such as biology and economics the problems are truly large, involving tens of thousands of variables.   The complications caused by uncertainty are also greater in these areas than in physical sciences.   Thus simulation has become an indispensable tool for a modern researcher in most social, biological and life sciences.

Simulation for business executive: There are many problems faced by management that cannot be solved by standard operations research tools like linear and dynamic programming, inventory and queueing theory. Therefore, a business executive had to make decisions based solely on his intuition and experience.   Now he can use computer simulation to make better and more meaningful decisions.   Utilizing the power of a digital computer, he can build and study a simulation model (of his system) containing arbitrarily high-order complexities and a huge number of interdependencies, as well as uncertainties.   Simulation has been used widely for inventory control, facility planning, production scheduling, and the like.

1-6.   Remarks and references

Simulation is a very powerful, problem-solving technique.   Its applicability is so general that it would be hard to point out disciplines or systems to which simulation has not been applied.   The basic idea behind simulation is simple, namely, model the given system by means of some equations and then determine its time-dependent behaviour.   The simplicity of approach when combined with the computational power of the high-speed digital computer makes simulation a powerful tool.   Normally, simulation is used when either an exact analytic expression for the behaviour of the system under investigation is not available, or the analytic solution is too time-consuming or expensive.

Since the popularity and usefulness of simulation is dependent on the capabilities and availability of the computer, the subject essentially started in the late 1950's.   It has grown—in its power, sophistication, and applicability—very rapidly in the past 15–20 years, and is still expanding at a rapid rate.   One of the early textbooks and still a good one is:

TOCHER, K.D., *The Art of Simulation*, Van Nostrand Co., Princeton, N.J., 19 63.

An extremely readable and elementary 100-page textbook on essentials of computer simulation is

SMITH, J., *Computer Simulation Models*, Hafner Publishing Company, New York, N.Y., 1968.

Some of the other general textbooks on simulation are:

EMSHOFF, J. R. and R. L. SISSON, *Design and Use of Computer Simulation Models*, Macmillan Co., New York, 1970.

GORDON, G., *System Simulation*, Prentice-Hall, Englewood Cliffs, N.J., 1969.

MARTIN, F.F., *Computer Modelling and Simulation*, John Wiley and Sons, New York, 1968.

MIZE, J. H. and J. G. COX, *Essentials of Simulation*, Prentice-Hall, Englewood Cliffs, N.J., 1968.

NAYLOR, T. H., J. L. BALINTFY, D. S. BURDICK, and K. CHU, *Computer Simulation Techniques*, John Wiley and Sons, New York, 1966.

SHANNON, R. E., *Systems Simulation: the Art and Science*, Prentice-Hall, Englewood Cliffs, N.Y., 1975.

FISHMAN, G. S., *Concepts and Methods in Discrete Event Digital Simulation*, John Wiley and Sons, New York, 1973.

ZEIGLER, B.P. *Theory of Modelling and Simulation*, Wiley-Interscience, New York, 1976.

MAISEL, H. and GNUGNOLI, *Simulation of Discrete Stochastic Systems*, Science Research Associates, Chicago, 1975.

The literature on simulation is vast. Numerous bibliographies and survey articles on simulation have been published, containing hundreds of references. Many of these references can be found in the textbooks given above.

Simulation requires several skills. You must be familiar with the system being simulated and know enough of system theory and modelling techniques to be able to make a realistic model of the system. The five different models of the pure-pursuit problem in Exercises 1-2 to 1-6 in the next section are included to emphasize the importance of modelling. Secondly, a certain amount of skill in computer programming is also required. Also, some knowledge of statistics is needed for designing the simulation experiment. Different textbooks lay different amounts of emphasis on these three aspects of simulation.

Besides general textbooks on simulation, there are a number of specialized texts devoted to application of simulation to a particular area such as economics, industrial systems, psychology, social sciences, international relations, ecology, and war games.

There have been a number of cases where more than a million dollars have been spent on a single simulation project. Many of the large successful simulation projects are never publicized because of their military application or their proprietary interest of private industry.

1-7. Exercises

1-1. Identify six different problems from your own experience that you think should be solved using digital simulation rather than analytically.

1-2. In the pure-pursuit problem of Sec. 1-1, suppose the initial (x, y) coordinates of the bomber at time 0 are $(0, 0)$ and of the fighter $(0, d)$. The bomber (the target) moves in a straight line along the x axis (east) at a constant velocity VB and the fighter at a velocity VF pointing itself continuously toward the target. Show that the path followed by the fighter can be described by the following equation:

$$x = \frac{1}{2}\left[\frac{y^{1+r}}{(1+r)\,d^r} - \frac{y^{1-r}}{(1-r)\,d^{-r}} \right] + \frac{r.d}{1-r^2},$$

where
$$r = \frac{VB}{VF},$$

and (x, y) are the coordinates of the fighter.

1-3. In the special case when the target moves along the x axis, using the FORTRAN program given in Sec. 1-1, find the point where the pursuer catches up with the target. Compare the simulation result with the one obtained using the analytic expression in Exercise 1-2. Explain the difference between the two results, if any.

1-4. The pure-pursuit situation in Sec. 1-1 can also be simulated in terms of polar coordinates (R, θ) instead of rectangular coordinates (x, y). The relevant equations (2-dimensional problem) are

$$\frac{dR}{dt} = VB \cdot \cos \theta - VF$$

$$R\frac{d\theta}{dt} = -VB \cdot \sin \theta$$

where R is the distance between the bomber and the fighter (denoted by DIST in Sec. 1-1) and θ is the angle of the line from the fighter to the bomber. Write a FORTRAN program using polar coordinates.

1-5. Write a program for simulating a 3-dimensional pure-pursuit problem.

1-6. In the pure-pursuit course the fighter flies directly toward the target. In a *lead-pursuit course* the fighter flies in a direction ahead of the line of sight by a lead angle φ. Write a computer program to simulate a 2-dimensional lead-pursuit course with a specified lead angle, the velocities, and the initial positions of the two aircraft.

1-7. In a field there are four animals—a dog, a mongoose, a snake, and a mouse. Dogs kill mongooses, mongooses kill snakes, and snakes kill mice. The speeds of the mouse, snake, mongoose and dog are, respectively, 8, 12, 18 and 30 km/hour. Simulate the chase with different starting positions to see which animal gets killed first.

1-8. Simulate on a computer the following game between two players (called the game of matching pennies). The two players simultaneously flip a coin each. If both sides are the same (both heads or both tails), player A wins a rupee from B, otherwise B wins a rupee from A. Each player starts with 10 rupees. By conducting the experiment 500 times, find out how long the game will last on the average before one of the players goes broke.

1-9. Suppose you are the manufacturer of a car which is in great demand. At present you make 1,000 cars per month and sell it easily at Rs. 20,000 each (ignore excise duty, sales tax, etc., for the time being). By using overtime, etc., you can increase the production, but you must also increase the price in order to make a profit (10 per cent on sale). The number of cars you can produce and the corresponding price (of all units) is given below:

Cars	Production	1,000	1,200	1,300	1,500	2,000
	Price	20,000	21,000	22,000	25,000	30,000

The demand for your cars is predicted to rise at 5 per cent per year provided the price stays at Rs. 20,000 each. As the price rises a certain number of customers will switch to other cars (or scooters). This switchover percentage is estimated to be as below:

Price	20,000	21,000	22,000	25,000	30,000
Percentage switched	0	5	10	25	50

By investing capital you can increase your production without increasing the cost per unit. But you must pay 8 per cent interest on the additional capital. The investments and the corresponding increases in production are as follows:

Investment in Rs.	1,000,000	2,000,000	5,000,000
Increase in production of cars	300	500	1,000

Simulate the company's situation over the next 20 years. By experimenting with the model find out which investment should be made and when (if any).

2

Simulation of Continuous Systems

From the viewpoint of simulation there are two fundamentally different types of systems: (i) systems in which the state changes smoothly or continuously with time are called *continuous systems*, and (ii) systems in which the state changes abruptly at discrete points in time are called *discrete systems*. The system of pure pursuit in Sec. 1-1 is an example of a continuous system, because the positions of the two aircraft can vary continuously with time. The inventory system in Sec. 1-3, on the other hand, is a discrete system because the addition to and the demand from the stock can occur only in discrete numbers. Hence the stock-level can change only discretely with time. A queueing situation is another example of a discrete system because the customers join or leave the queue only in discrete numbers. Usually, the simulation of most systems in engineering and physical sciences turns out to be continuous, whereas most systems encountered in operations research and management science are discrete. Most studies of communication, transportation, and computer systems also involve discrete system simulation. As we will see in this and subsequent chapters, the methodologies of discrete and continuous simulations are inherently different. In this chapter we will deal with continuous systems only.

Continuous dynamic systems, those systems in which the state or the variables vary continously with time, can generally be described by means of differential equations. If the set of (simultaneous) differential equations describing a system are ordinary, linear, and time-invariant (i.e., have constant coefficients), an analytic solution is usually easy to obtain. In general, differential equations of a more difficult nature can only be solved numerically. Simulating the system often gives added insight into the problem besides giving the required numerical solution. As an elementary example of a continuous dynamic system let us consider the following simple chemical plant.

2-1. A chemical reactor

In a certain chemical reaction when two substances A and B are brought together they produce a third chemical substance C. It is known that 1 gram of A combines with 1 gram of B to produce 2 grams of C. Furthermore, the rate of formation of C is proportional to the product of the amounts of A and B present. In addition to this *forward reaction* there is also a *backward reaction* decomposing C back into A and B. The rate of decomposi-

15

tion of C is proportional to the amount of C present in the mixer.   In other words, at any time t if a, b, and c are the quantities of the chemicals A, B and C present, respectively, then their rates of increases are described by the following three differential equations:

$$\frac{da}{dt} = k_2 c - k_1 ab, \qquad \ldots(2\text{-}1)$$

$$\frac{db}{dt} = k_2 c - k_1 ab, \qquad \ldots(2\text{-}2)$$

$$\frac{dc}{dt} = 2k_1 ab - 2k_2 c, \qquad \ldots(2\text{-}3)$$

where k_1 and k_2 are the *rate constants*. (These constants will vary with temperature and pressure, but we do not allow the temperature or pressure of the reaction to vary.)   Given the values of the constants k_1 and k_2 and the initial quantities of the chemicals A and B (and $c = 0$), we wish to determine how much of C has been produced as a function of time.   Determination of the rate of such chemical reactions is important in many industrial processes.

A straightforward method of simulating this system is to start at time zero and increment time in small steps of $\triangle t$. We assume that the quantities of chemicals remain unaltered during each step and only change 'instantaneously' at the end of the step.   Thus the quantity of A (or B or C) at the end of one such step is given in terms of the quantity at the beginning of the step as

$$a(t + \triangle t) = a(t) + \frac{da(t)}{dt} \cdot \triangle t \qquad \ldots(2\text{-}4)$$

If $\triangle t$ is sufficiently small Eq. (2-4) is a reasonable representation.   Identical equations can be written for $b(t + \triangle t)$ and $c(t + \triangle t)$.

Suppose we wish to simulate the system for a period T.   We will divide this period T into a large number N of small periods $\triangle t$.   That is

$$T = N . \triangle t$$

At time zero, we know $a(0)$, $b(0)$, $c(0)$.   From these initial values and the values k_1 and k_2 we compute the amounts of chemicals at time $\triangle t$ as

$$a(\triangle t) = a(0) + [k_2 . c(0) - k_1 . a(0).b(0)] \triangle t$$
$$b(\triangle t) = b(0) + [k_2 . c(0) - k_1 . a(0).b(0)] \triangle t$$
$$c(\triangle t) = c(0) + [2k_1 . a(0).b(0) - 2k_2 . c(0)] \triangle t$$

Using these values we calculate the next state of the system, i.e., at time $2t$ as

$$a(2 \triangle t) = a(\triangle t) + [k_2 . c(\triangle t) - k_1 a(\triangle t).b(\triangle t)] . \triangle t$$
$$b(2 \triangle t) = b(\triangle t) + [k_2 . c(\triangle t) - k_1 a(\triangle t).b(\triangle t)] . \triangle t$$
$$c(2 \triangle t) = c(\triangle t) + [2k_1 . a(\triangle t).b(\triangle t) - 2k_2 . c(\triangle t)] . \triangle t$$

Using the state of the system at $2 \triangle t$, we determine its state at $3 \triangle t$, and so on.   We continue in this vein, moving time forward by $\triangle t$ and determining the state of the system from the previous state, for N steps, at the end of which we have the desired result.   This procedure is shown in the form of a flow-chart in Fig. 2-1.

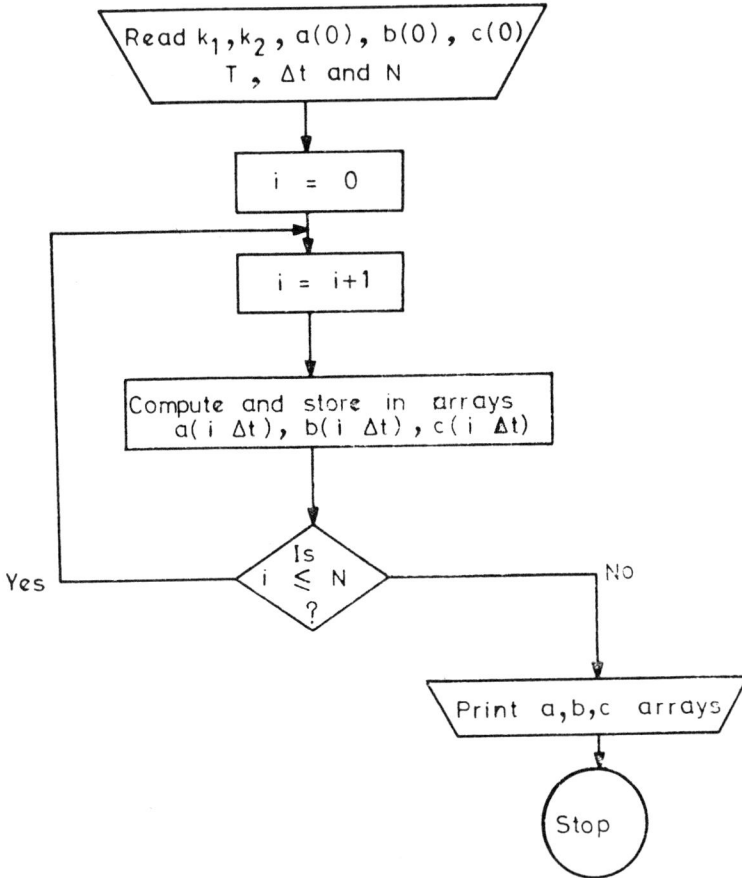

Fig. 2-1:   Flowchart of a chemical reaction simulator.

A FORTRAN (format free) program which simulates the system with $k_1 = 0.008$ gram^{-1} min^{-1}, $k_2 = 0.002$ min^{-1}, and $a(0) = 100$ grams, $b(0) = 50$ grams, $c(0) = 0$ grams, for a period of $T = 5$ minutes in steps of $\triangle t = 0.1$ min. is as follows ($N = 50$).

```
DIMENSION A (52), B (52), C(52),
REAL K1, K2
A (1) = 100.0
B (1) = 50.0
C (1) = 0.0
```

```
      DELTA = 0.1
      T = 0
      K1 = 0.008
      K2 = 0.002
      DO 3 I = 1,51
      PRINT, T, A(I), B(I), C(I)
      A(I + 1) = A(I) + (K2*C(I) − K1*A(I)*B(I))*DELTA
      B(I + 1) = B(I) + (K2*C(I) − K1*A(I)*B(I))*DELTA
      C(I + 1) = C(I) + 2.*(K1*A(I)*B(I) − K2*C(I))*DELTA
      T = T + DELTA
    3 CONTINUE
      STOP
      END
```

The following is the output of this program, which gives the state of the system (i.e., the values of a, b, and c) for 5 minutes at the intervals of 0.1 minute.

TIME	A(I)	B(I)	C(I)
0.00	100.00	50.00	0.00
0.10	96.00	46.00	8.00
0.20	92.47	42.47	15.06
0.30	89.33	39.33	21.34
0.40	86.52	36.52	26.95
0.50	84.00	34.00	32.00
0.60	81.72	31.72	36.55
0.70	79.66	29.66	40.69
0.80	77.77	27.77	44.45
0.90	76.05	26.05	47.89
1.00	74.48	24.48	51.04
1.10	73.03	23.03	53.94
1.20	71.70	21.70	56.61
1.30	70.46	20.46	59.07
1.40	69.32	19.32	61.36
1.50	68.26	18.26	63.48
1.60	67.28	17.28	65.44
1.70	66.36	16.36	67.28
1.80	65.51	15.51	68.99
1.90	64.71	14.71	70.59
2.00	63.96	13.96	72.08

(*Continued...*)

(. . . Continued)

TIME	A(I)	B(I)	C(I)
2.10	63.26	13.26	73.48
2.20	62.60	12.60	74.79
2.30	61.99	11.99	76.03
2.40	61.41	11.41	77.18
2.50	60.86	10.86	78.27
2.60	60.35	10.35	79.30
2.70	59.87	9.87	80.27
2.80	59.41	9.41	81.18
2.90	58.98	8.98	82.04
3.00	58.57	8.57	82.86
3.10	58.19	8.19	83.63
3.20	57.82	7.82	84.36
3.30	57.48	7.48	85.05
3.40	57.15	7.15	85.70
3.50	56.84	6.84	86.32
3.60	56.55	6.55	86.91
3.70	56.27	6.27	87.46
3.80	56.00	6.00	87.99
3.90	55.75	5.75	88.50
4.00	55.51	5.51	88.97
4.10	55.29	5.29	89.43
4.20	55.07	5.07	89.86
4.30	54.86	4.86	90.27
4.40	54.67	4.67	90.66
4.50	54.48	4.48	91.03
4.60	54.31	4.31	91.39
4.70	54.14	4.14	91.73
4.80	53.98	3.98	92.05
4.90	53.82	3.82	92.35
5.00	53.68	3.68	92.65

2-2. Numerical integration vs. continuous system simulation

Some of you may have recognized that all we have done for studying the dynamics of the reaction rates in Sec. 2-1 is to use Euler formula to perform numerical integration of three simultaneous differential equations, Eqs.

(2-1)–(2-3). What then, you might ask, is the difference between an ordinary numerical integration and a continuous system simulation? What is it that makes one study of a dynamic system a computation and another study, a simulation? Although the dividing line between simulation and ordinary computation often becomes quite thin, there are two distinctive features of simulation : (i) In simulation, we always keep track of the state of the system explicitly. The outcome of each step (of numerical calculations) in a simulation experiment can be interpreted directly as the state of the system at some point in time. Simulation, essentially, consists of constructing a state history of the system—a succession of explicit state descriptions at each instant as we move forward in time. Thus there is a one-to-one correspondence between what the computer does and what takes place in the system. In a numerical solution of equations no such correspondence is preserved. Usually in pure computations shortcuts are taken, parameters are lumped and mathematical equations manipulated before the computer program is developed. These destroy the one-to-one correspondence between the computer steps and the original system from which the equations were derived. Consequently the output data have to be interpreted in the light of earlier manipulations before conclusions can be drawn about the system. (ii) Secondly, there is also a difference of attitude. In case of a pure numerical calculation we only see the given set of differential equations as a mathematical object and proceed to integrate them. In simulation we look upon the equations as one of the steps in the entire process. We know the real-life system, and we are aware of the approximations in the model that is being simulated. Finally, by looking at the output data (which directly represent the dynamics of the system) we are also prepared to modify the model, if necessary.

2-3.   Selection of an integration formula

As we observed earlier, continuous dynamic systems are generally represented by means of differential equations. Numerical solution of these differential equations involves some integrating procedure. Many different integration formulas are available for this purpose, and the selection of an appropriate formula for integration is the most crucial decision to be made in a continuous system simulation. In Sec. 2-1 we used the simplest possible integration formula, which is known as Euler formula. There are much more efficient ways of performing numerical integration which do not rely simply on the last known values of the variables. Instead, some of them use several previous values to predict the rate at which the variables are changing and also in some formulas the integration step size Δt is adjusted to match the rate at which the variables are changing. As a matter of fact, the simple Euler formula employed in Sec. 2-1 is rarely used in practice because of the rapid accumulation of errors (to be discussed shortly). There are improved versions of the Euler formula available, such as, Euler-

Richardson formula, Euler-Gauss formula. Some of the integration formulas commonly used in simulation are: Simpson's rule ($\frac{1}{3}$ rule, 3/8 rule); trapezoidal rule; the Runge-Kutta family of formulas (second, third or fourth order); predictor-corrector methods; and so on. Many of these are available as standard subroutines. There is no integration method which is the best for simulations. One has to consider several factors when choosing an integration formula. Accuracy and the speed of computation are the most important considerations. Other factors are self-starting ability, solution stability, presence or absence of discontinuity, and ease with which error can be estimated. Any detailed discussion of these is beyond the scope of this book. The following is a very brief excursion.

Errors: There are basically two types of computation errors that occur at each step of integration: (i) *Round off* errors are introduced because of the limited size of the computer word. Every number has to be represented within this size. For example, suppose a number obtained as a product of two 4-digit numbers

$$.2102 \times .8534 = .17938468$$

has to be accommodated within 4-digits. It is therefore rounded off to .1794, introducing thereby an error. Some computer systems (compilers such as ALPS, BASIC and some versions of FORTRAN) have automatic rounding built into them, but many systems do not round off; they simply *chop off*; which is even worse. Thus the product in the foregoing example would end up being 0.1793. (ii) *Truncation errors* are caused when an infinite mathematical series is approximated by a finite number of terms. In continuous system simulation truncation errors arise mainly due to the inadequacy of an integration formula being used. For example, when Euler integration formula is used we are using only the first two terms of the Taylor series (which is infinite).

$$f(t + \Delta t) = f(t) + \frac{df(t)}{dt} \cdot \Delta t + \frac{d^2 f(t)}{dt^2} \cdot \frac{(\Delta t)^2}{2!} + \frac{d^3 f(t)}{dt^3} \frac{(\Delta t)^3}{3!} + \cdots$$

when Δt is sufficiently small the truncation error in Euler formula can be approximated with

$$\frac{d^2 f(t)}{dt^2} \cdot \frac{(\Delta t)^2}{2}$$

The second derivative can be approximated to

$$\frac{d^2 f(t)}{dt^2} = \frac{1}{\Delta t} \left[\frac{df(t + \Delta t)}{dt} - \frac{df(t)}{dt} \right]$$

On dividing the error term with value of $f(t)$ to get a relative error and on getting rid of the sign, we get

$$\text{Relative error} = Er = \left[\frac{df(t + \Delta t)}{dt} - \frac{df(t)}{dt} \right] \frac{\Delta t}{2 f(t)} \qquad (2\text{-}5)$$

In each individual step *Er* may be small but when accumulated over hundreds of consecutive steps in an integration the truncation error could make the simulation results meaningless.

Integration step: Choice of the step size $\triangle t$ of integration is another very important decision. The smaller the integration step the smaller is the error. The relative integration error in using Euler formula, for example, is given by Eq. (2-5). Clearly *Er* can be made as small as we please by making $\triangle t$ sufficiently small. But the number of computation steps and therefore the computation time will increase inversely in proportion to $\triangle t$. More steps would also accumulate an increased amount of round off errors. A compromise has to be made between the conflicting requirements of speed and accuracy. For a given accuracy, it is often possible to arrive at an optimal combination of an integration formula and the step size.

Sometimes, when the error varies widely, it is advisable to use a *varying-step integration* formula. That is, the error is evaluated at each integration step and the step size $\triangle t$ for the next step automatically adjusted accordingly.

It often happens that the time intervals for which we require the output of integration are much larger than the integration step size. In that case the program is so written that values of the variables are saved once, say, every 100 steps of integration. This will be illustrated in Sec. 2-5.

2-4. Runge-Kutta integration formulas

In Euler formula (used in Sec. 2-1) to estimate the value of the variable at time $(t + \triangle t)$ we used its slope at time *t*,

$$y(t + \triangle t) = y(t) + \frac{dy(t)}{dt} \cdot \triangle t.$$

In other words, the value of *y* at $(i + 1)$th instant is estimated in terms of its value and slope at the *i*th instant. That is,

$$y_{i+1} = y_i + \dot{y} \cdot \triangle t$$

where $\dot{y}$ is the usual short-hand notation for the first derivative of *y*.

As mentioned earlier, Eular formula is the simplest and crudest method of numerical integration. It is not very efficient because it requires a very small step-size $\triangle t$ for reasonable accuracy.

A much more refined, accurate, and commonly used method is the Runge-Kutta method. It is a method designed to approximate the Taylor series without our having to evaluate the higher order derivatives. The main idea is to compute the first derivate $f(t, y)$ of *y* at several carefully chosen points in the interval $(t, t + \triangle t)$, and to combine these values in such a way as to get good accuracy in the computed increment $y_{i+1} - y_i$. Based on this strategy, a family of formulas have been derived, known as Runge-Kutta formulas. The best amongst these, and by far the most popularly used integration formula, is the fourth-order Runge-Kutta formula, defined by the following equations:

$$u_1 = h \cdot f(t_i, y_i)$$
$$u_2 = h \cdot f(t_i + h/2, y_i + u_1/2)$$
$$u_3 = h \cdot f(t_i + h/2, y_i + u_2/2) \qquad \qquad \dots (2\text{-}6)$$
$$u_4 = h \cdot f(t_i + h, y_i + u_3)$$
$$y_{i+1} = y_i + \tfrac{1}{6} \cdot (u_1 + 2u_2 + 2u_3 + u_4)$$

where function f is the first derivative of y at various points, and h denotes the integration step-size $\triangle t$.

The equations in (2-6) appear quite complicated at first sight, but they are in fact easy to program. The function f is computed four times in each integration step. The truncation error in using the 4-th order Runge-Kutta method is of the order of h^5, which is far better than order h^2, the error Er in the case of the Euler formula. We can, therefore, use a larger step-size with Eq. (2-6). The price we pay for reduction in error is that four additional function evaluations are required per step. This price may be considerable in computer time if the function $f(t, y)$ is complicated. Like the Euler method, Runge-Kutta methods are *self-starting* (i.e., the computation of the solution can be started with no values other than the initial conditions of the differential equations). The derivation of the Runge-Kutta formulas or any further discussion is outside the scope of this book. There are several good texts on numerical analysis that treat this topic in detail. We will simply illustrate its use in continuous simulation with two examples.

An R-C amplifying circuit: Consider an electronic circuit of Fig. 2-2 where Amp is an ideal voltage amplifier with infinite input impedance and zero output impedance, and amplification factor A. The input capacitor C_1 is a coupling capacitor of a large value, say, $C_1 = 1\mu f$. Capacitor C_2 is a stray capacitance, of a small value, say, $C_2 = .005\ \mu F$. The values of the three resistors are $R_1 = 10^4$ ohms, $R_2 = 10^3$ ohms and $R_3 = 8 \times 10^3$ ohms. Let $A = 100$.

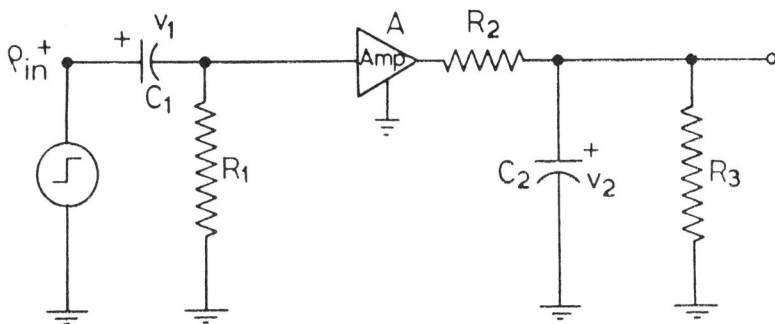

Fig. 2-2: R-C amplifying circuit.

This system is described by the following two equations: The current entering the capacitor C_1 is given by

$$C_1 \frac{dv_1}{dt} = (e_{in} - v_1) \cdot \frac{1}{R_1},$$

and the current entering capacitor C_2 is

$$C_2 \frac{dv_2}{dt} = \frac{A}{R_2}(e_{in} - v_1) - \frac{v_2(R_2 + R_3)}{R_2 R_3}$$

Hence

$$\dot{v}_1 = A_{11}v_1 + B_1 e_{in} \qquad \qquad ...(2\text{-}7)$$

$$\dot{v}_2 = A_{21}v_1 + A_{22}v_2 + B_2 e_{in}, \qquad ...(2\text{-}8)$$

where constants

$$A_{11} = -\frac{1}{R_1 C_1} = -100 \text{ sec}^{-1} = -B_1$$

$$A_{21} = -\frac{A}{R_2 C_2} = -2 \times 10^7 \text{ sec}^{-1} = -B_2$$

$$A_{22} = -\frac{R_2 + R_3}{R_2 R_3 C_2} = -2.25 \times 10^5 \text{ sec}^{-1}$$

The state of the system is given by the voltages v_1 and v_2.

Let us simulate the system and solve the two simultaneous equations, Eq. (2-7), (2-8).   Assume that initially $v_1(0) = v_2(0) = 0$ and at time $t = 0$ a unit step voltage is applied at the input terminal.   That is, $e_{in} = 1$ for $t \geqslant 0$ and $e_{in} = 0$ for $t < 0$.

As discussed in Sec. 2-3, there are two crucial decisions to be made when using numerical integration: about the integration formula and about the step-size Δt.   Let us in this case choose the Runge-Kutta 4th order integration method.   Regarding the step-size, since $C_1 \gg C_2$ initially the exponential rise in the output voltage (voltage v_2) will be very fast, at a time constant of

$$C_2 \left(\frac{R_2 R_3}{R_2 + R_3} \right) = 4.4 \ \mu \text{ sec},$$

whereas the output voltage will decay at a time constant of

$$C_1 R_1 = 10 \text{ m sec}.$$

Thus the ratio of the time constants is more than 2200.   Let us therefore choose the step-size initially to be $h = \Delta t = 0.5 \ \mu$ sec (about 1/9th of the time constant).   After, say, 200 iterations (about 23 time constants), we can increase the integration step-size.   Can we increase h by, say, a factor of 2000?   The investigation of this problem is left as an exercise for you.   The following is a FORTRAN program which simulates this system, using the 4th order Runge-Kutta integration method: (Note that initially the step-size is set to a smaller value HS, and after N1 steps it is increased to a larger value HL and then run for N2 steps):

```
      READ, A11, A21, A22, B1, B2, N1, N2, HS, HL
      T = 0.
      V1 = 0.
      V2 = 0.
      H = HS
      N = N1 + N2
      DO 130 I = 1, N
      IF(I.GT.N1) GO TO 120
C     EVALUATE RUNGE-KUTTA TERMS —4 FOR EACH EQUATION
100   U11 = H*((A11* V1) + E1)
      U12 = H*((A21* V1) + (A22*V2) + B2)
      U21 = H*(A11*(V1 + .5*U11) + B1)
      U22 = H*(A21*(V1 + .5*U11) + A22*(V2 + .5*U12) + B2)
      U31 = H*(A11*(V1 + .5*U21) + B1)
      U32 = H*(A21*(V1 + .5*U21) + A22*(V2 + .5*U22) + B2)
      U41 = H*(A11*(V1 + U31) + B1)
      U42 = H*(A21*(V1 + U31) + A22*(V2 + U32) + B2)
C     EVALUATE VOLTAGES
      V1 = V1+(U11+2.*U21+2.*U31+U41)/6.
      V2 = V2 + (U12 + 2.*U22 + 2.*U32 + U42)/6.
      T = T + H
110   PRINT, I, T, V1, V2
      GO TO 130
C     STEP-SIZE INCREASES
120   H = HL
      GO TO 100
130   CONTINUE
      STOP
      END
```

2-5. Simulation of a servo system

A very important application of continuous system simulation is in design and analysis of control systems. Let us study the behaviour of a second-order nonlinear feedback system represented by the following block diagram.

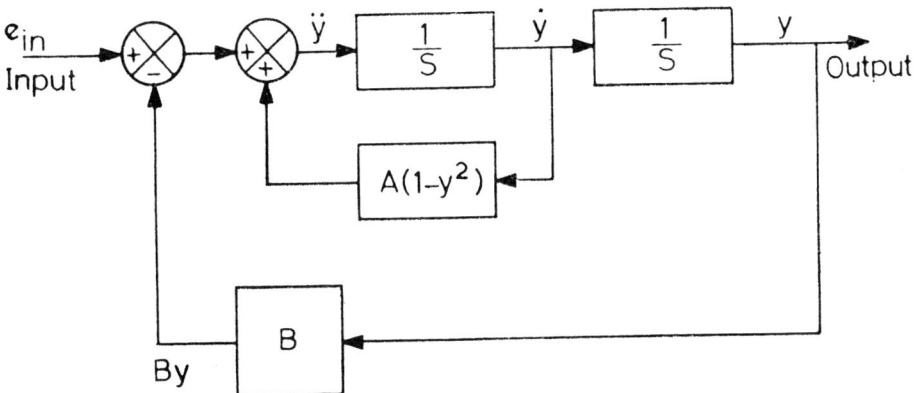

Fig. 2-3: A nonlinear second-order servo system.

(Those of you not familiar with the control theory symbols may ignore the diagram and simply start from the differential equation.)

This block diagram represents many natural as well as man-made servo systems. Some examples are: beating of the heart, periodic opening and closing of flowers in response to the sunlight, rate of variation of prices, squeaking of door with rusty hinges, dripping of a leaky tap, a neon-lamp oscillator, to name a few.

The system of Fig. 2-3 can also be described by the following differential equation

$$\ddot{y} = A(1 - y^2)\dot{y} - By + e_{in}$$

where A and B are positive constants.

In the case of zero input signal, the equation becomes

$$\ddot{y} = A(1 - y^2)\dot{y} - By \qquad \qquad ...(2\text{-}9)$$

This is the well-known Van der Pol non-linear equation. (It can be seen that when the amplitude y is small, the damping term $A(1 - y^2)$ is negative, but when y becomes large the damping becomes positive. Thus small-amplitude oscillations will tend to build up, while large-amplitude oscillations will be damped out.)

Let us simulate this system. The second-order differential equation can be written as a set of two simultaneous equations of first order. We replace Eq. (2-9) with (using the variable y_1 in place of y)

$$\dot{y}_1 = y_2$$
$$\dot{y}_2 = A(1 - y_1^2)y_2 - By_1$$

To be more specific let constants $A = 0.1$, $B = 1.0$ and let the initial conditions be

$$y_1(0) = 1.0$$
and
$$y_2(0) = 0.$$

Our equations therefore become

$$\dot{y}_1 = y_2$$
and
$$\dot{y}_2 = 0.1(1 - y_1^2)y_2 - y_1 \qquad \qquad ...(2\text{-}10)$$

An instantaneous description of the state of the system is given by the outputs of the two integrators, i.e., by variables y_1 and y_2. We will use, once again, the fourth-order Runge-Kutta method to obtain the values of y_1 and y_2 as a function of time. We will choose the step-size $\Delta t = H = .001$ second and simulate the system for 5 seconds. Thus the number of steps will be $N = 5,000$. This is too large a number of outputs to be plotted or examined. We will, therefore, print out the values of y_1 and y_2 only once every 100 integration steps. This can be implemented by keeping a counter K which is decremented by 1 for each integration step. Every time K equals zero,

y_1 and y_2 are printed and K is reset to 100. The following FORTRAN program performs the simulation.

```
C      H IS TIME STEP, N IS NO. OF STEPS, Y1, Y2 INITIAL VALUES
       T = 0.
       Y1 = 1.
       Y2 = 0.
       H = .001
       N = 5000
       K = 1
       DO 120 I = 1, N
       K = K - 1
       IF (K.NE.0) GO TO 110
C      PRINT ONCE IN 100 STEPS
       PRINT, T, Y1, Y2
       K = 100
C      CALCULATE THE RUNGE-KUTTA TERMS
  110  U11 = H*Y2
       U12 = H*(.1*(1. - Y1*Y1)*Y2 - Y1)
       U21 = H*(Y2*+.5*U12)
       U22 = H*(.1*(1.-(Y1+.5*U11)*(Y1+.5*U11))*(Y2+.5*U12)-(Y1+.5*U11))
       U31 = H*(Y2 + .5*U22)
       U32 = H*(.1*(1. - (Y1+.5*U21)*(Y1+.5*U21))*(Y2+.5*U22)-(Y1+.5*U21))
       U41 = H*(Y2 + U32)
       U42 = H*(.1*(1. - (Y1 + U31)*(Y1 + U31))*(Y2 + U32) - (Y1 + U31))
C      CALCULATE Y1 AND Y2
       Y1 = Y1 + (U11 + 2.*U21 + 2.*U31 + U41)/6.
       Y2 = Y2 + (U12 + 2.*U22 + 2.*U32 + U42)/6.
       T = T + H
  120  CONTINUE
       PRINT, T, Y1, Y2
       STOP
       END
```

By studying the three examples in this chapter so far, you may have acquired the incorrect impression that (i) every dynamic continuous system must first be expressed as a set of simultaneous differential equations before being simulated and, that (ii) such a system is always deterministic. The next example is meant precisely to dispel this notion. Moreover, in this example we are simulating a system which is too large and expensive to experiment with and where an incorrect design could become very costly.

2-6. Simulation of a water reservoir system

Let us consider the following proposal for constructing a dam across a river to create a reservoir. The reservoir is to be constructed at a specified site. The curve of the projected demand for the water from the reservoir has been determined (from the expected growth pattern and the seasonal fluctuations). The input to the reservoir is from the river inflow and from the rainfall directly over the reservoir. The output consists of the seepage and evaporation losses, in addition to the water supplied to meet the projected demand. This system (called a simple run-of-river storage demand system) is represented symbolically in Fig. 2-4.

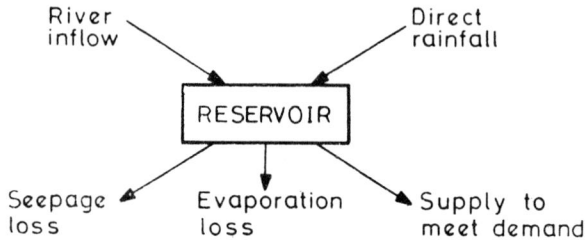

Fig. 2-4:   A simple run-of-river storage demand system.

The amount of seepage loss is not a constant but depends on the volume of the water stored. We have been given a curve (converted into a table) showing the seepage loss as a function of volume for the proposed reservoir. Likewise, the evaporation loss depends on the area of the exposed surface and the coefficient of evaporation. We are given another curve showing the surface area as a function of volume as well as the seasonal variation of the coefficient of evaporation. Therefore, for a given volume of water in the reservoir at a particular time of the year we can calculate the two losses.

In reality no reasonable finite-sized reservoir can provide an absolute guarantee of meeting the demand 100% of the time because the river inflow, the rainfall, the losses, the demand are all random variables. To build such a large dam which will never fail (to meet the demand) through its entire life will generally be uneconomical. Therefore, in practice one determines the reservoir size which will meet the demand with a specified risk of failure (of water shortage). For example, a 2% failure means that once in 50 years the reservoir would become empty before meeting the demand for water. The objective of the study is to determine the size of the reservoir with a specified risk of failure.

There is a single state variable in this system, namely, the volume of water in the reservoir. Since the volume varies continuously with time, we are dealing with a continuous system. It is reasonable to take one month as the basic time interval for the simulation study. Thus, for example, if we wish to simulate the system for 100 years, the simulation run length will be 1200. The simulation will be repeated assuming several different capacities of the reservoir. The output will be in series of ranked shortages for each capacity.

The basic procedure, to be repeated for each time step, may be expressed in terms of the following steps:

(1) For the current month M of the current year IY determine the total amount of river inflow and the total rainfall directly over the reservoir. Let the sum of two inputs be denoted by VIN (= RAIN + RFLOW).

(2) Add the input volume VIN to the volume left over in the reservoir at the end of the last month, VOL $(m-1)$.   This gives us the gross volume, GROSSV $=$ VIN $+$ VOL $(m-1)$.

(3) On the basis of the last month's volume VOL $(m-1)$ calculate this month's seepage and evaporation losses and add them as total loss TLOSS $=$ SEEP $+$ EVAP.

(4) From the demand curve (stored as a table in the computer memory) determine the demand of water for the current month DEM.

(5) If the TLOSS $\geqslant$ GROSSV, then the reservoir runs dry without supplying any water and therefore shortage, SHORT $=$ DEM.   The volume of water left at the end of the current month VOL $(m)=0$. Spillage SPILL $=0$ and go to Step 8; else if TLOSS $<$ GROSSV then the net water volume available to satisfy the demand is VNET $=$ GROSSV $-$ TLOSS.

(6) If DEM $\geqslant$ VNET the reservoir runs dry and the shortage is given by SHORT $=$ DEM $-$ VNET, and SPILL $=0$.   Go to Step 8; else if DEM $<$ VNET, then the difference DIFF $=$ VNET $-$ DEM is the water left over.

(7) If this leftover water exceeds the capacity CAP of the reservoir there will be a spill over, i.e., if DIFF $>$ CAP then SPILL $=$ DIFF $-$ CAP and VOL $(m)=$ CAP; else if DIFF $\leqslant$ CAP then SPILL $=0$ and VOL $(m)=$ DIFF.

(8) Print out SPILL and SHORT for this month, and move to the next month.   If the period exceeds the intended simulation length stop, else go to Step 1.

The following format-free FORTRAN program implements these steps:

```
READ, N, VOL, CAP
IY = 1
M = 1
DO 30 IY = 1, N
DO 30 M = 1, 12
SPILL = 0.
SHORT = 0.
CALL RIVFLO (IY,M,RFLOW)
CALL RAINF (IY,M,RAIN)
VIN = RFLOW + RAIN
GROSSV = VOL + VIN
CALL SEPEJ (VOL,SEEP)
CALL EVPRSN (M,VOL, EVAP)
TLOSS = SEEP + EVAP
CALL DEMAND (IY,M,DEM)
VNET = GROSSV - TLOSS
IF (VNET .LE. O.) VNET = 0.
DIFF = VNET - DEM
IF (DIFF .GE. O.) GO TO 10
SHORT = -DIFF
```

```
        VOL = 0.
        GO TO 20
   10   VOL = DIFF
        IF (CAP .GT. DIFF) GO TO 20
        SPILL = DIFF — CAP
        VOL = CAP
   20   PRINT, FLOW, RAIN, TLOSS, SHORT, SPILL, VOL
   30   CONTINUE
        STOP
        END
```

Subroutines

The foregoing program contains five subroutines requiring data about the riverflow, rainfall and the demand as a function of time; the seepage loss as a function of water stored in the reservoir; and the evaporation loss as a function of the volume (and hence the exposed surface) and the particular month of the year. The long sequence of data for river inflow and the rainfall could either be obtained from historical records or generated using suitable pseudorandom number generators. Similarly we can design the other subroutines, from an intimate knowledge of the system. As an example, we will write down the subroutine EVPRSN, for computing the evaporation loss.

Let the unit of measuring the volume be a million cubic meters. Suppose the highest possible dam at this site will create a reservoir of capacity 1000 units. Also suppose that we have a curve that gives the exposed surface area as a function of volume from 0 to 1000 units. Let the x-axis be divided into 100 equispaced ranges; and the data be stored in the form of a table (SURTBL) with 100 columns giving the surface area at volume 10, 20, …, 1000 units. The surface area SAREA for any intermediate value of VOL can be computed using an appropriate interpolation formula. Let us assume that a linear interpolation will suffice. We are also given 12 values for the coefficient of evaporation COEF—one for each month of the year. Then the following subroutine will yield the evaporation loss.

```
        SUBROUTINE EVPRSN (M, VOL, EVAP)
        REAL SURTBL (100), COEF (12)
        DATA SURTBL /…, …, … /
        DATA COEF /…, …, … /
        IVOL = VOL/10.
        RVOL = IVOL
        FRAC = VOL/10. — RVOL
        SAREA = SURTBL (IVOL) + FRAC* (SURTBL(IVOL+1)—SURTBL(IVOL))
        EVAP = SAREA * COEF (M)
        RETURN
        END
```

Note that the third statement requires 100 values and the fourth statement requires 12 values. Other subroutines can be written down similarly.

Output: The output will be a series of monthly shortages and spills.

The shortages could be combined into total annual shortages.   These annual shortages can be ranked according to the amount of shortage involved. From this ranked series of shortages for each capacity of the reservoir we would determine the acceptable reservoir size.

In the foregoing model no distinction was made regarding how the shortage is distributed month-wise within a particular year.   For example, the total failure to meet any demand for one month may be more serious than a 10 per cent shortage for ten consecutive months.   Such refinement can be easily incorporated by a procedure of assigning weights to different types of failures within a particular year.

There is another refinement which should be made in our computation. The losses for the entire current month were computed on the basis of the volume in storage at the end of last month.   If a large change in volume takes place between two consecutive time steps, this would lead to errors. This could be corrected by first finding a temporary value of VOL (m) on the basis of given VOL $(m - 1)$ (as usual) and then recalculating the losses on the basis of the average value

$$\frac{\text{VOL}(m) + \text{VOL}(m-1)}{2}$$

of the two volumes.

2-7. Analog vs. digital simulation

Block-diagram programming system: Let us once again consider the continuous, dynamic nonlinear system described by the van der Pol equation in Sec. 2-5.   The simulation program for that system can be expressed by means of the following block diagram.

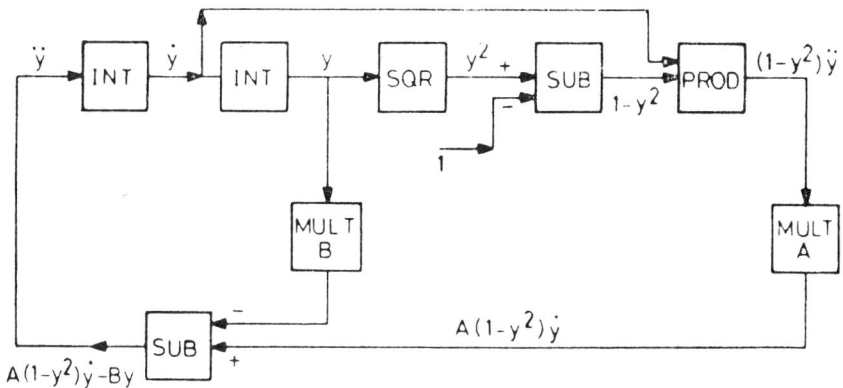

Fig. 2-5:   Block diagram for $y = A(1 - y^2)\dot{y} - By$.

Each of the blocks performs a mathematical operation.   Block INT performs integration, SQR squares, PROD takes the product, MULT multiplies with a constant, and SUB subtracts.   The blocks may be looked upon as subroutines.   The interconnection of the blocks is self-explanatory.   Note that the variables $\ddot{y}$, $\dot{y}$, y, y^2, etc., vary with time and must be updated every H (i.e., $\triangle t$) seconds.   The complete sequence of operations (by these blocks) is, therefore, repeated every H seconds if we use Euler integration (or four times every H seconds if we employ the 4th order Runge-Kutta integration).

Block-diagram oriented languages: Any continuous system (requiring numerical solution of differential equations), however complex, can be simulated by suitably 'patching' together a number of blocks such as these. Different systems will vary only in the number of blocks required and in their interconnections.   Since the same few types of blocks are used again and again for simulation of all continuous systems, it would be very useful to provide a package of standard subroutines to perform the operations of these blocks.   It would be even more convenient to have a special-purpose programming language which allowed direct implementation of block diagrams such as the one in Fig. 2-5.   Development in the simulation area has taken place precisely in this direction.   A large number of such continuous system simulation languages have been designed and implemented.   One or more of these languages are available at almost every computing centre. These languages will be discussed in greater detail in Chapter 9.

Analog implementation: Theoretically speaking, the means by which each of the blocks is actually implemented is immaterial, as long as it does its assigned task so that the entire set-up gives us the state of the system as a function of time.   These block functions may all be performed by one digital computer or by, say, different microprocessors—each specially programmed to do a specific job.

A block diagram, such as in Fig. 2-5, can also be simulated on an (electronic) analog computer, which consists of special-purpose elements such as integrators, multipliers, adders, function generation, and nonlinear elements. These elements are interconnected to imitate the system under study. The variables and their derivatives are represented by means of voltages (which vary according to the equations governing the given system).   The voltages can be monitored continuously at suitable points in the set-up to get the state of the system as a function of time.

Historically analog computers came into being years before digital computers did, and have played a major role in simulation of continuous dynamic systems.   Although analog computers are giving way to digital computers at an increasing pace, they are still in occasional use.   The following are some of the disadvantages of analog computers.

1. **Inadequate accuracy:**   In general, the result from a digital simulation is more accurate than that from an analog simulation.   The accuracy of analog simulation depends on the accuracy of the components being used, which can vary from .01% to 2%.   When accuracy required of components is more than 0.1%, the cost of components increases rapidly.   An accuracy

of about 1 % for a simulation of system with modest complexity is considered good. This limited accuracy cannot meet the need in simulating
systems like missiles and space vehicles.

2. **Scaling needed:** The magnitudes of dependant variables are represented in an analog computer by voltages. For a 10-volt analog computer
the maximum range of voltages is from -10 to $+10$. All program variables
must be scaled carefully so that none exceeds the maximum voltage. If a
variable exceeds the maximum voltage, then the corresponding amplifier
becomes saturated and results become inaccurate. This magnitude scaling
is a tedious task in an analog simulation, because there are usually many
variables and their maximum values are not known in advance.

In a digital computer with floating point arithmetic the magnitude scaling problem does not arise, because the quantities that can be represented
on a digital computer have a very large range. For the IBM 360, for example,
the range is from -10^{75} to $+10^{75}$. It has a precision of 7 decimal digits.
Therefore, normally no magnitude scaling is needed.

In addition to magnitude scaling, analog computers also require time
scaling. The maximum computing time for an analog computer is limited
because of drifts affecting the accuracy of the results. The time scale factor,
i.e., the ratio of computing-time to problem-time has to be determined.
(If this ratio is 1, simulation is *real time*.) Since there is only one time scale
factor, the task of time scaling is much easier. In digital computer simulation time scaling is generally not needed.

3. **Hardware set up necessary:** In analog simulation input constants
and initial conditions are incorporated by setting up voltages and potentio-
meters. Then the various elements (amplifiers, multipliers, voltmeters, etc.)
have to be connected on a patch board. Such setting up is not needed in a
digital simulation.

A simulation program on a digital computer can be easily stored for re-
use. Availability of various mathematical functions on a digital computer
is another advantage. Since in a digital simulation no set up is required
nor any calibration and accuracy test is needed, rapid switching from one
simulation to another can be made. This results in a better machine utilization.

The two main advantages of analog simulation have been higher speed of
solution (necessary for certain applications) and direct access to and immediate display of the computed results. Both these advantages are vanishing
in the presence of superspeed digital computers available in a multiprogram-
ming environment with on-line CRT displays.

We will not discuss analog simulation any further. The reader may
refer to any of several excellent textbooks available on analog computers.

2-8. Remarks and references

Electronic analog computers became available soon after World War II and they were found to be extremely valuable in analysis and design of numerous engineering systems.   Analog computers were used for simulating various continuous dynamic systems which were too difficult to lend themselves to analytic studies.   About ten years later, in the mid 1950's, when digital computers became commercially available, their advantages (such as greater accuracy, no need of scaling, greater flexibility, etc., as discussed in Sec. 2-7) over analog computers in simulating complex continuous systems were recognized, and they began to be used for this purpose.

A general purpose digital computer was required to have certain minimum hardware facilities if it was to be used successfully for simulating large continuous systems; such as hardware floating point arithmetic, long word length to reduce round-off errors, and a reasonably large random-access memory for handling a large amount of intermediate data.   As the hardware (and software) of the digital computers became increasingly better and cheaper during the last twenty years, the digital computer began to be used more and more for simulating continuous dynamic systems.

The most comprehensive and an early textbook dealing with the simulation of continuous systems on a digital computer is

CHU, Y., *Digital Simulation of Continuous Systems*, McGraw-Hill, New York, 1969.

Some more recent books on this topic are

ORD-SMITH, R. J. and J. STEPHENSON, *Computer Simulation of Continuous Systems*, Cambridge University Press, Cambridge, U.K., 1975.
STEPHENSON, R. E., *Computer Simulation for Engineers*, Harcourt, Brace, Jovanovich, New York, 1971.
SHAH, M. J., *Engineering Simulation Using Small Scientific Computers*, Prentice-Hall, Englewood Cliffs, N.J., 1976.

A journal devoted entirely to computer simulation was started in 1963 and is called SIMULATION.   A good collection of articles, dealing exclusively with simulation of continuous systems, from this journal can be found in

McLEOD, J. (ed.)., *SIMULATION : The dynamic Modeling of Ideas and Systems with Computers*, McGraw-Hill, New York, 1968.

As pointed out in the beginning of this chapter, continuous system simulation is encountered mostly in engineering and physical sciences.   For example, simulation has played a crucial role in the development of modern aerospace industry and chemical-process industries.   A few applications in these areas have already been illustrated, namely, a chemical reactor, an aircraft pursuit system, an electrical network, a feedback control system, and a water reservoir system.   Some additional applications are pointed out in the form of exercises.   These are trajectory calculations, the multibody problem, vibration and shock absorbers, and econometric models.   This list of continuous dynamic systems where simulation has been applied profitably is indeed very large. The examples we chose in this chapter were simplified to keep the problems manageable. A real problem is more involved computationally (but not conceptually).

The examples of simulation applied to various engineering and other disciplines can best be found in journals, technical reports, and textbooks in respective fields. For instance, the following provides a good reference for simulation of water resource systems (a simple example of which was given in Sec. 2-6).

> HUFSCHMIDT, M. and M. B. FIERING, *Simulation Techniques for the Design of Water Resources Systems,* Harvard University Press, Cambridge, Mass., 1966.

Likewise an excellent treatment on digital simulation of chemical engineering plants can be found in Chapter 5 of

> LUYBEN, W. L., *Process Modeling, Simulation and Control for Chemical Engineers,* McGraw-Hill, New York, 1973.

An integrator is the heart of an analog simulation. Likewise, the selection of an appropriate integration subroutine (from amongst several available on your computer system or at least in the literature) is of central importance to the program for simulation of a continuous system. There are a number of excellent textbooks on numerical analysis that discuss various integration formulas and their merits from the viewpoint of speed, accuracy, etc. A few of these are:

> ACTON, F. S., *Numerical Methods that Work,* Harper and Row, New York, 1970.
> CONTE, S. D. and C. De BOOR, *Elementary Numerical Analysis : An Algorithmic Approach,* (2nd Ed.), McGraw-Hill, New York, 1968.
> DAHLQUIST G. and A. BJÖRCK, *Numerical Methods,* Prentice-Hall, Englewood Cliffs, N.J., 1974.
> RALSTON, A., *A First Course in Numerical Analysis,* McGraw-Hill, New York, 1965.
> RAJARAMAN, V., *Computer Oriented Numerical Methods.* Prentice-Hall of India, New Delhi, 1971.

It is the technology of electronic devices which has tilted the balance overwhelmingly in favour of digital simulation for continuous systems, although analog simulation appears more natural. In view of the advancing technology, particularly of microprocessors, the field is far from having been stabilized. An interesting article on the effect of electronic technology on continuous system simulation is

> AUS, H. M. and G. A. KORN, *The Future of Continuous-System Simulation.* Proc. AFIPS/FJCSS, 1969.

2-9. Exercises

I. TRAJECTORY SIMULATION

Simulation has been used in computing trajectories of various types of rockets, bullets, space vehicles, etc. Because of the drag (air-resistance) the equations of motion get sufficiently complicated for a closed form mathematical solution. In the case of a rocket the mass itself does not remain constant but reduces as the fuel is used up.

2-1. Given a cannon that fires spherical balls of mass m, you are asked to produce a range table, i.e., a table that gives ranges for various values of muzzle velocity and gun elevation (firing angle). You are also asked to investigate the sensitivity of range to small changes in muzzle velocity and gun elevation. For simplicity assume that the drag is proportional to the square of the instantaneous velocity of the cannon ball, and it is purely along the direction of flight. Making use of the following four equations, write a computer program to produce a range table:

$$m \frac{dy}{dt} + mg \sin \theta + cv^2 = 0$$

$$mv \frac{d\theta}{dt} + mg \cos \theta = 0$$

$$\frac{dx}{dt} = v \cos \theta$$

$$\frac{dy}{dt} = v \cos \theta$$

Constant c is the drag coefficient for the cannon ball. Variables v and θ are the instantaneous velocity and angle of elevation of the cannon ball, and x, y are the coordinates of its instantaneous position. For various values of the starting conditions, i,e., muzzle velocity v_0, elevation θ_0, and $x_0 = y_0 = 0$, the program should yield the range.

2-2. A missile is fired vertically up. It has a rocket motor that produces a certain constant upward thrust F for as long as the fuel-burning motor is on. The motor burns the fuel at a constant rate b. Assume that the missile does not go so high as to vary the gravity constant g nor does the drag coefficient vary during the flight. Set up the equation of the vertical motion. Write a program which gives the vertical distance y at any time t.

2-3. Modify the simulation program in Exercise 2.2 in order to make it valid for higher altitudes. That is, take into account the reduction in the air resistance and change in the value of the gravitational constant g as the missile rises higher.

2-4. Suppose a 50-kg. heat-seeking missile is fired at a jet bomber flying at a constant speed of 1,200 Km/hour. The missile has a rocket motor that produces a thrust of 5000 Kg. for a period of 4 minutes. Simulate the missile system to test its effectiveness and to estimate how close the target should be before a missile is fired. Assume the drag coefficient $c = .04$ Kg/Km^2 and the weight of liquid fuel is 20 Kg. (which is burned in 4 minutes at a constant rate).

2-5. Assuming that the drag force is proportional to the square of the speed and proportional to the cross-sectional area of a moving body, how will you simulate the experiment of the Tower of Pisa by dropping two lead balls of diameter 1 cm and 20 cm from a 400 meter tower?

Notice that in all trajectory calculations any refinements, such as, (i) making the air-resistance more complicated than just proportional to v^2, and also including a non-zero component perpendicular to the velocity vector, and (ii) taking into account the effects of the earth's rotation, can be easily accommodated. These refinements require only additional computation and not any increased analytical ability. This is one of the fundamental advantages of simulation.

II. THE MULTIBODY PROBLEM

When there are two bodies in space, it is easy to compute their paths analytically using Newton's laws of motion. But if there are three (or more) bodies influencing each other (such as the sun-earth-moon system), it has not been possible to obtain their paths of motion in a closed analytic form. It is, in fact, one of the oldest unsolved problems in physics. A great deal of effort has been spent in solving this problem. We can, however, simulate any N-body system for any required period given an initial set of coordinates.

2-6. Assuming that there are N heavenly bodies in a plane, write a FORTRAN program to compute their paths for a specified period T. (Divide T into N small periods. Compute the position at each of these instants using the fact that there are only two forces acting on a body—sum of the $N-1$ gravitational forces due to the other $N-1$ bodies and the forces due to acceleration.)

2-7. After gathering the relevant data for the sun-earth-moon system, simulate the motion of this 3-body system for the period of a month.

III. SUSPENSION SYSTEM

In trajectory problems the external forces (drag and gravity) either remain constant or vary slowly. Consequently the trajectory is a smooth curve. In contrast, the suspension system of an automobile is subjected to abruptly changing forces due to potholes in the road. The purpose of a suspension system is to damp out the effect of vibrations, caused by sudden changes in the road surface.

2-8. Each wheel with a mass m in an automobile has an independent suspension system, consisting of a spring and a shock absorber, as shown in Fig. 2-6. The resistance force of the spring is proportional to the displacement (i.e., compression) and the resistive force of the shock absorber is mostly proportional to the rate of change of displacement. The exact equation of motion for the system is

$$m\ddot{y} + k_1(\dot{y} - k_2\ddot{y}) + k_3 y = k_3 . F(t) \qquad \qquad ...(2\text{-}11)$$

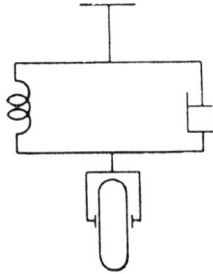

Fig. 2-6.

We wish to find the transient behaviour of this system with the following values of the constants:

$$\text{mass } m = 1.0, \quad k_1 = 5.0, \quad k_2 = 0.05$$

spring stiffness $k_3 = 700$, to two types of forces

(i) step function $F(t) = 0, \quad (t \leqslant 0)$
$$a, \quad (t > 0)$$

(ii) ramp function $F(t) = 0, \quad (t \leqslant 0)$
$$a\,t, \ (t > 0)$$

Write a program to simulate the system. Observe, in particular, the time required for the wheel to return to normal after it runs over a square pothole and the amount of overshoot.

2-9.   Simulate the suspension system described in Exercise 2-8, with an added requirement that there is a physical stopper that prevents the maximum displacement from exceeding a value of 2 units.

2-10.   Write a computer program to analyze the behaviour of the suspension system in Exercise 2-8 when it runs over a series of equispaced potholes on the road.

2-11.   How will you decide on the constants of the spring k_3, and of the shock absorber k_1 (assume k_2 to be one-hundredth of k_1), given m, $F(t)$, the maximum tolerable displacement, and the maximum time allowed to return to normal?

IV.   ECONOMETRIC MODELS

Simulation has been used widely to study the dynamic behaviour of large economic systems—of industries, of farms, of nations. The purpose is to determine economic variables of interest as a function of time in response to different actions taken. The following is an extremely elementary model of a nation's economy.

2-12.   The gross national product $GNP(t)$ during time t can be expressed as a sum

$$GNP(t) = GS(t) + IN(t) + C(t) \qquad \ldots(2\text{-}12)$$

Where $GS(t)$ is the government spending during time t, $IN(t)$ is the investment during t, and $C(t)$ is the consumption. Two of these three quantities can themselves be expressed as

$$IN(t) = m + c[GNP(t-1) - GNP(t-2)] \qquad \ldots(2\text{-}13)$$
$$C(t) = a + b.GNP(t-1) + d.GNP(t-2) \qquad \ldots(2\text{-}14)$$

where a, b, c, m, d are constants which have been determined for this system. At time t the previous year's GNP is known. Simulate the system for predicting the current year's GNP, given that the government spending has been announced.

3

Discrete System Simulation

In the last chapter our objects of simulation were continuous systems—those systems in which the state changed smoothly with time. In this chapter (and in all subsequent chapters) we will deal with discrete systems—systems in which the changes are discontinuous. Each change in the state of the system is called an *event*. For example, arrival or departure of a customer in a queue is an event. Likewise, sale of an item from the stock or arrival of an order to replenish the stock is an event in an inventory system. Arrival of a car at an intersection is an event if we are simulating street traffic. Therefore, the simulation of a discrete system is often referred to as *discrete-event simulation*.

Discrete-event simulation is commonly used by operations research workers to study large, complex systems which do not lend themselves to a conventional analytic approach. The very simple inventory problem simulated in Sec. 1-3 is an example. Some other examples are the study of sea and airports, steel melting shops, telephone exchanges, production line, stock of goods, scheduling of projects, to name a few. Discrete system simulation is more diverse and has less of a theory than continuous system simulation. There are no overall sets of equations to be solved in discrete-event simulation.

3-1. Fixed time-step vs. event-to-event model

In simulating any dynamic system—continuous or discrete—there must be a mechanism for the flow of time. For we must advance time, keep track of the total elapsed time, determine the state of the system at the new point in time, and terminate the simulation when the total elapsed time equals or exceeds the simulation period. For continuous systems, in Chapter 2, we advanced time in small increments of Δt for as long as was needed. In simulation of discrete systems, there are two fundamentally different models for moving a system through time : the *fixed time-step* model and the *event-to-event* (or *next event*) model. In a fixed time-step model a "timer" or "clock" is simulated by the computer. This clock is up-dated by a fixed time interval τ, and the system is examined to see if any event has taken place during this time interval (minutes, hours, days, whatever). All events that take place during this period are treated as if they occurred simultaneously at the tail end of this interval. In a next-event simulation model the computer advances time to the occurrence of the next event. It shifts from event to event. The system state does not change in between. Only those points in time are kept track of when something of interest happens to the system.

Flowcharts for these two methods of simulating a discrete system in their most general forms are shown in Fig. 3-1.

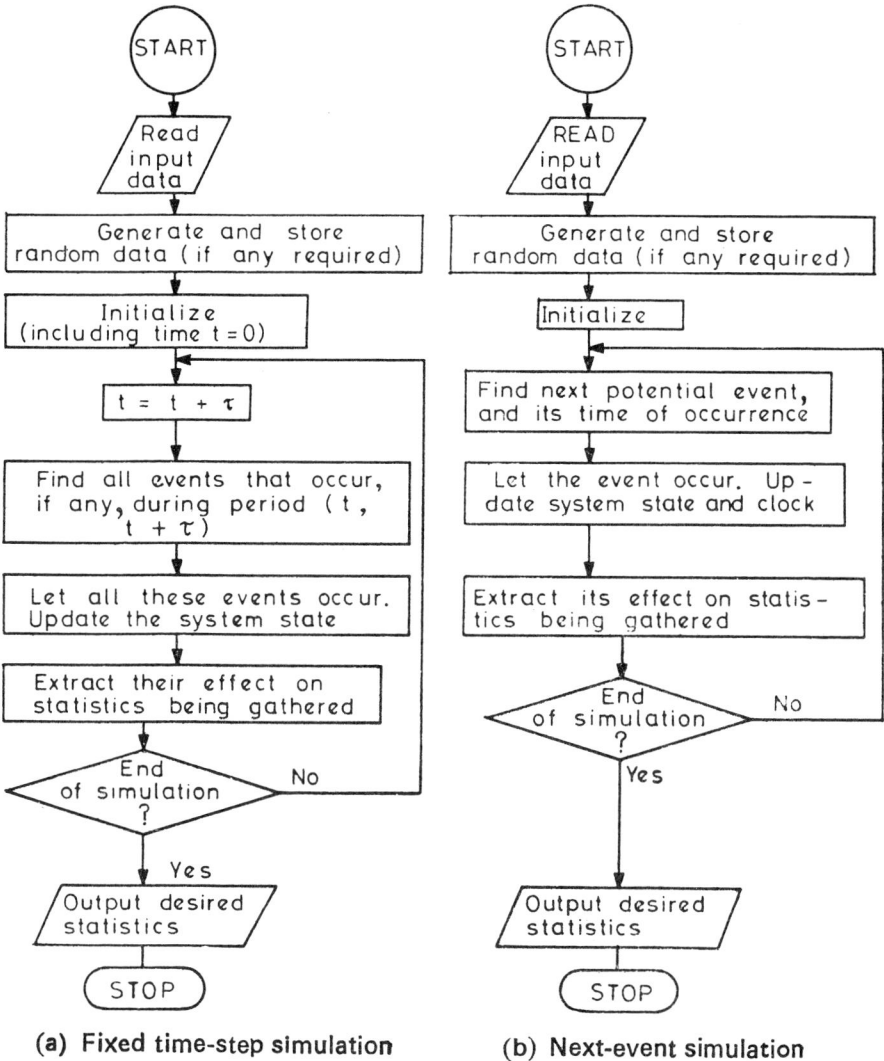

(a) Fixed time-step simulation   (b) Next-event simulation

Fig. 3-1:   Flowcharts for discrete system simulation.

To illustrate the difference between the two models, let us assume that we are simulating the dynamics of the population in a fish bowl, starting with, say, 10 fish.   If we used the fixed time-step model with, say, $\tau = 1$ day, then we would scan the fish-bowl (figuratively speaking) once every 24 hours, and any births and deaths that take place are presumed to be during the last moment of this period.   On the other hand, if we use a next-event model then we will first find out when the next-event (birth or death) is to take place and then advance the clock exactly to that time.

In general, the next-event model is preferred, (except when we may be forced to use the fixed time-step model) because we do not waste any computer time in scanning those points in time when nothing takes place.   This waste is bound to occur if we pick a reasonably small value for τ.   On the other hand, if τ is so large that one or more events must take place during each interval then our model becomes unrealistic and may not yield meaningful results.   Therefore in most simulations of discrete systems the next-event model is used.   The only drawback of the next-event model is that usually its implementation (programming for it) turns out to be more complicated than the fixed time-step model.   To construct these two applications, in Chapter 4 we will use these two different models to simulate a queueing system.   However, except for that case, in the rest of this book we will employ only next-event models of discrete systems.

3-2.   On simulating randomness

There are numerous natural as well as man-made systems where chance plays some part.   These are called *stochastic* systems.   There is inherent randomness or unpredictability in their behaviour.   We have already encountered two such examples, namely, the inventory system in Chapter 1 and the water reservoir system in Chapter 2.   Some other examples of randomness that are frequently simulated are: arrival of customers in a store, arrival of vehicles at a traffic light, request for telephone lines at a telephone exchange, births and deaths in a population, collision of particles in a nuclear reactor, arrival of an elevator on a given floor, etc.

Discrete dynamic systems could be classified as deterministic or stochastic.   The former are less demanding computationally than the latter and are frequently solved analytically. Hence simulation in the study of discrete dynamic systems is used almost exclusively for stochastic systems—systems in which at least one of the variables is given by a probability function. Complex discrete, dynamic, stochastic systems often defy an analytic solution and are therefore studied through simulation.

To simulate such random variables, we require a source of randomness. In simulation experiments, this is achieved through a source of *uniformly distributed random numbers*.   These numbers are samples from a uniformly distributed random variable between some specified interval, and they have equal probability of occurrence in the same manner as all six faces of an unbiased die have equal chance of occurrence. A random number generator and its appropriate use form the heart of any simulation experiment involving a stochastic system. Before discussing methods of generating random numbers, let us see how they are used.

Use of random numbers: an example: Suppose a situation has three possible outcomes. For example, the price of a certain commodity can go up, down, or stay at the same level at the end of a particular day. Suppose the probabilities of these three outcomes are 0.3, 0.5, and 0.2, respectively. Then we need a random selector which reproduces the outcome, in the long run, with relative frequencies of 0.3, 0.5, and 0.2. They can be obtained with a device generating 10 uniform random numbers 0, 1, 2, ..., 9 with equal probability, and associating the sets of numbers {0, 1, 2} with the first outcome (i.e., price going up); {3, 4, 5, 6, 7} with the second outcome (i.e., price coming down), and {8, 9} with the third outcome (i.e., price remaining unchanged). Thus, we have a device that simulates the stochastic phenomenon of the price going up, down or remaining unchanged with the specified probabilities (of 0.3, 0.5, and 0.2, respectively). Using this device we can now conduct experiments. Thus, in general, the procedure for choosing a single random element from the range of all possible values consists of two steps. First a number is obtained (say 4) from a random number source, then it is transformed to correspond to an appropriate outcome of the experiment (number 4 corresponds to the price going up, in this case).

3-3. Generation of random numbers

Random numbers could be obtained from a sack of numbered beads as in bingo; or from rotations of a roulette wheel; or from any other randomizing device. However, such physical generators of random numbers are not suitable for simulation experiments on computers for two reasons: (i) The generation and feeding into the computer of thousands of such numbers is excessively laborious and time consuming, and more importantly, (ii) a sequence of numbers generated cannot be reproduced at a later time or by another person for repeating a simulation run. Such repetitive runs are required for debugging computer programs as well as for studying the effect of changes in the model.

We would, therefore, like to have some fast and deterministic method of generating a sequence of numbers which have the property of being random. Such deterministically generated numbers which appear to be random are called *pseudorandom* numbers.

Numerous arithmetic methods of generating pseudo-random numbers have been suggested, studied, and used on computers in the past thirty years or so. These methods are usually based on some recurrence relation. Each new number is generated from the previous one by applying some simple 'scrambling' operation. A fast, and the most commonly used method (or generator) is the so-called *multiplicative congruential generator* (some-times also called the *power-residue generator*).   It consists of computing

$$x_{i+1} = x_i . a \text{ (modulo } m), \qquad \qquad ...(3\text{-}1)$$

where x_i is the ith pseudo-random number, x_{i+1} is the next pseudo-random number, a is a constant multiplier, and, modulo m means that the number $(x_i . a)$ is divided by m repeatedly till the remainder is less than m.   The remainder is then set equal to the next number x_{i+1}.   The process is started with an initial value x_0, called the *seed*.   To illustrate, suppose we start with the seed $x_0 = 3$ and parameters $a = 7$ and $m = 15$.   Then the successive random numbers generated are:

$$x_1 = \ 3 \times 7 = 21 \equiv \ \ 6$$

$$x_2 = \ 6 \times 7 = 42 \equiv 12$$

$$x_3 = 12 \times 7 = 84 \equiv \ \ 9$$

$$x_4 = \ 9 \times 7 = 63 \equiv \ \ 3$$

and so on, all between 0 and 14.

Clearly, because of the modulus arithmetic each of the numbers genera-ted by Eq. (3-1) must be one of the integers 0, 1, 2, ..., $m-1$.   Thus even-tually the series will repeat itself.   The period of this generator will never be greater than m (but it can be much shorter than m, if a and x_0 are not chosen properly).   With a proper choice of m, a, and x_0 it is possible to obtain a generator with period almost equal to m.

A great deal of analytic and experimental study has been conducted on sequences generated by the congruential generator [Eq. (3-1)] with various combinations of m, a, and the seed x_0.   [It can be shown that if x_0 is odd, and $m = 2^r$ $(r > 2)$ and $a = k.8 \pm 3$ (k being any non-negative integer), then the period of the sequence generated is maximum and is equal to 2^{r-2}.] The following choice of the three parameters leads to a good random se-quence.

(1) Choose m be one more than the largest integer that can be held in one word of the computer being used.   For example, in the IBM 360/370 system a word is 32 bits long, of which the most significant bit is reserved for the sign.   Thus the largest integer one computer word can hold is $2^{31} - 1 = 2,147,483,647$, and therefore, m should be 2,147,483,648.   In case we are using an IBM 1130/1800 system, (which has 16-bit words), we would choose $m = (2^{15} - 1) + 1$ $= 32,768$.

This choice of m makes the division of the product $x_i . a$ in Eq. (3-1) unnecessary, for the modulo operation.   A machine word cannot hold an integer larger than $(m - 1)$.   Therefore, as soon as the product exceeds $(m - 1)$ an overflow would automatically occur, and we would be left with only the remainder. (For most FOR-TRAN environments no action is taken when an integer overflow occurs.)

(2) The seed x_0 must be relatively prime to m. Since m is a power of 2, any odd positive integer for x_0 would do. (It is not difficult to see that if x_0 is even, every x_i would also be even.)

(3) Lastly, the *constant multiplier a* must be properly selected. Clearly, a must also be relatively prime to m, i.e., a must also be an odd number. It has been found that the best choice for a is that it satisfies the relation

$$a = k.8 \pm 3 \qquad \qquad \dots (3\text{-}2)$$

and is close to the integer $2^{b/2}$, where b is the number of bits in the computer word. Thus for an IBM 360/370 system, a 32-bit binary machine, we might pick

$$a = 2^{16} + 3 = 65,539.$$

The subprogram to generate random numbers should be tailored to the machine being used. The following FORTRAN Function (actually an assembly-laguage equivalent of it) has been used throughout this book for generating uniformly distributed pseudo-random numbers in the range (0, 1), on the IBM 7044 computer—a 36-bit binary machine.

```
FUNCTION RNDY1 (DUM)
INTEGER A, X
DATA A, X/189277, 11750920161/
X = A*X
AX = X
RNDY1 = AX/34359738368.0
RETURN
END
```

Notice that the seed x_0 is supplied by the program itself. The user must, however, put some dummy argument (DUM) just to comply with the FORTRAN requirement for using and defining a function. The third statement in this program assigns a value 189277 (which is equal to $23,660 \times 8 - 3$ and lies between 2^{17} and 2^{18}) to the multiplier A. The same statement sets the value of the seed as 11,750,920,161, a large odd number. The fifth statement converts an INTEGER variable into a REAL one. The sixth statement simply puts a decimal point behind the most significant bit, by dividing the generated number with $2^{35} = 34,359,738,368$. Thus all generated integers (which lie between 0 and $2^{35}-1$) are put into the range (0, 1). The sequence of the first 250 numbers (each 8-digit long) produced by this program on the IBM 7044 is shown in Table 3-1 (page 46).

It should be noted that the least significant digits of the pseudo-random number generated by the multiplicative congruential method are not random. Therefore, low-order digits should not be used as random numbers.

0.12605673	0.63945656	0.41933851	0.13560773	0.42469418
0.84082449	0.74020635	0.03859064	0.32124565	0.41372764
0.12712769	0.34750068	0.88700985	0.56569849	0.71384876
0.15439663	0.73127418	0.38438318	0.89630192	0.34040167
0.20715574	0.81669794	0.13634698	0.34709622	0.33082132
0.86722385	0.52967285	0.88980526	0.67189881	0.99240244
0.95817188	0.90184278	0.09789246	0.79209450	0.27209922
0.12377563	0.88041454	0.22506470	0.57232984	0.87676947
0.29604600	0.69995449	0.28802593	0.68407930	0.47963840
0.51830582	0.37002663	0.52974694	0.91286987	0.27119800
0.54527316	0.66856805	0.55586741	0.91606059	0.20258154
0.02639124	0.25470810	0.38522433	0.10507539	0.35481164
0.68261174	0.70277291	0.74959149	0.42932156	0.69763737
0.71125819	0.81837045	0.70498065	0.62469626	0.63484096
0.79334503	0.96866811	0.59469365	0.83042011	0.42833864
0.65197936	0.69861210	0.20331260	0.39948643	0.59382989
0.33934862	0.88904662	0.07919170	0.16682845	0.78911820
0.92783065	0.00392972	0.80648247	0.58523636	0.78326067
0.23121197	0.10729789	0.02209292	0.68182824	0.40602278
0.77483593	0.62212986	0.87479187	0.98204138	0.84778971
0.09363551	0.04897409	0.66796139	0.72914251	0.90816759
0.23804685	0.79422058	0.69047086	0.25541778	0.71086777
0.92045329	0.63845453	0.75833005	0.43842954	0.62897794
0.05765601	0.95628558	0.86598516	0.07463225	0.16863216
0.18916636	0.84191151	0.48626862	0.46544028	0.14011042
0.67987362	0.44022211	0.92160124	0.91977078	0.45585227
0.35106367	0.27858218	0.19989099	0.76659736	0.24995090
0.95586113	0.52900933	0.30106957	0.54588907	0.24663635
0.58810474	0.70143276	0.09021481	0.58824246	0.76899630
0.31515973	0.48961480	0.82133635	0.08330946	0.56481367
0.23799234	0.47691497	0.03482086	0.78706795	0.86249388
0.25522759	0.71299479	0.51752671	0.90400832	0.98564532
0.99052353	0.32290863	0.17745147	0.48154996	0.33268388
0.40715661	0.38214801	0.82930494	0.35132289	0.34303564
0.75762388	0.77537080	0.86128480	0.40578150	0.10512107
0.00062777	0.82209201	0.11036270	0.12014770	0.19596767
0.17269229	0.67891822	0.60637572	0.97821812	0.19208509
0.28993362	0.76619879	0.81046108	0.64363914	0.08571769
0.38826279	0.21580850	0.58591397	0.03974269	0.37728143
0.69869744	0.35779788	0.91041011	0.69644971	0.91276737
0.87077474	0.63280492	0.41776729	0.73938178	0.96613230
0.62500039	0.20058468	0.06585702	0.21992429	0.61047640
0.14368453	0.17746056	0.20349902	0.68321339	0.58121061
0.80224132	0.83240682	0.46702461	0.01775690	0.97275453
0.06149900	0.34568924	0.02292932	0.99374360	0.80903049
0.86544868	0.53069273	0.92984154	0.61757918	0.53642869
0.61381547	0.15235440	0.18459393	0.38454978	0.42872409
0.60918928	0.52038404	0.73048838	0.65108073	0.60698931
0.11636278	0.79725136	0.34739572	0.01953820	0.13135707
0.87292619	0.85298774	0.96149679	0.22879631	0.88016954

Table 3-1:   First 250 pseudo-random numbers generated by RNDY1.

Random number generators are used so frequently that almost every computer manufacturer provides one or more subprograms tailored to this particular system.   For example, RANDU is an IBM supplied subroutine that forms part of their Scientific Subroutine Package.   FPMCRV is supplied by ICL as a PLAN scientific subroutine.   On the GE 225 computer RAND is the system pseudo-random number generator.   And so on. Even some pocket calculators have a built-in function that generates random numbers.

For the purposes of illustration, for sampling, or for hand simulation many textbooks on statistics or simulation provide tables of random numbers.

The tables of random numbers encountered frequently in textbooks are of two-digit integers in the range of 00 to 99.   Tables of five-digit random numbers would range from 00000 to 99999.   Actually the number of digits in a random number table is not too important.   If there are too many digits the numbers can be truncated.   If there are too few, the successive numbers can be run together to give the required number of digits.

Tests for randomness.   It is obvious that the sequence of numbers generated by the multiplicative congruence method (by any arithmetic method for that matter) is not truly 'random' in the sense that the entire sequence is predetermined and predictable.   If the process is started with the same x_0, exactly the same sequence would result.   Since m is finite, one of the numbers generated will eventually be exactly the same as a previously generated number.   Once this happens the subsequence of numbers will also be repeated.   For these reasons the name pseudo-random is used for these generators.

This lack of true unpredictability is not a serious drawback for computer simulation provided the generated sequence possesses some of the important 'random like' characteristics.   How random is a given sequence of random numbers is a difficult question to answer and one that has been discussed at great lengths.   A bewildering variety of tests have been proposed in the literature for testing the randomness of a sequence.   For most simulation purposes a random number sequence is adequate if (i) its uniformity is assured, and (ii) the successive numbers in the sequence are independent. For these characteristics the following two tests would suffice.

(i) **Frequency test:**   The *frequency test* or *uniformity test* counts how often numbers in a given range occur in the sequence to ensure that the numbers are uniformly distributed.   There should be no favoured numbers, that is, no number should occur more frequently than what is expected from chance variation.   For example, if we have a sequence of 5,000 3-digit numbers (from 000 to 999), we should expect that in the range 00 to 99 there are about 500 numbers; similarly in the range 100 to 199 there should be about 500 numbers, and so on.   Clearly, we do not expect that there be exactly 500 numbers in each of the 10 ranges (namely, 00 to 99, 100 to 199, ..., 900 to 999).   In fact, if we found that there are exactly 500 numbers in each range, we should suspect some nonrandomness. On the other hand, deviation from 500 should not be too much, otherwise we would suspect some nonuniformity. Then how much deviation should we allow from the expected value of 500 and still accept the sequence as uniformly distributed? A neat quantitative answer to this question is provided by the *chi-square goodness of fit test* (or simply *chi-square test*).

Chi-square test: The chi-square test is a very important and useful statistical test for determining how well certain observed data fit the theoretically expected data. The testing is performed by first dividing the observed data (in our case, the generated random numbers) into k non-overlapping classes; k must be 3 or more (in our example, $k = 10$). Then we count O_i, the number of times the observed data falls in each class i, for i, $i = 1, 2, ..., k$. Next, we determine the expected number of occurrences E_i in each class i. Then to measure how far the observed frequency deviates from the expected we compute the chi-square statistic, defined by

$$\text{chi}^2 = \sum_{i=1}^{k} \frac{(O_i - E_i)^2}{E_i} \qquad \ldots (3\text{-}3)$$

Intuitively we can see that this sum measures the discrepancy between the observed frequencies and their expected values. The more the actual occurrences depart from their expected values the larger the values of chi^2. Conversely, the closer the O_i's are to E_i's the smaller the values of chi^2, becoming zero when the two sets of frequencies are identically equal.

In our example, $E_i = 500$, for $i = 1, 2, ..., 10$. Suppose by actual frequency count of numbers generated we found the occurrences as shown in the third column of the table below. Then the chi^2 statistic can be calculated as follows:

i	Range	O_i No. of observed occurrences	No. of expected occurrences	$(O_i - E_i)^2$	$\dfrac{(O_i - E_i)^2}{E_i}$
1	000–099	468	500	1024	2.048
2	100–199	519	500	361	.722
3	200–299	480	500	400	.800
4	300–399	495	500	25	.050
5	400–499	508	500	64	.128
6	500–599	426	500	5476	10.952
7	600–699	497	500	9	.018
8	700–799	515	500	225	.450
9	800–899	463	500	1369	2.738
10	900–999	529	500	841	1.682

Total = chi^2 = 19.588.

The question now arises : how large or small a computed value of chi^2 can we accept before concluding that the discrepancy between the observed frequency and those expected is too great (or too small) to have arisen by mere chance?   For this purpose there are statistical tables which give those critical values of chi^2 which can be exceeded by chance with various probabilities, such as .001, .01, .05, .1, etc.   These are called chi^2-tables.   To read a chi^2-table we must have another parameter, called the *degree of freedom*. The degree of freedom is defined by

$$v = k - 1,$$

where k is the number of sets into which data is divided.   For our example, $v = 9$.

Now we read the chi^2 tables and find the following row of entries for $v = 9$.

.995	.99	.95	.90	.75	.50	.25	.10	.05	.01	.005
1.73	2.09	3.33	4.17	5.90	8.34	11.4	14.7	16.9	21.7	23.6

This means that there is a 99.5% probability of chi^2 exceeding 1.73; a 99% probability of chi^2 exceeding 2.09, ..., and a .5% probability of chi^2 exceeding 23.6.   Thus the probability of the chi^2 statistic (for $v = 9$) falling below 1.73 and above 23.6% is only 1%.   That is, 990 out of 1,000 sequences from a perfectly uniform random number generator would have given

$$1.73 \leqslant \text{chi}^2 \leqslant 23.6.$$

Likewise, if we take 1 as the cutoff point, we would reject all sequences with chi^2 below 2.09 and above 21.7.   In particular, the random-number sequence whose chi^2 we have just calculated and found to be 19.588, is barely acceptable.

The frequency test can be performed on the occurrence of each digit also. The test can be repeated on several sets of N (say 10,000) numbers.   We can then obtain a value of the chi-square for each set, and see if these values themselves pass a chi-square test.

(ii) **Independence test:** A sequence may be uniformly distributed and yet be far from being random because the adjacent terms may be related. One of the most effective method of determining correlation between adjacent terms is the poker test, which can be explained as follows:

Suppose we are given five independent decimal digits.   We could treat these digits as a hand of poker in a card game and classify accordingly, i.e., five of a kind (*a a a a a*); four of a kind (*a a a a b*); full house (*a a a b b*); three of a kind (*a a a b c*); two pairs (*a a b b c*); one pair (*a a b c d*); and bust (*a b c d e*).   It is fairly easy to compute the probabilities associated with these seven hands.   They are approximately 0.0001, 0.0045, 0.0090, 0.0720,

0.1080, 0.5040, 0.3024, respectively. If we generated $5n$ random digits we can form n random poker hands and then compare the observed frequencies of these seven types of poker hands with the expected distribution. To measure the amount of deviation between the expected and actual distribution we once again use the chi-square test, with degree of freedom $\nu = 6$.

Although there are a very large number of tests for randomness, for most simulation purposes, a sequence of pseudorandom numbers that passes both the frequency test and poker test will be adequate. The multiplicative congruential generator, with the values of a, m, and x_0 suggested has been found to pass both these tests.

3-4. Generation of non-uniformly distributed random numbers

In the last section we learned how to generate numbers which had randomness properties and were uniformly distributed between 0 and 1. These numbers were referred to as pseudorandom numbers. From these numbers we can readily obtain uniformly distributed random numbers y_i's between any arbitrary interval (A, B), using the relation

$$y_i = A + (B - A).u_i \qquad \qquad ...(3\text{-}4)$$

where u_i's are the previously generated uniform radom numbers in the interval (0, 1).

Many simulation experiments require random samples from nonuniform distributions, such as, normal, exponential, beta, gamma, chi-square, lognormal, Cauchy, and Weibull distributions. It can be shown that samples from any arbitrary distribution can be generated using the uniformly distributed random numbers in the interval (0, 1) $r_1, r_2, \ldots$. In fact, at present there are no fast practical methods of generating samples from arbitrary distributions on the computer, except via the uniform random numbers. There are many special techniques and tricks for converting uniform random numbers into samples from various other distributions. We will briefly discuss two most commonly used general methods:

The inverse transformation method: Suppose we are given a probability distribution function $F(z)$, which is continuous, and we wish to generate n random samples $z_1, z_2, \ldots, z_n$ from this distribution. By definition, every probability distribution function increases monotonically from 0 to 1, and the probability that a random sample z lies in the interval (z_1, z_2) is equal to $F(z_2) - F(z_1)$ for all pairs $z_1 \leqslant z_2$. Moreover, since $F(z)$ is continuous it takes all values between 0 and 1; and therefore for any number u, $0 \leqslant u \leqslant 1$, there exists a unique z_u such that $F(z_u) = u$. Symbolically this value of z may be represented by $F^{-1}(u)$, the inverse function. (See Fig. 3-2.)

Let us generate n uniformly distributed random numbers $u_1, u_2, \ldots, u_n$ in the interval (0, 1), using the method given in Sec. 3-3. Next we take their inverse transforms $F^{-1}(u_1)$, $F^{-1}(u_2)$, $\ldots$, $F^{-1}(u_n)$. That these are the

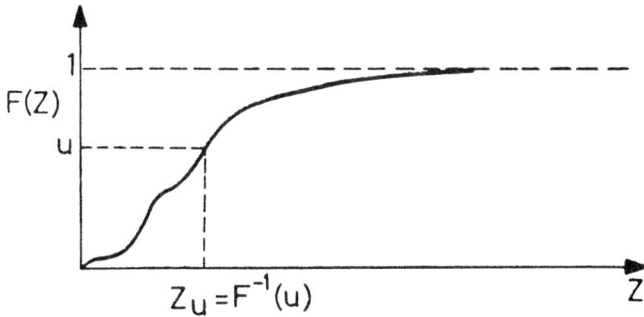

Fig. 3-2: A continuous probability distribution function $F(z)$.

desired numbers $z_i = F^{-1}(u_i)$, for $i = 1, 2, \ldots, n$ can be seen as follows:

Consider any two numbers a and b in the range $(0, 1)$ such that $a \leqslant b$. By definition, the probability that a uniform random number in the range $(0, 1)$ lies between a and b is $(b - a)$ for all $0 \leqslant a \leqslant b \leqslant 1$. Let $F^{-1}(a) = z_a$ and $F^{-1}(b) = z_b$. The inverse transform method would hold if the actual probability of the random variable z lying between z_a and z_b equals the generated probability $(b - a)$. That is, the actual probability of z lying between z_a and z_b should be $F(z_b) - F(z_a)$, which indeed is the case because $(b - a) = F(z_b) - F(z_a)$.

Thus, to generate n samples from any continuous probability distribution function $F(z)$, all we need to do is to generate n uniform random numbers $u_1, u_2, \ldots, u_n$ in the interval $(0, 1)$ and apply inverse transform $F^{-1}(u_i)$ to each. To illustrate how the inverse transform method works, let us generate a random sample from an exponential distribution function.

Exponential distribution function: There are many phenomena that are governed by the exponential probability function. For example, the probability that the waiting time w of a telephone call exceeds time t is given by

$$Pr[w > t] = \lambda e^{-\lambda t} \qquad \ldots(3\text{-}5)$$

where λ is a positive constant depending on characteristics of the telephone system. For a radioactive material expression (3-5) describes the probability that no particle is emitted from the radioactive substance during time t. Constant λ depends on the property of the particular radioactive material. We will see in Chapter 4 that the probability of a nonarrival of a customer in a queueing system is also given by Eq. (3-5). The *probability density function* and the *probability distribution function* (also called the *cumulative probability distribution function*) of this distribution is given in Fig. 3-3. You may recall that the cumulative distribution function $F(t)$ by definition is the integral of the density function, i.e., $F(t) = \int_0^t \lambda e^{-\lambda t}\, dt = 1 - e^{-\lambda t}$. The average or expected value of t is given by

$$Ave = \int_0^\infty t . \lambda\, e^{-\lambda t} . dt = \frac{1}{\lambda}.$$

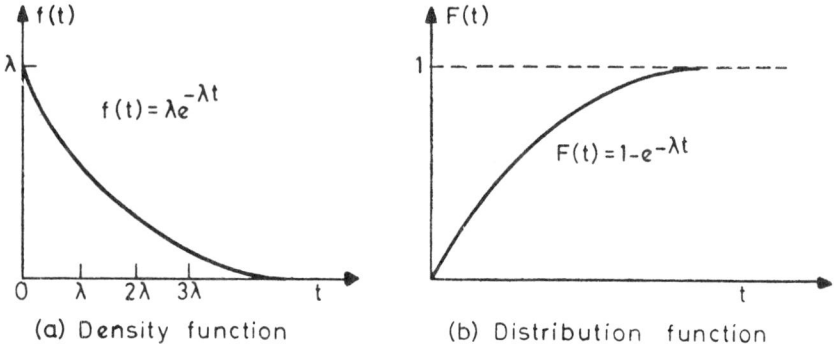

(a) Density function   (b) Distribution function

Fig. 3-3   The exponential distribution.

Now suppose that in order to perform a simulation experiment on some stochastic system governed by an exponential distribution function we require n random samples t_1, t_2, ..., t_n from the curve in Fig. 3-3(b).   The inverse of F can be obtained by equating u, a generated uniform random number, to

$$u = 1 - e^{-\lambda t}$$

so that

$$-\lambda t = \log_e (1 - u)$$

which gives the corresponding sample t as

$$t = -\frac{\log_e (1 - u)}{\lambda} = F^{-1}(u).$$

Since $(1 - u)$ is as good a uniformly distributed random number between 0 and 1 as u is, we can replace $(1 - u)$ with u itself.   That is,

$$t_k = -\frac{1}{\lambda} \log_e u_k. \qquad \qquad ...(3\text{-}6)$$

We obtain the required n samples t_1, t_2, ..., t_n from the exponential distribution $(1 - e^{-\lambda t})$ by transforming n uniform random numbers u_1, u_2, ..., u_n in the interval (0, 1), according to Eq. (3-6).   To take a specific set of numbers, suppose we need 5 random samples from an exponential distribution with the expected value $\lambda = 3.80$.   First we generate 5 random numbers u_k's in the range (0, 1).   Suppose these turn out to be .135, .639, .424, .010, .843. Then we take their natural logarithms, $\log_e u_k$, which are -2.00, $-.448$, $-.858$, -4.61, $-.171$.   On multiplying these with $-1/3.8$ we get the desired samples, which are:

.526, .118, .226, 1.213, .045.

A pair of FORTRAN statements is sufficient to generate samples (T) from an exponential distribution with any specified LAMDA, λ:

```
RN = RNDY1 (DUM)
T = -1.0/LAMDA*ALOG (RN)
```

where RANDY is the uniform random number generator in the range (0, 1) as described in Sec. 3-3, and ALOG is the FORTRAN-supplied function for the natural logarithm of a floating-point number.

Look-up tables: Although the two FORTRAN statements for generating samples from an exponential distribution appear to be extremely simple, in reality the computation of the natural logarithm on a digital computer can be time consuming, if thousands of such samples are required. Therefore, sometimes it is more convenient to store the values of $\log_e (1 - u)$ for many values of u; $0 \leqslant u \leqslant 1$ along with its slope in the form of a look-up table. In doing so we are trading off memory space for speed of execution. How justified the trade-off is depends on the length of the simulation run, the frequency with which the samples are required, and on the computer being used.

The inverse transformation method (also called the *probability-integral transformation method*), although simple in principle, is often difficult to apply for many probability distributions because we cannot find a mathematical expression for the inverse function F^{-1}. In such cases, the so-called *rejection method* (which does not require an explicit expression for F^{-1}) can be used.

The rejection method: The rejection method for obtaining samples from a given nonuniform distribution basically works by generating uniform random numbers repeatedly and accepting only those that meet a certain condition. This condition of acceptance is so designed that the accepted numbers appear to be drawn from the given distribution. For the rejection method to be applicable, the probability density function $f(t)$ of the distribution must be nonzero only over a finite interval, say (A, B). Let $f(t)$ be bounded by an upper limit C. See Fig. 3-4.

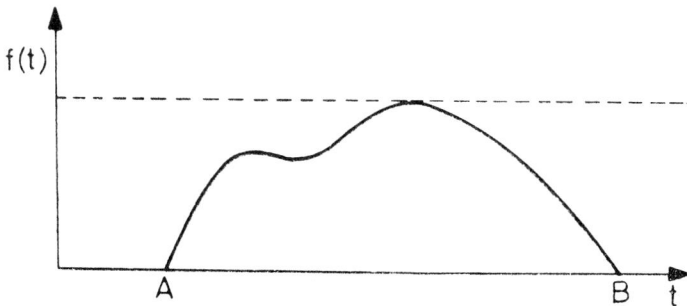

Fig. 3-4: Probability density function.

The rejection procedure consists of the following steps:

(1) Generate a pair of uniform random numbers u_1, u_2 in the interval (0, 1).

(2) Using u_1 locate a point p on the horizontal axis as

$$p = A + (B - A).u_1.$$

(3) Using u_2 locate a point q on the vertical axis as $q = C.u_2$.

(4) If $q > f(p)$ reject the pair and go to the Step (1), othwewise, accept p as the value of a sample from the desired distribution.

The procedure is repeated till the required number of samples have been generated. Fig. 3-5 illustrates how the rejection technique can be used to generate samples from a probability density function.

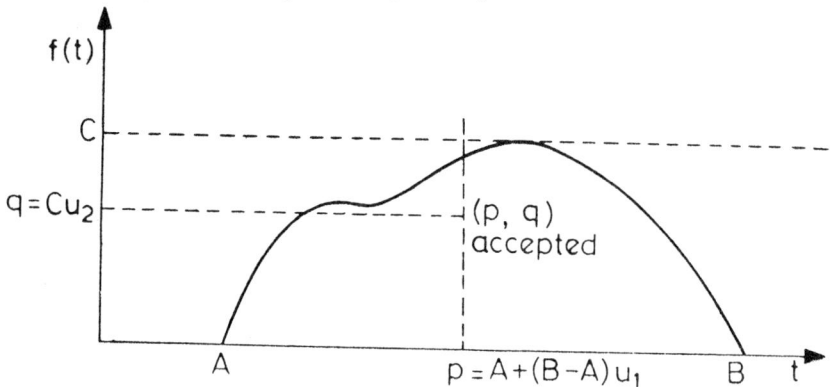

Fig. 3-5: Rejection method.

It is not difficult to see that this procedure does indeed work because all the points above the curve $f(t)$ in the interval (A, B) are rejected. The points that are accepted are within the boundary of the curve and therefore are distributed according to the density function $f(t)$. The restriction that this method works only for a finite interval should be noted.

There are several other methods available for sampling nonuniform distribution functions, and they are chosen according to the requirements of speed, accuracy and the function being sampled. Some of these are applicable for sampling only a specific distribution. Let us consider one such special method, used for the normal distribution only.

Normal distribution: The *normal* or *Gaussian* distribution is the most familiar and frequently encountered probability distribution. Its density function is a bell-shaped curve given by the expression

$$f(x) = \frac{1}{\sigma \sqrt{2\pi}} e^{-\frac{1}{2} \left(\frac{x - \mu}{\sigma} \right)^2} \qquad \ldots(3\text{-}7)$$

for $-\infty < x < \infty$.

The parameter μ is the expected value and σ is the standard deviation. Note that while a single parameter (λ) was sufficient to specify an exponential distribution, a normal distribution requires two parameters, μ and σ.

If the parameters of the normal distribution have values $\mu = 0$ and $\sigma = 1$, we call it the *standardized normal distribution*. It is expressed by

$$f(s) = \frac{1}{\sqrt{2\pi}} e^{-\frac{s^2}{2}} \qquad \qquad ...(3\text{-}8)$$

The density function and its integral, i.e., the (cumulative) distribution function are shown in Fig. 3-6.

There does not exist an explicit expression for the cumulative distribution function $F(s)$, although very extensive tables are available in handbooks of statistics.

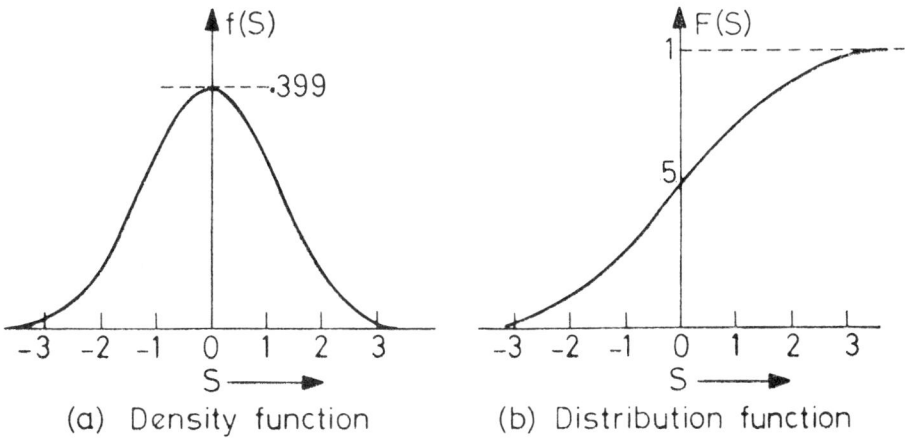

(a) Density function   (b) Distribution function

Fig. 3-6:   Standardized normal distribution.

One of the commonly used methods for generating random samples from a standardized normal distribution is to use the following relation, called the *Box-Muller transformation*.

$$s = (-2 \log_e r_1)^{1/2} \cos(2\pi r_2) \qquad \qquad ...(3\text{-}9)$$

where r_1 and r_2 are two uniform random numbers in the range (0, 1), and s is the desired sample from the standardized normal distribution. We will not derive Eq. (3-9) here; its derivation can be found in many textbooks on statistics.

A sample x from any normal distribution with specified μ and σ can be obtained from s, (a sample from the standardized normal distribution), as follows:

$$x = \sigma.s + \mu \qquad \qquad ...(3\text{-}10)$$

The following FORTRAN subroutine will generate a random sample from a normal distribution using Eqs. (3-9) and (3-10).

```
SUBROUTINE NORMAL (MU, SIGMA, X)
REAL MU, SIGMA, X, R1, R2, V
R1 = RNDY1 (DUM)
R2 = RNDY2 (DUM)
V = (−2.*ALOG (R1))**0.5*COS(6.283*R2)
X = SIGMA*V + MU
RETURN
END
```

Parameters μ and σ are MU and SIGMA in the subroutine. Functions RNDY1 and RNDY2 are two uniform pseudo-random number generators —each with its own seed. Observe that as in the case of exponential distribution, the generation of random samples may become quite time-consuming because of the evaluation of logarithmic and cosine functions. One may therefore resort to look-up tables.

Another commonly used procedure for generating normal samples, which is based on the Central Limit Theorem, will be given in a later chapter.

Multiple Sources of Randomness: In simulation experiments it is often necessary to deal simultaneously with several random variables which are independent. For example, in a queueing situation (with a single server) there may be one random variable for the arrival times of the customer and another one for the service times. Sometimes we need to add two random variables (e.g., two independent sources of delays) with different or same distribution. In all such cases it is best to employ different random number generators, such as RNDY1 and RNDY2 used in SUBROUTINE NORMAL. These different generators may sometimes have the same multiplier, a, and the same modulo, m, but differ only in their seeds, x_0.

3-5.   Monte Carlo computation vs. stochastic simulation

The term *Monte-Carlo computation* (or method or technique) was coined during World War II by S. Ulam and J. von Neumann at the Los Alamos Scientific Laboratory. In order to design nuclear shields they needed to know how far neutrons would travel through various materials. The problem was too difficult to solve analytically and too hazardous and time consuming to solve experimentally. Therefore, they simulated the experiment on a high-speed computer using random numbers. This technique was given the code name Monte Carlo, because it was based on a gambling-like principle.

Some people use the term Monte Carlo method to mean any computatation that involves random numbers. However, a more generally accepted meaning of Monte Carlo is restricted only to those computations in which random numbers are used to obtain solutions of problems which are inherently deterministic. And for those computations that employ random numbers to solve inherently stochastic problems the term 'stochastic simulation' is used. For example, the inventory problem in Chapter 1 would be a case of stochastic simulation and not Monte Carlo. But the following method of evaluating the constant π by making use of random numbers would be called a Monte Carlo method.

Deterministic problem through random numbers: Consider a quadrant of a unit circle as shown in Fig. 3-7 below. All points satisfying the equation $x^2 + y^2 \leqslant 1$; $x, y \geqslant 0$ lie in this quadrant. This equation can be rewritten as $y \leqslant \sqrt{1 - x^2}$.

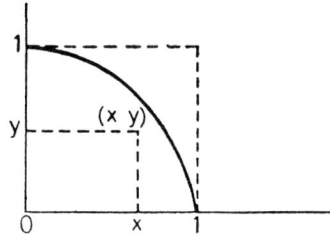

Fig. 3-7:   Monte Carlo evaluation of π.

Let us now generate a pair of uniform random numbers u_1 and u_2 in the range $(0, 1)$. We call this pair *acceptable* if

$$u_2 \leqslant \sqrt{1 - u_1^2}$$

else we will reject the pair; and generate and test another pair of uniformly distributed random numbers. Clearly all the rejected points like above the curve in Fig. 3-7 and those accepted lie below. If we generate a large number of random pairs and compute the ratio of the number of pairs accepted to those generated, the ratio will approach the area under the curve, which is $\pi/4$.

Thus by using random numbers we have solved a completely deterministic problem. Such an application is called a Monte Carlo technique. (Notice that we have used the rejection technique here; and the area under any curve can be evaluated by this method.)

3-6.   Remarks and references

In this chapter we started out with discussing simulation of those dynamic systems in which the changes occur at discrete moments in time. These changes are called events, and our object has been to simulate a sequence of these events and their effect on the state of the system. The passage of time is recorded by a number in the computer called CLOCK. At the beginning of the simulation CLOCK is set to zero and then allowed to run. There are two distinct methods of advancing the clock—(i) steps of fixed lengths or (ii) by updating the value of CLOCK each time an event takes place. In most simulations of discrete systems the latter strategy, called the next-event simulation model, is used.

We also observed that simulation in the study of discrete dynamic systems is used almost exclusively for stochastic systems—systems in which at least one of the variables is given by a probability function.   Complex, discrete, dynamic, stochastic systems (which defy an analytic solution) frequently arise in operations research, transportation and traffic engineering, econometrics, etc.

Simulation of a stochastic system requires one or more sequences of random numbers.   The idea of generating 'pseudorandom' numbers by means of an (deterministic) arithmetic process was first proposed by J. von Neumann and N. Metropolis in 1946.   It was D. H. Lehmer who first proposed the multiplicative congruential method in 1948.   Since that time an enormous amount of work has been done in generation, analysis, and testing of pseudorandom numbers.   A good account of these techniques can be found in

KNUTH, D. E., *The Art of Computer Programming, Vol. 2, Seminumerical Algorithms*, Addison-Wesley, Reading, Mass., 1969 (Chapter 3).

HULL, T. E. and A. R. DOBELL, 'Random Number Generators,' *SIAM Review*, 4, (July 1962), pp. 230–254.

JANSSON, B., *Random Number Generators*, Victor Pettersons, Stockholm, 1966.

REITMAN, J., *Computer Simulation Applications*, John Wiley and Sons, New York, 1971 (Chapter 4).

In many simulation experiments one needs random samples from distributions other than the uniform.   The generation of nonuniform stochastic variates from some of the commonly encountered distributions, along with flowcharts and FORTRAN programs, is given in Chapter 4 of

NAYLOR, T. H., J. L. BALINTFY, D. S. BURDICK, and K. CHU, *Computer Simulation Techniques*, John Wiley and Sons, New York, 1966.

Another good source of algorithms for stochastic variate generation is Chapter 8 of

FISHMAN, G. S., *Concepts and Methods in Discrete Event Digital Simulation*, John Wiley, New York, 1973.

The *Communications of the ACM* is a good source of lists for algorithms for generation of different stochastic variates.   For example, *CACM* Algorithm Numbers 121 (Sept. 1962), 200 (Aug. 1963), 267 (Oct. 1965), 334 (July 1968), give ALGOL procedures for generation of random normal deviates.   Likewise, Algorithm Numbers 342 (Dec. 1968) and 369 (Jan. 1970) give listings for random samples from a Poisson distribution.

A distinction is usually made between Monte Carlo techniques and the simulation methods.   The former is applied to the use of random numbers in estimating some quantity which is inherently deterministic, such as evaluation of π.   The term simulation (of a discrete dynamic, stochastic system) on the other hand is used when random numbers are used to study a system which is inherently stochastic, such as a queueing system, vehicular traffic pattern, etc.   Sometimes the dividing line between the two becomes fuzzy.

The concept of the Monte Carlo technique is quite old.   The first Monte Carlo method was proposed in 1777 by Comte de Buffon.   The application of the Monte Carlo method (as well as the discrete system simulation) to solve real problems began only since World War II.   A thorough survey of mathematical aspects of the Monte Carlo method with a comprehensive bibliography is given in

HALTON, J. H., 'A Retrospective and Prospective Survey of the Monte Carlo Method.' *SIAM Review*, 12, (January 1970), pp. 1–63.

3-7. Exercises

3-1.   Write a program to generate and print 5,000 uniformly distributed random numbers between .000 and .999 (3 significant digits).   Test the numbers for uniformity by dividing them into 10 ranges and using the chi-square test, as described in Sec. 3-3.

3-2.   Write a program to generate uniformly distributed random numbers between 0 and 1 (with as many significant digits as your computer word can hold).   Study and comment on the behaviour of the least significant digit of these numbers generated.

3-3.   Using a random number generator, write a program to simulate the following game of dice: A pair of six-sided fair dice, each carrying spots 1, 2, 3, 4, 5, and 6 are rolled.   If on the first roll the sum of the two dice faces is 7 or 11 the person rolling the dice wins.   If this sum is 2, 3, or 12, then the person rolling the dice loses.   If the sum is any of the other six numbers (4, 5, 6, 8, 9, 10) this number becomes the 'point' of the person rolling the dice, and the rolling continues till either (i) the 'point' is rolled again, in which case the person rolling the dice wins, or (ii) a 7 is rolled in which case he loses.   Run the program to simulate 100 rolls and find who won how man times.

3-4.   Write a computer program to simulate 10 dealings of the game of bridge, using random numbers.   Neatly print the cards (A, K, Q, J, 10, 9, 8, 7, 6, 5, 4, 3, 2, of clubs, diamonds, hearts and spades) of the four players—North, East, South and West, for each of the 10 dealings.

3-5.   The Prisoner's Dilemma (in its various forms) is probably the most frequently used game for live behavioural experiments.   Two prisoners A and B are charged with a joint crime and are held incommunicado.   If A confesses and B does not, A is given a reduced sentence of two years for cooperating with the authorities, and B gets a 10-year prison term, and vice versa.   If both confess each gets six years.   If neither confesses, each will receive only a one-year sentence.   Neither can control or even know the behaviour of the other.   Simulate this game on a computer and study the total penalty under varying probabilities of prisoners taking different actions. [Ref. Emshoff, J., "A Simulation Model of Prisoner's Dilemma," *Behavioral Science*, Vol. 15, No. 4, July 1970.]

3-6. The probability distribution function of the Weibull distribution is defined by

$$F(y) = 1 - e^{-\lambda y^c}, \quad y \geqslant 0, \quad c > 1, \quad \lambda \geqslant 0$$

Using the inverse transformation method, write a FUNCTION subprogram WEIB to generate N random samples from the Weibull distribution.

3-7. Write a FUNCTION subprogram ERLANG that uses the rejection technique to obtain random samples from an (a) Erlang distribution, described by the density function

$$g(y) = \frac{\lambda (\lambda y)^{n-1} e^{-\lambda y}}{(n-1)!}, \quad \lambda > 0, y \geqslant 0,$$

and n is a positive integer.

(Observe that when $n = 1$, Erlang distribution is the same as the exponential distribution. When n is allowed to have any fractional (positive) value, the more general distribution is called the *gamma* distribution. As n increases, the gamma distribution asymptotically approaches the normal distribution.)

3-8. Write a FUNCTION subprogram BETA that uses the rejection technique to generate random variates from a beta distribution.

3-9. A particle moves along a straight line from some initial position 0 and takes a sequence of N steps. Each step is of unit length and can go left or right, each with probability $1/2$. Simulate this experiment for various values of N (say 10, 25, 50, 100, 500), and determine how far the particle is from the origin at the end of each run. This problem, known as the *random-walk problem*, can be solved by statistical techniques, but we prefer to simulate.

3-10. Experiment with the random-walk problem in Exercise 3-9 by making the left and right steps non-equiprobable (.75 and .25; or .6 and .4; etc).

3-11. Instead of keeping the random-walk confined along a straight line (as in Exercises 3-9 and 3-10), let it take place along a 2-dimensional rectangular grid, and simulate.

3-12. Repeat the random-walk simulation on a 3-dimensional (cubic) grid.

3-13. The following is a simplified model of the molecular mixing of two different gases, due to T. Ehrenfest. There are two compartments, separated by a permeable membrane, and each contains M molecules initially. One transfer consists of picking one molecule from each side at random and exchanging them. With $M = 100$, find out what happens after N successive transfers, for various values of N. This problem can also be solved analytically, but we prefer a simulation.

3-14. Write a program to determine the approximate value of $\sqrt{3}$ using 1,000 random numbers. (Hint: Choose 1,000 random numbers x_i's uniformly distributed between 1 and 2. Determine p, the number of these numbers for which $x_i{}^2 < 3$.   Then estimate the value of 3 as $1 + p/1000$.

3-15.   We wish to study the effect of birth rate and death rate on growth of a population, year by year for a given period of N years.   We start with a fixed population P_0 (say, 1,000).   The birth rate B is constant (say, 20 per thousand per year).   The death rate D, on the other hand, is proportional to the current population (say, 15 per thousand, per thousand per year).

Assume that the population is constant throughout the year except on January 1, when all the births and deaths take place.   The number of births on January 1 is equal to the integer closest to the birth rate times the number of people alive on December 31.   Likewise, the number of deaths is determined by the number of people alive on December 31.   Write a computer program to simulate this model of population growth, and plot the population for a 20-year period for several values of parameters, B and D.

3-16.   Write a program to simulate the population-growth problem using the following next-event model (instead of the fixed-time-step model of Exercise 3-15): Let $P(t)$ denote the population at time t.   Suppose the last birth occurred at time t_B; then since the time between births is inversely proportional to the population and the birth rate B, the next birth would occur at time

$$t_B + \frac{1}{B \times P(T_B)}.$$

Likewise, if the last death occurred at time t_D, the next death would occur at time

$$t_D + \frac{1}{D \times [P(t_D)]^2}.$$

Move the clock from event to event (births and deaths), and trace through a period of 20 years.

4

Simulation of Queueing Systems

A queue is a waiting line for service.   People, cars, trucks, ships, T.V.'s,
arrive at a certain place to be serviced in some way.   People form queues
to be served in banks, post offices, ships, and railway ticket counters; T.V.'s
form queues in repair shops to be serviced; etc.   When the arrival rate and
service rate do not exactly correspond, queues are likely to develop or the
service facility remains idle.   While long queues mean wastage of time,
indiscriminate duplication of sercive facilities to eliminate all queueing is
obviously not a solution because of the loss in terms of the idle time of the
service facilities. A queueing problem is essentially a problem of balancing
the cost of waiting against the cost of idle time for the service facilities in the
system.   This balancing requires an analysis of the queueing system, which
means determining various statistics such as the facility, idle time, average
waiting time, queue length, etc., for various conditions.   The problem arises
due to the stochastic nature of the times between the arrivals of customers
as well as the time it takes to serve each customer.   (The term 'customer'
in the queueing context does not necessarily mean a person.   A customer
could, for example, be a machine waiting for the setter in a workshop.)

Since waiting lines and servicing play such a prominent role in our daily
lives (including numerous business and industrial situations), a great deal
of research has been done on mathematical analysis of queues.   There are
dozens of text-books on queueing theory.   Unfortunately, there are so many
different combinations of parameters that one often finds that the existing
formulas are inadequate.   One therefore usually ends up solving most
queueing problems in practice by simulation.

The important parameters in a queueing system are: (i) The arrival
pattern of customers, i.e., frequency distribution of interarrival times;
(ii) The service pattern, i.e, frequency distribution of service times; (iii) The
number of *servers* (or *service counters* or *service channels*); and (iv) the *queue*
discipline, i.e., the order in which service is provided, such as, first-come-
first-served, last-come-first-served (in a stack of dishes the last dish put is
picked first), or some priority system (such as, giving hospital beds to emer-
gency patients ahead of regular patients, unloading a ship carrying perishable
goods ahead of other ships, etc.).

The earliest work on mathematical theory of queueing was done by
A. K. Erlang around 1918, in connection with telephone traffic.   Erlang
investigated the arrival rate of telephone calls, the time they took, and how

the number of subscribers waiting varied with the number of lines. Since then a great deal of analytical work on queueing theory (as a branch of statistics) has accumulated. In order to get an idea of the type of mathematical formulas available and the approach taken in their development, we will make an analytical study of a very elementary queueing situation.

4-1. Rudiments of queuing theory

In the simplest model of a queue, we assume that customers arrive randomly. There is only one service counter, which can serve only one customer at a time. The amount of time it takes to serve a customer also varies randomly. If the service counter is busy, arriving customers join the queue. From the queue the customers are served on a first-come-first-served basis. As soon as a customer is served he gets out of the system.

Poisson arrival pattern: To facilitate the analysis, let us assume that the interarrival times of the customers are such that there is a fixed long-term average time gap between two arrivals. Let this time be α. Let us further assume that the customers arrive independently, and that the probability of and arrival during any period depends only on the length of that period.

Therefore, the probability of a customer arriving during a very small slice of time h is h/α. Hence the probability of a customer not arriving during time h is $(1 - h/\alpha)$. Now let us define that

$f(t) =$ Probability that the next customer does not arrive during the interval t given that the previous customer arrived at $t = 0$, and likewise;

$f(t + h) =$ Probability that the next customer does not arrive during the interval $(t + h)$ given that the previous customer arrived at $t = 0$.

Since the arrivals of customers in different periods are independent events (i.e., the queue has no memory), we can write

$$f(t + h) = f(t) \cdot \left(1 - \frac{h}{\alpha}\right)$$

or

$$\frac{f(t + h) - f(t)}{h} = - \frac{f(t)}{\alpha}$$

Taking limits on both sides as h tends to zero, we get

$$\frac{df(t)}{dt} = - \frac{f(t)}{\alpha}$$

The solution of this differential equation is

$$f(t) = ce^{-t/\alpha} \qquad \qquad \ldots(4\text{-}1)$$

Since at time $t = 0$ an arrival has just taken place, the probability of a nonarrival at $t = 0$ is 1.   That is, $f(0) = 1$, and therefore the constant c in Eq. (4-1) is unity.   Thus

$$f(t) = e^{-t/\alpha} \qquad \qquad \dots(4\text{-}2)$$

Thus two very simple assumptions, namely, (i) constancy of a long-term average and (ii) statistical independence of arrivals have led to Eq. (4-2) which gives the probability that the next customer does not arrive before time t has elapsed since the arrival of the last customer.

The probability that a customer arrives during an infinitesimal interval between t and $t + \delta t$ is given by the product of (i) the probability that no customer arrives before time t and (ii) the probability that exactly one customer arrives during δt.   This product is

$$(e^{-t/\alpha}) \cdot \left(\frac{\delta t}{\alpha}\right)$$

In other words, the probability density function of the interarrival time is

$$\frac{1}{\alpha} \cdot e^{-t/\alpha} \qquad \qquad \dots(4\text{-}3)$$

The integral

$$\frac{1}{\alpha} \int_0^t e^{-t/\alpha} \, dt = 1 - e^{-t/\alpha} \qquad \qquad \dots(4\text{-}4)$$

is the probability distribution function.

The curves for Eqs. (4-3) and (4-4) are shown in Fig. 4-1.   These are the curves for the exponential distribution, discussed in Chapter 2.   The curve in Fig. 4-1(b) gives the probability that the next customer arrives by time t, given that the preceding customer arrived at time zero.   Customarily the inverse of the average interarrival time is denoted by λ, which is nothing but the average number of customers arriving at the system per unit time.

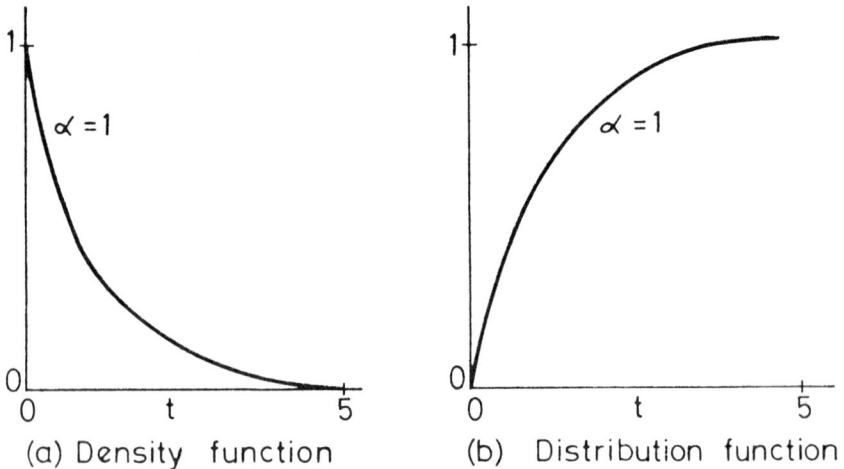

(a) Density function   (b) Distribution function

Fig. 4-1:   Interarrival time of customers.

Having found that the interarrival time is governed by exponential distribution, we will now find the probability that exactly k customers have arrived during the time interval t (assuming that no customer had arrived by time $t = 0$).

Let $q_k(t)$ be the probability that exactly k arrivals take place between the start time zero and t, for $k = 1, 2, 3, \ldots$. Then we can write

$q_1(t + h) =$ (Probability that no arrivals take place between time zero and t).(probability that one arrival takes place during time h) + (probability that one arrival takes place between time zero and t) . (probability that no arrivals take place during time h)

$$= f(t) \cdot \frac{h}{\alpha} + q_1(t) \cdot \left(1 - \frac{h}{\alpha}\right)$$

where $f(t)$, as previously determined, is $e^{-t/\alpha}$. Therefore,

$$\frac{q_1(t + h) - q_1(t)}{h} = \frac{1}{\alpha} [f(t) - q_1(t)]$$

as $h \to 0$ this expression becomes

$$\frac{dq_1(t)}{dt} = \frac{1}{\alpha} [f(t) - q_1(t)]$$

The solution of this differential equation can easily be seen to be

$$q_1(t) = \frac{t}{\alpha} e^{-t/\alpha} = \frac{t}{\alpha} f(t)$$

Extending the same argument (since at most one arrival can take place in the interval h) we get

$$q_2(t) = \left(\frac{t}{\alpha}\right)^2 \frac{1}{2!} \cdot f(t).$$

It can be seen that, in general

$$\frac{dq_k(t)}{dt} = \frac{q_{k-1}(t) - q_k(t)}{\alpha}.$$

We have already solved this differential equation for $k = 1$ and 2 (for $k = 0$, $q_0(t) = f(t)$). Solving it successively for $k = 3, 4, \ldots$, we will get

$$q_k(t) = \left(\frac{t}{\alpha}\right)^k \frac{1}{k!} e^{-t/\alpha} \qquad \ldots(4\text{-}5)$$

Expression (4-5) is known as the Poisson distribution formula. It is one of the most important and widely encountered distributions. Curves for $q_k(t)$ for several values of k are shown in Fig. 4-2. Note that for $k = 0$, we get the negative exponential curve,

$$q_0(t) = e^{-t/\alpha} = f(t)$$

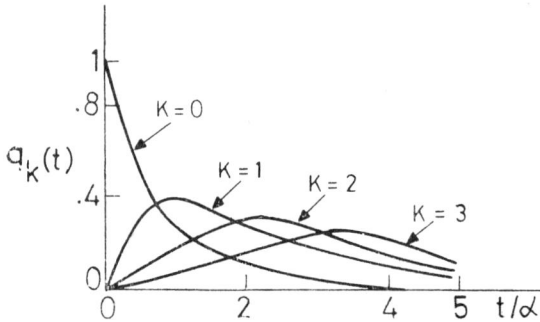

Fig. 4-2: Poisson distribution.

We have thus seen that if the interarrival time is distributed exponentially, the number of arrivals is given by Poisson distribution. Therefore, the two terms negative exponential arrival or Poisson arrival are often used interchangeably. It should be emphasized here that Poisson arrival pattern is just one of many possible arrival patterns in a queueing situation. It results from the three assumptions that (i) the successive arrivals are statistically independent of each other, that (ii) there is a long-term inter-arrival time constant α, and that (iii) the probability of an arrival taking place during a time interval h is directly proportional to h.

Exponential service time: Let us make similar assumptions about the servicing process, namely, (i) the statistical independence of successive servicings, (ii) the long-term constancy of service time, and (iii) the probability of completing the service for a customer during a time interval h is proportional to h. Therefore, as in the case of interarrival time, we will get

$$g(t) = e^{-t/\beta} \qquad \qquad \ldots (4\text{-}6)$$

where $g(t)$ is the probability that a customer's service could not be completed in time t, (given that the previous customer's service was completed at time zero) and β is the long-term average service time.

Operating characteristics: Now we have completely defined the four parameters of the queueing system. These are (i) Poisson arrival pattern, (ii) negative exponential service times, (iii) a single server, and (iv) the first-come-first-served queue discipline. For this particular queueing system we will now derive some interesting and useful statistics about the system:

Clearly, at any given time t the probability of the service counter being busy is

$$\frac{\text{average service time}}{\text{average arrival gap}} = \frac{\beta}{\alpha} = \rho \qquad \qquad \ldots (4\text{-}7)$$

ρ is an important ratio. It is called the *utilization factor* of the service facility.

It immediately follows from Eq. (4-7) that the probability of finding the service counter free is

$$(1 - \rho) \qquad \qquad \dots(4\text{-}8)$$

Let $P_n(t)$ be the probability of exactly n customers being in the system at time t.   Let $h > 0$ be a very small slice of time.   The probability of one customer arriving and no customer departing during interval h is

$$\frac{h}{\alpha} \cdot \left(1 - \frac{h}{\beta}\right)$$

Likewise, the probability of one customer arriving and one customer departing during interval h is

$$\frac{h}{\alpha} \cdot \frac{h}{\beta}$$

The probability of no customer arriving and one customer departing is

$$\left(1 - \frac{h}{\alpha}\right) \cdot \frac{h}{\beta}$$

and finally of no customer arriving and no customer departing is

$$\left(1 - \frac{h}{\alpha}\right) \cdot \left(1 - \frac{h}{\beta}\right)$$

Since h is so small that no more than one departure and no more than one arrival can take place, these are the only possible changes that could occur during an interval h.

For the queueing system to have n customers at time $(t + h)$, it must have had either n or $(n + 1)$ or $(n - 1)$ customers at time t.   The probability that there are n customers in the system at time $(t + h)$ can therefore be expressed as the sum of these three probabilities.   Thus for any $n > 0$ we can write

$$P_n(t + h) = P_n(t) \cdot \left(1 - \frac{h}{\alpha}\right) \cdot \left(1 - \frac{h}{\beta}\right) + P_n(t) \cdot \frac{h}{\alpha} \cdot \frac{h}{\beta}$$

$$+ P_{n+1}(t)\left(1 - \frac{h}{\alpha}\right) \cdot \frac{h}{\beta} + P_{n-1}(t) \cdot \frac{h}{\alpha} \cdot \left(1 - \frac{h}{\beta}\right)$$

From this we get

$$\frac{P_n(t + h) - P_n(t)}{h} = \frac{1}{\beta} P_{n+1}(t) + \frac{1}{\alpha} P_{n-1}(t) - \left(\frac{1}{\alpha} + \frac{1}{\beta}\right) P_n(t)$$

$$+ \frac{h}{\alpha\beta} [2P_n(t) - P_{n+1}(t) - P_{n-1}(t)]$$

Taking the limits of both sides of this equation when h tends to zero

$$\lim_{h \to 0} \frac{P_n(t + h) - P_n(t)}{h} = \frac{1}{\beta} P_{n+1}(t) - \left(\frac{1}{\alpha} + \frac{1}{\beta}\right) P_n(t) + \frac{1}{\alpha} P_{n-1}$$

that is

$$\frac{dP_n(t)}{dt} = \frac{1}{\beta} P_{n+1}(t) - \left(\frac{1}{\alpha} + \frac{1}{\beta}\right) P_n(t) + \frac{1}{\alpha} P_{n-1} \qquad \dots(4\text{-}9)$$

Equation (4-9) holds for all $n > 0$. When $n = 0$, the contributions made by the P_{n-1} terms would be zero. Therefore

$$\frac{dP_0(t)}{dt} = \frac{1}{\beta} P_1(t) - \frac{1}{\alpha} P_0(t) \qquad \dots(4\text{-}10)$$

$P_n(t)$ can be obtained by solving the two differential Equations (4-9) and (4-10). We are most interested in a steady state solution. If $\rho < 1$, after the passage of a sufficiently long time the queue would reach an equilibrium, and $P_n(t)$ would converge to a constant. Thus we can set

$$\frac{dP_n}{dt} = 0$$

Applying this to Eq. (4-10) and (4-9) gives, respectively

$$P_1 = \frac{\beta}{\alpha} P_0(t) = \rho P_0 \qquad \dots(4\text{-}11)$$

and

$$P_{n+1} = (1 + \rho) \cdot P_n - \rho \cdot P_{n-1} \qquad \dots(4\text{-}12)$$
$$= P_n + (P_n \cdot \rho - \rho \cdot P_{n-1})$$

Repeated substitution of Eq. (4-11) into (4-12) gives

$$P_n = \rho^n P_0,$$

for all $n > 0$ and $\rho < 1$. $\qquad \dots(4\text{-}13)$

Clearly

$$\sum_{n=0}^{\infty} P_n = 1$$

Therefore

$$P_0 \sum_{n=0}^{\infty} \rho^n = 1$$

or

$$P_0 \frac{1}{1 - \rho} = 1, \text{ since } \rho < 1$$

Therefore,

$$P_0 = (1 - \rho),$$

the same result as in Eq. (4-8).

The average number of customers in the system is given by

$$\sum_{n=0}^{\infty} n \cdot P_n = P_0 \sum n \cdot \rho^n = \frac{\rho}{1 - \rho} \qquad \dots(4\text{-}14)$$

The average number of customers in the system but not being served (i.e., the average *queue length*) is the difference of the average number of customers in the system and the probability that at least one customer is in the system (which is nothing but ρ). Thus

$$\text{average queue length} = \frac{\rho}{1 - \rho} - \rho$$

$$= \frac{\rho^2}{1 - \rho} \qquad \qquad .. (4.15)$$

Substituting Eq. (4-9) into (4-13), the probability of n customers being in the system can also be expressed as

$$P_n = \rho^n (1 - \rho) \qquad \qquad ...(4\text{-}16)$$

Probability of n customers being in the queue is the same as the probability of $(n + 1)$ customers being in the system which is

$$\rho^{n+1} (1 - \rho), \quad \text{for } n > 0 \qquad \qquad ...(4.17)$$

Probability of more than n customers being in the system

$$= 1 \sum_{i=0}^{n} \rho^i (1 - \rho)$$

$$= 1 - [(1 - \rho) + \rho(1 - \rho) + \rho^2(1 - \rho)$$

$$+ \ldots + \rho^{n-1}(1 - \rho) + \rho^n (1 - \rho)]$$

$$= 1 - [1 - \rho^{n+1}]$$

$$= \rho^{n+1} \qquad \qquad ...(4.18)$$

These and similar other statistics about the queue are called the *operating characteristics* of the queueing system. Derivation of some of the other characteristics are left as exercises. Usually one is interested in only some of these quantities. As an illustration of how a particular formula from queueing theory can be put to use, let us consider the following design problem.

Problem: Suppose you are to design a roller conveyor system for baling and strapping large jute bundles, as shown in Fig. 4-3. The number of

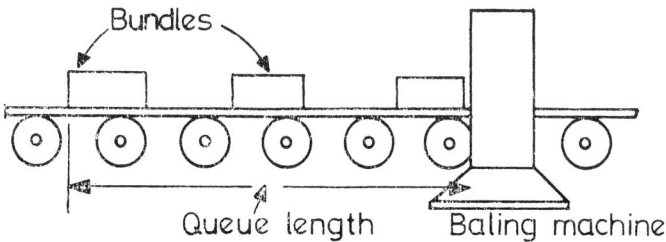

Fig. 4-3: Baling of bundles.

bundles arriving per unit time is not fixed, but it obeys the Poisson distribution law with average interarrival time α of 3 minutes. The time taken
by the baling machine is also not fixed but obeys the negative exponential
distribution with average service time β of 2.5 minutes. How long should
the conveyor be built so that it is sufficient to hold the bundles waiting to
be baled, if each bundle is 1.5 meters long?

Solution: The utilization factor in this case is

$$\rho = \frac{\beta}{\alpha} = \frac{2.5}{3.0} = \frac{5}{6},$$

and therefore

$$\text{Average number of bundles on the conveyor} = \frac{\rho}{1-\rho} = 5.$$

A conveyor just long enough to hold only 5 bundles would not do, because
this is only the average number of bundles. On the other hand, we ask
the question : What is the maximum number of bundles that can build up
on the conveyor? Theoretically the answer is an infinite number. For
design purposes, however, we can use formula (4-18), and then by setting a
reasonable limit on the probability figure we can evaluate n as follows:

Suppose we build the conveyor so that 99 per cent of the time it is sufficient to hold the bundles waiting to be baled. Thus the probability of
having more than n bundles being in the system is

$$(5/6)^{n+1} = .01,$$

and yields

$$n = 24.26$$

Thus if the conveyor is made $24 \times 1.5 = 36$ meters long, with 99 per cent
assurance we can say that it is long enough. This would be an acceptable
risk.

Birth and death process: A lot of early research in queueing theory was
related to the studies of epidemics and population. Customers arriving for
service can be thought of as *births* and those whose service is completed as
deaths. Once a customer is served he leaves the system and is of no further
concern to us. Nor is he of any concern to us before his arrival to the
system. If the average interarrival time is smaller than the average service
time (i.e., if customers are arriving faster than being served) the births exceed
the deaths, and the population grows unbounded. Preventing arrivals
corresponds to a *pure death process*. Stopping service corresponds to the
achievement of immortality by the entire population. And so on.

More complex queueing models: The queueing system we just considered was of the simplest kind. We assumed Poisson arrivals, exponential
service time, and only a single service counter. Customers keep coming
and joining the queue regardless of the length of the queue. Every customer is treated alike—no priority is given to anyone. In reality such

queues rarely occur. The arrivals may not be governed by Poisson distribution; service time may not be exponentially distributed; there may be a priority system amongst the customers; there may be several service counters operating in parallel and/or in series; the average arrival rate may not be a constant throughout the day but vary from hour to hour; there may be *balking* (customers' reluctance to enter the system as the queue length increases); there may be *reneging* (customers leaving the system without being served if the waiting time increases); there may be an upper limit imposed on the length of the queue; arrivals or servicing may occur in *bulk* instead of one by one.

A few of these complications can be handled analytically. A number of mathematical formulas are available in books and papers on queueing theory to incorporate some of these variations. For example, it can be shown that if the service time is a constant T, instead of exponentially distributed, then the probability P_n of having n customers in the system becomes

$$P_n = (1 - \rho) \sum_{k=1}^{n} (-1)^{n-k} \, e^{k\rho} \left[\frac{(k\rho)^{n-k}}{(n-k)!} + \frac{(k\rho)^{n-k-1}}{(n-k-1)!} \right] \quad \ldots (4\text{-}19)$$

for all $n > 1$, and the utilization factor $\rho = T/\alpha < 1$, as usual.

It is interesting to contrast this expression for P_n with the one given in Eq. (4-16) and observe how complicated the expression has become with the introduction of a very simple variation in the service pattern. Does it surprise you to find that a constant service time makes the expression for P_n much more complicated than an exponentially distributed service time!

There are many such formulas available. (See, for example, Houlden's book *Some Techniques of Operations Research* which gives appropriate formulas for eleven different types of queueing situations.) However, in spite of a great deal of analytic results available in queueing theory, it is generally found that for a particular managerial application, none of the formulas apply exactly. The simplified situation which is amenable to an analytic attack will not, usually, model a real queueing situation. Therefore for a complete study of a queueing sysem in any industrial or business application, one almost invariably resorts to simulation. The primary use of the queueing theory formulas is for getting a general insight into the situation and for determining how sensitive the operating characteristics of a system are to alternative decisions

We will illustrate the general technique of simulating a queueing system by means of two relatively simple and idealized examples. In the first example we will simulate a single-server, first-come-first-served type of queueing situation in which the interarrival times as well as the service times are not distributed uniformly. In the second example, we will simulate a system with the same arrival and service patterns and the queue discipline as example 1, but with two servers instead of one.

4-2. Simulation of a single-server queue

Let us simulate the arrival and servicing of N customers by a single server. Let these customers be marked 1, 2, ..., N. Let the interarrival time AT_k denote the time gap between the arrivals of the $(k-1)$th customer and the kth customer into the system. These times will be generated, as samples from some specified probability distribution, by means of an appropriate random number generator. Similarly, let ST_k denote the service time of the kth customer, $k = 1, 2, ..., N$. The service times are also generated as samples from some specified probability distribution. We will use CAT_k to denote the cumulative arrival time of the kth customer.

We will assume that initially there is no queue, and the server is free. As the first customer arrives, at time zero, he goes directly to the service counter. After the service, this customer departs from the service counter (and, therefore, from the system) at time ST_1. The second customer will arrive at

$$CAT_2 = AT_2.$$

If $ST_1 > CAT_2$, the second customer has to wait (forming a queue of length 1) for a period

$$WT_2 = ST_1 = CAT_2.$$

(WT_k denotes the waiting time of the kth customer in the queue.) On the other hand, if $CAT_2 > ST_1$ then the departure of the first customer takes place before the arrival of the second. Thus the service counter remains idle awaiting the arrival of the second customer for a period

$$IDT_2 = CAT_2 - ST_1.$$

(IDT_k denotes the idle time of the server awaiting the arrival of the $k$tl customer.)

To consider the general situation let us assume that so far $(i - 1)$ customers have arrived into the system and $(j - 1)$ customers have left. That is, the next customer due to arrive is the ith and the next customer due to depart is the jth. Clearly,

$$1 \leqslant j \leqslant i \leqslant N$$

and the queue length is given by $(i - j - 1)$, if $i > j$. The next arrival time $NAT = CAT_i$. The next departure time, i.e., the cumulated departure time CDT_j of the jth customer is given by

$$NDT = CDT_j = \text{cumulative arrival time of } j + \text{waiting time of } j + \text{service time of } j$$

$$= CAT_j + WT_j + ST_j.$$

We must now determine which event would take place—whether i would arrive first or j would depart first.   This is decided by comparing NAT with NDT.   If the difference

$$DIF = NAT - NDT$$

is negative, an arrival would take place first, and the length of the queue would increase by 1.   If DIF is positive and the queue length $(i - j - 1)$ is also positive then a departure would take place first, reducing the length of queue by 1.   In both these cases there is no idle time for the service counter.   However, if DIF is positive and the queue length is zero, then the service counter will lie idle waiting for the ith customer for the duration

$$IDT_i = DIF.$$

Finally, $DIF = 0$ implies that both events—the next arrival and departure— will take place simultaneously, leaving the queue length unaltered.

This next-event simulation procedure for this simple queueing situation is shown in the flowchart on page 74.

In the flowchart, the interarrival times AT_i's and the service times ST_i's can be generated by calling the suitable subroutines.   From the inter- arrival times, the cumulative arrival times are easily calculated using the relationship

$$CAT_k = CAT_{k-1} + AT_k,$$

and $$CAT_1 = AT_1 = 0.$$

The event times are indicated by the variable CLOCK.

As regards the output, one can calculate many different statistics.   Some of these are:

1.   Maximum queue length
2.   Average queue length (averaged over all queue lengths, including zero)
3.   Average length of nonempty queue (averaged over only non-zero queue lengths)
4.   Average number of customers in the system
5.   Probability that there are m customers in the system
6.   Average waiting time (averaged over all customers)
7.   Average waiting time of customers that wait (averaged over only those customers that wait in the queue)
8.   Maximum waiting time
9.   Average time spent by a customer in the system
10.   Total idle time
11.   Percentage of the time the service counter is idle
12.   Percentage of the time the service counter is busy (utilization)
13.   Average fraction of the time a customer spends waiting in the queue.

Because of the very divergent nature of statistics required, they have not been included in the flowchart.   These are easy to compute.

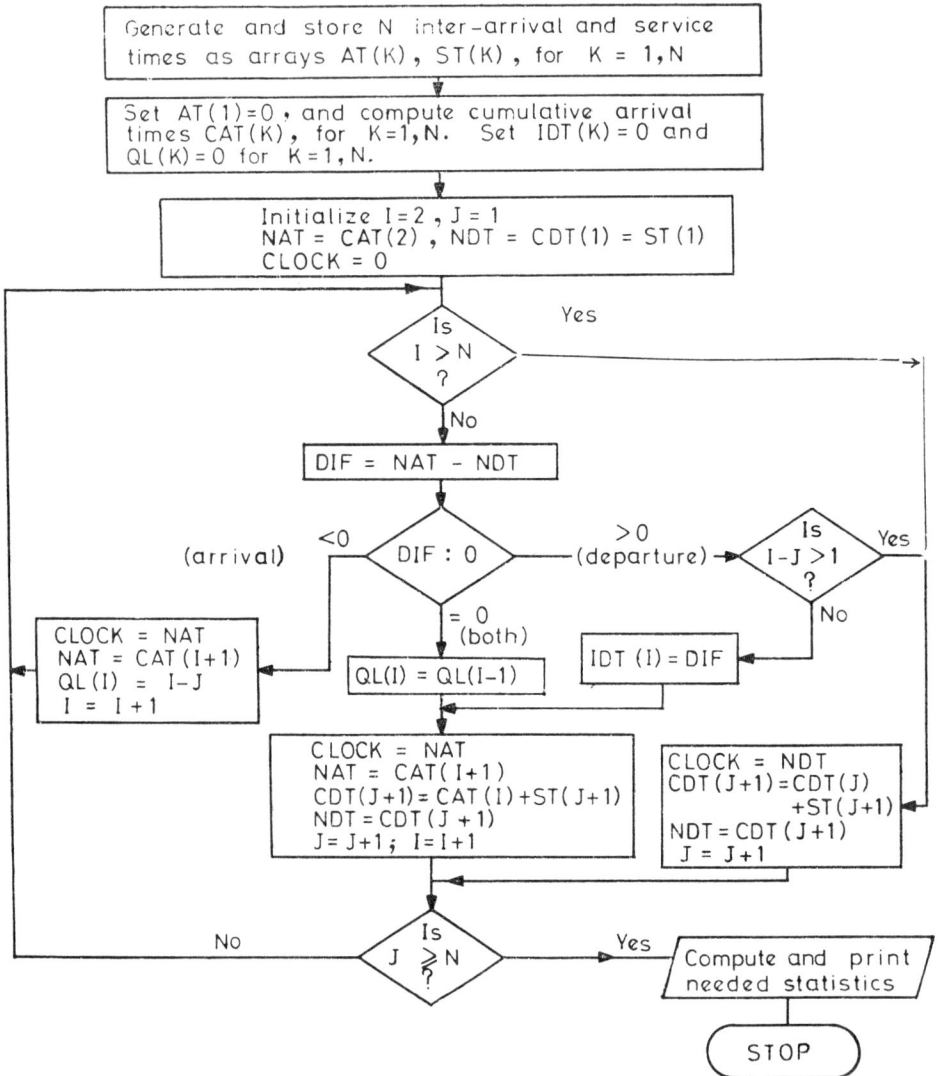

$F^{\text{ig}}.\,4\text{-}4$:   Flowchart for 1-server queue simulation.

In the flowchart we have obtained the vector $QL(I)$ the queue length immediately after the ith arrival, for $i = 1, 2, \ldots, N$. From this one could compute the average queue length, and the maximum queue length. Similarly, we have produced an array $IDT(I)$, giving the idle time of the service counter while waiting for the ith arrival $i = 1, 2, \ldots, N$. From the array one could get the maximum idle time, the total idle time, or the average idle time. The waiting time of the ith customer is given by

$$WT_i = CDT_i - ST_i - CAT_i.$$

Since the three terms on the right-hand side are available to us, the left-hand side can be easily computed. From WT_i's we can find the total waiting time, or maximum waiting time, or average waiting time. The average may be computed over all customers, or over only those customers that had to wait in the queue. In some experiments we may be interested not in the waiting time, but the total time spent by the customer in the system, i.e., in quantity $WT_i + ST_i$.

If several of the statistics are required, it is best to write a separate subroutine and call it at the completion of the portion of the program shown in the flowchart. Details of such subroutines are left as exercises.

An example: To illustrate the procedure for simulating this simple queueing situation let us consider the following trivial example.

Let $N = 8$, and let the generated interarrival times and service times be

$$AT_i\text{'s} = (0, 10, 15, 35, 30, 10, 5, 5)$$
$$ST_i\text{'s} = (20, 15, 10, 5, 15, 15, 10, 10)$$

Therefore

$$CAT_i\text{'s} = (0, 10, 25, 60, 90, 100, 105, 110)$$

The realization of this queueing process is depicted in Fig. 4-5 (page 76). Each arrival event is shown as a cross and each departure as a dot on the time axis. The figure is self-explanatory.

Arrays generated by the procedure are:
Cumulative departure times,

$$CDT_i\text{'s} = (20, 35, 45, 65, 105, 120, 130, 140);$$

queue lengths immediately after each arrival,

$$QL_i\text{'s} = (0, 1, 1, 0, 0, 1, 1, 2)$$

and the idle times,

$$IDT_i\text{'s} = (0, 0, 0, 15, 25, 0, 0, 0).$$

The program terminates at time 140, when the last departure takes place.

Note that on one occasion two events occur simultaneously—the departure of customer No. 5 and the arrival of customer No. 7, at time 105.

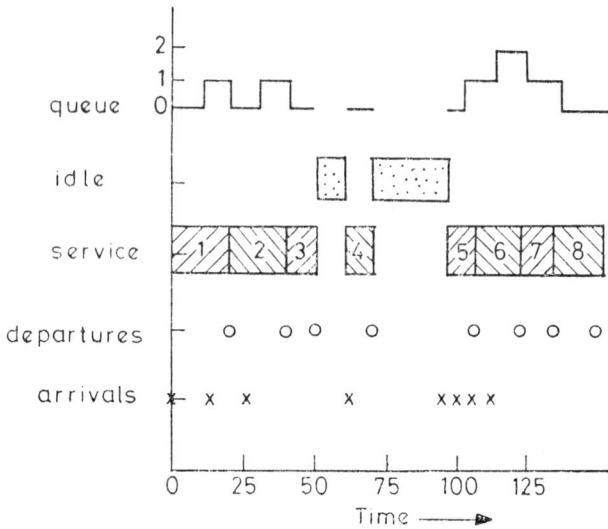

Fig. 4-5: 1-Server queue.

4-3. Simulation of a two-server queue

Since many queueing systems in real life have more than one server, the study of multi-server queues is of much practical importance. Let us consider the following situation: Ships arrive at a harbour according to the given probability distribution for interarrival times. There are two docking facilities, 1 and 2, at the harbour. When a ship arrives at the system both facilities are checked to determine if either of them is free. The ship goes directly to whichever facility is free. If both are free then the ship goes to the facility that has been idle for a longer period. If both are occupied then the ship joins the common queue, causing a waiting time for itself and increasing the queue length by one. The ships in the queue are serviced (unloaded, loaded, and dispatched) on a first-come-first-served basis. The service times for each docking facility can be viewed as independent samples from some specified distributions. Neither the interarrival time nor the service time distribution need be exponential. When a service facility becomes vacant before the next ship arrives, idle time occurs until a ship arrives and enters the vacant docking facility. This queueing system, although simple to describe, is difficult to study analytically. We are interested in determining the ·usual operating characteristics (such as queue lengths, waiting times, idle times, etc.) of this system through simulation.

Before formulating the general problem let us first acquire an understanding of this system through a small example given in a tabular form below (Table 4-1).

We have six ships arriving at times 0, 10, 48, 55, 65, 85 hours. The simulation starts at time zero. At that time there are no ships in the system.

k	AT_k	CAT_k	Facility 1			Facility 2			WT_k	QL_k
			$ST_{k,1}$	$CDT_{k,1}$	$IDT_{k,1}$	$ST_{k,2}$	$CDT_{k,2}$	$IDT_{k,2}$		
1	0	0	25	25	0	—	—	—	0	0
2	10	10	—	—	—	30	40	10	0	0
3	38	48	22	70	23	—	—	—	0	0
4	7	55	—	—	—	50	105	15	0	0
5	10	65	45	115	0	—	—	—	5	1
6	20	85	—	—	—	15	120	0	20	1

Table 4-1.

The first column in the table is ships serial number, k. The second column gives the AT_k's, the interarrival times. That is, AT_k = time gap between the arrival of $(k-1)$th ship and the kth ship. Obviously,

$$AT_1 = 0.$$

The third column contains the cumulative arrival times CAT_k's of the ships. Clearly,

$$CAT_k = CAT_{k-1} + AT_k$$

and $$CAT_1 = AT_1 = 0.$$

As the first ship arrives at time zero, it goes directly to Facility 1. The service time of Ship 1 at Facility 1 turns out to be 25 hours. Therefore, at 25 hours Ship 1 leaves the system. Column 4 gives $ST_{k,1}$ the service time for the kth ship at Facility 1. Column 5 contains the cumulative departure time, that is, the time elapsed (since time 0) at the departure of the kth ship from Facility 1. This time is denoted by $CDT_{k,1}$. In the sixth column is the idle time $IDT_{k,1}$ of Facility 1, while waiting for Ship k to arrive. The next three columns give the corresponding three numbers for Facility 2. The tenth column gives the waiting time (in the queue) WT_k for the kth ship. The last column contains the queue length QL_k immediately after the arrival of ship K.

At time 10 hours, the second ship arrives and goes directly to Facility 2. Since the service time of Ship No. 2 at Facility 2 is 30 hours, it leaves the system at time 40, i.e., $CDT_{2,2} = 40$. Before Ship No. 2 arrived, Facility 2 was idle for 10 hours.

When the third ship arrives, we check to see which of the two facilities is vacant or will fall vacant earlier. This is done by comparing the latest values of the cumulative departure times $CDT_{1,1}$ and $CDT_{2,2}$. For these are the instants when the facilities would be free next. The smaller of the two indicates the time when the next earliest departure from the system would take place. Thus the next departure time is

$$MNDT = \min \{25, 40\}$$
$$= 25$$

This gives the earliest time when the service for the Ship No. 3 can be started. Since

$$CAT_3 > MNDT$$

Ship No. 3 has not arrived at time 25, and therefore

$$CAT_3 - MNDT = 48 - 25 = 23 = IDT_{3,1}$$

is the amount of idle time Facility 1 spends while waiting for Ship No. 3 to arrive.

The cumulative departure time at Facility 1 of Ship No. 3 is given by

$$CDT_{3,1} = \text{Cumulative arrival time for Ship No. 3}$$
$$+ \text{ Service time for Ship No. 3}$$
$$= CAT_3 + ST_{3,1}$$
$$= 48 + 22 = 70$$

Before Ship No. 4 arrives at time 55, Facility 2 would have been released at time 40, because

$$\min \{70, 40\} = 40$$

and therefore the idle time $IDT_{4,2} = 55 - 40 = 15$. Since the service time $ST_{4,2} = 50$, Ship No. 4 departs from Facility $2t$ at

$$CDT_{4,2} = CAT_4 + ST_{4,2}$$
$$= 55 + 50 = 105$$

Next, Ship No. 5 arrives and both facilities are busy. For

$$MNDT = \min \{70, 105\} = 70 \quad \text{and} \quad CAT_5 = 65.$$

Therefore, Ship No. 5 will form a queue and wait there for a period

$$MNDT - CAT_5 = 70 - 65 = 5 \text{ hours.}$$

At the end of this period it would be serviced by Facility 1.

From time 70 to 105 hours, Facilities 1 and 2 will both be busy servicing Ship No. 5 and 4, respectively. Therefore Ship No. 6, arriving at $CAT_6 = 85$, will have to wait in the queue for 20 hours to be serviced by Facility 2 at time 105.

It is left as an exercise for you to draw a diagram similar to Fig. 4-5 for this 6-customer queueing example. The flowchart for the simulation of a 2-server queueing system is shown in Fig. 4-6.

It is instructive to compare the flowchart of the 1-server system with that of the 2-server system. In the former case we needed only one variable NDT to denote the next departure time. In the case of a 2-server queue we require two next departure times $NDT(1)$ and $NDT(2)$, one for each server. The minimum of these two, $MNDT$, tells us the time when a server would be free next. It is $MNDT$ that has to be compared with the next arrival time NAT to determine whether an arrival or a departure takes place.

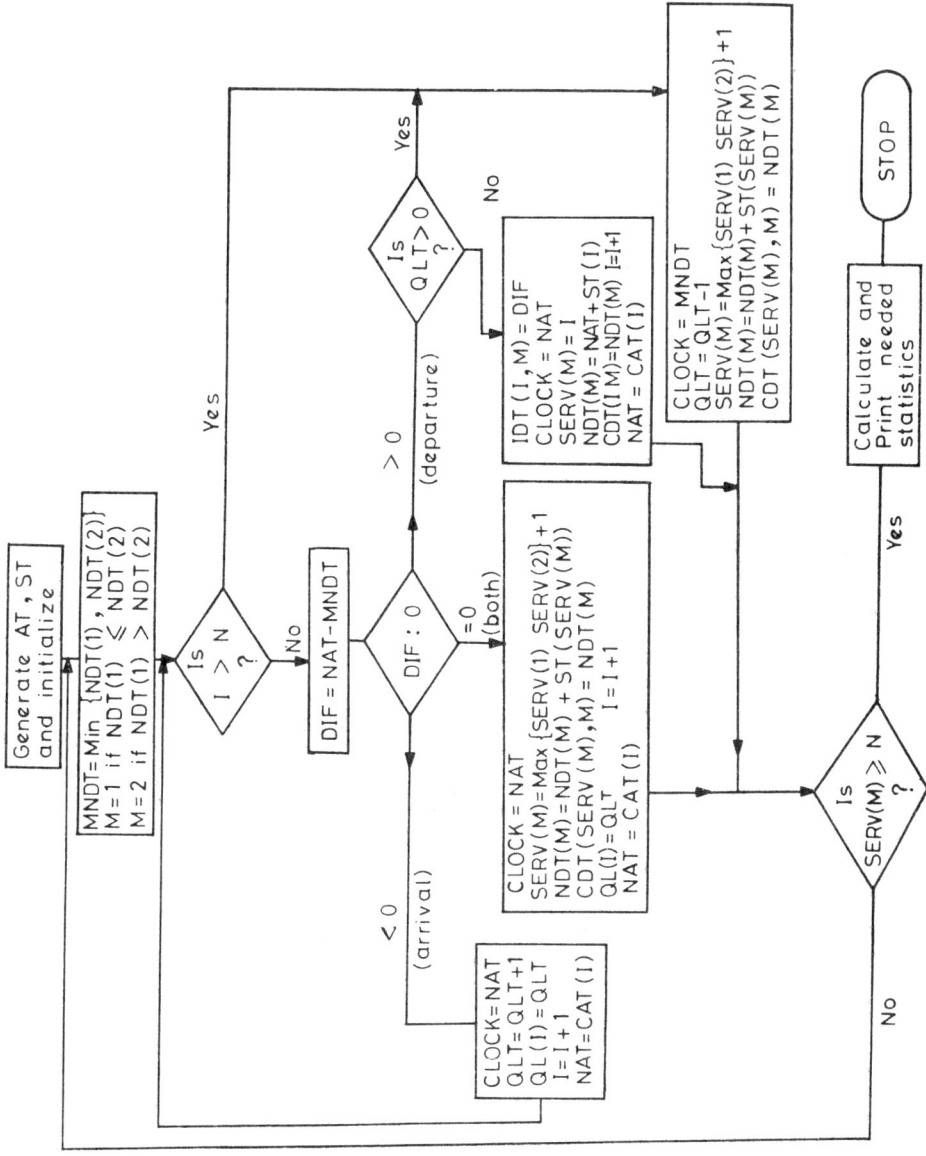

Fig. 4-6: Simulation of a 2-server queue.

Moreover, we must know not only $MNDT$, the time of the next departure, but also which of the two facilities will fall vacant at time $MNDT$. This is denoted by a variable M.

In case of a 1-server queue, it was sufficient to know the serial number of the customer due to arrive next, i, and the serial number of the customer due to depart next, j, in order to determine queue length as $i - j - 1$. This simple relationship does not hold in the case of a multiserver queue, because the customers need not depart in the same order in which they arrived. We therefore keep another pair of variables $SERV(1)$ and $SERV(2)$ to tell us which customer is currently being served by Server 1 and Server 2, respectively. The larger of these two numbers plus 1 is the customer to be served next (i.e., customer at the head of the queue). This is taken care of by setting

$$SERV(M) = MAX\{SERV(1), SERV(2)\} + 1$$

in case of a departure in the presence of a queue.

The current queue length is denoted by the variable QLT, which is incremented by 1 if the next event is an arrival; decremented by 1 (if positive) if the next event is a departure; and left unaltered if both arrival and departure occur simultaneously. As in the case of a 1-server, the queue lengths $QL(I)$'s are stored as a vector of size N for computation of needed statistics at the end.

The rest of the logic in this flowchart is the same as in the case of the 1-server queue.

Data generation and initialization: The interarrival times and service times can be generated from any desired distribution by means of an appropriate subroutine, GENRAT (AT, ST). Initialization and computation of cumulative arrival time $AT(I)$'s can also be done by calling another subroutine $INIT$. Initialization consists of the following:

$$IDT(K, L) = 0 \text{ and } CDT(K, L) = 0, \text{ for } K = 1, N \text{ and } L = 1, 2$$

$$QL(K) = 0 \text{ for } K = 1, N$$

$$QLT = 0.$$

Since the first ship goes to Facility 1 and the second to Facility 2, the next ship due to arrive is the third. Therefore, we set

$$I = 3$$

and

$$NAT = CAT(3).$$

The next departure time from Facility 1 is the service time of Ship 1, and this is also the cumulative departure time of Ship 1 from Facility 1. Thus

$$NDT(1) = CDT(1, 1) = ST(1).$$

Likewise, $NDT(2) = CDT(2, 2) = CAT(2) + ST(2)$

Initial idle time for Facility 2 (in waiting for the arrival of Ship 2) is

$$IDT(2, 2) = CAT(2)$$

Also initially, $SERV(1) = 1$

$$SERV(2) = 2$$

Like the initialization, and data generation, the required statistics for the queueing system can also be obtained by means of a subroutine

$$STAT \ (CAT, \ CDT, \ IDT, \ QL)$$

which uses the four arrays produced by the main program $CAT(I)$, $CDT(I,J)$, $IDT(I, J)$ and $QL(I)$ for $I = 1$, N and $J = 1, 2$.

The following is a format-free FORTRAN program for simulating this 2-server queueing system. The arrays have dimensions to handle up to 500 customers, but this could be changed to any number desired.

```
      INTEGER AT(500), ST(500), CAT(500), CDT(500, 2),QL(500), SERV(2)
      INTEGER IDT(500, 2), NDT(2), ISER(500), QLT
C     DATA GENERATION AND INITIALIZATION
      CALL GENRAT (AT, ST)
      CALL INIT (CAT, AT, QL, QLT, IDT, CDT, NAT, NDT, SERV, ISER)
      I = 1
      READ, N
   10 M = 1
      MNDT = NDT(1)
      IF (NDT(1) . LE . NDT(2)) GO TO 20
      M = 2
      MNDT = NDT(2)
   20 IF (I . GT . N) GO TO 60
      DIF = NAT - MNDT
      IF (DIF) 30, 40, 50
C     ARRIVAL TAKES PLACE
   30 CLOCK = NAT
      QLT = QLT + 1
      QL(I) = QLT
      I = I + 1
      NAT = CAT(I)
      GO TO 70
C     SIMULTANEOUS ARRIVAL AND DEPARTURE
   40 CLOCK = NAT
      SERV(M) = SERV(1) + 1
      IF (SERV(2) . GT . SERV(1)) SERV(M) = SERV(2) + 1
      IJ = SERV(M)
      ISER(IJ) = M
      NDT(M) = NAT + ST(IJ)
      CDT(IJ, M) = NDT(M)
      I = I + 1
      NAT = CAT(I)
      GO TO 70
C     DEPARTURE TAKES PLACE
   50 IF(QLT . GT . O) GO TO 60
```

```
C      FACILITY IDLES TILL NEXT ARRIVAL
       IDT(I, M) = DIF
       CLOCK = NAT
       SERV(M) = I
       ISER(I) = M
       NDT(M) = NAT + ST(I)
       CDT(I, M) = NDT(M)
       I = I + 1
       NAT = CAT(I)
       GO TO 70
C      HEAD OF THE QUEUE IS SERVED
   60  CLOCK = MNDT
       QLT = QLT - 1
       SERV(M) = SERV(1) + 1
       IF (SERV(2) . GT . SERV(1)) SERV(M) = SERV(2) + 1
       II = SERV(M)
       ISER(II) = M
       NDT(M) = NDT(M) + ST(II)
       CDT(II, M) = NDT(M)
C      END OF SIMULATION RUN
   70  IF (SERV(M) . LT . N) GO TO 10
       CALL STAT (CAT, CDT, IDT, QL)
       STOP
       END
```

4-4. Simulation of more general queues

More than two servers: The program for simulation of the 2-server queueing system can be easily converted to include any number of servers, say S. The value of J will be changed from 1 to S rather than 1 and 2. Similarly, vector *SERV* will be of size S instead of 2. Variable *MNDT* would be the minimum of S departures instead of just two departure times. And so on. It is left as an exercise to generalize the program from 2-server to an S-server situation.

More complex arrival and service patterns: In both 1-server and 2-server queue simulations it is not necessary that the interarrival times have the same pattern throughout the simulation period: In many systems there are rush hours and slack hours. For example, the interarrival time of customers could be exponential but with values of mean, α, which vary from hour to hour. (See Exercise 4-11.) Likewise, all servers in the system may not be equally efficient. Thus the average value of the service times of different servers may have different values. The first of these factors can be easily accommodated in the subroutine GENRAT. For the second factor, we would have to defer generating service time ST_i till it is determined which of the servers is assigned to the ith customer. (See Exercise 4-10.)

Priority: In the queueing systems simulated so far all customers were served on a first-come-first-served basis. In practice, however, there are many queueing situations where some customers are given priority over others. There may, for example, be three classes of customers (say, ships carrying perishable goods of different types) I, II and III—each with its own Poisson arrival pattern. Class I gets priority over II and III, and Class II gets priority over III. In case of arrival of a higher priority customer at a moment when a lower priority customer is being served, there are two possibilities. In the case of a *non-pre-emptive* priority any customer which is currently being served is first finished before the server undertakes to serve a higher priority waiting customer. In the case of *pre-emptive* priority the servicing of a customer is interrupted as soon as a higher-priority customer arrives. The interrupted customer goes back to the head of the queue. Within the pre-emptive priority discipline, there are various possibilities depending on what happens to the partially served customer. For example, the service may resume where it was interrupted without any loss in service time, or the server may have to start all over again, with a new service time or with the old service time. It is possible to imagine practical situations where each of these conditions hold. It is impossible to exhaustively describe all possible priority schemes.

Batch arrivals: There are cases where customers arrive in batches (in bus loads, say) rather than individually. We can have for instance the case of random arrivals (Poisson process) of batches of random sizes (say, 1 to 30 customers per bus).

Batch service: The servicing may also be performed in batches (regardless of how the arrival took place). For instance, visitors arrive individually at a museum according to Poisson process, but are given guided tours in batches of random sizes with minimum and maximum limits on the batch size.

Balking and reneging: There are queueing situations in which there is balking i.e., a tendency for the customer not to enter the system if the queue length is large. Similarly, a customer may leave the system without being served if the waiting time becomes too long. Both these factors can be taken into account with relatively minor modifications.

Multiple queues: In the case of the 2-server queue we assumed a common queue. In many situations each server has its own queue; customers join the shorter queue and either stay in the same queue or change queues if the difference between queue lengths becomes large.

Queues in tandem: In some queueing situations a customer has to be served by a number of servers in tandem or series (rather than by any one of several servers in parallel). For example, machines for testing and repair go through several stations one after another, with a possibility of forming queues for service at each of these stations.

These are just a few of the complications possible in a real-life queueing situation. It is not possible to discuss and give details of simulation for each variation in a single volume, let alone in a single chapter. You can, however, expand the simple 2-server flowchart and program to incorporate many of these complications. The program will, of course, grow in size, but conceptually it would not be much more difficult.

4-5. Remarks and references

Queues and congestions occur in all walks of life. In many industrial and business environments the queues are of sufficient economic significance to warrant expenditure on their scientific studies. The mathematical foundation for queueing theory was laid by A. K. Erlang about 50 years ago, through his study of telephone service systems. A vigorous and systematic development as well as applications of queueing theory to other areas—vehicular traffic, workshops, inventories, medical care, data handling, etc.—began only since the 1950's.

In spite of a large body of elegant formulas in queueing theory, it is found that in most practical cases the situation is so complex as to preclude an analytic solution. (This does not mean that the theory is useless. It often provides a valuable insight into the functioning of the system.) In such complicated cases one uses computer simulation—the method of the ultimate power.

There are a large number of good textbooks dealing with queueing theory, such as

KLEINROCK, L., *Queueing Systems, Volume 1: Theory*, Wiley Interscience, New York, 1975.
COX, D. R. and W. L. SMITH, *Queues,* John Wiley and Sons, New York, 1961.
KOSTEN, L., *Stochastic Theory of Service Systems*, Pergamon Press, Oxford, 1973.
LEE, A. M., *Applied Queueing Theory,* MacMillan and Co., London, 1967.
MORSE, P. M., *Queues, Inventories and Maintenance*, John Wiley and Sons, New York, 1958.
NEWELL, G. F., *Applications of Queueing Theory,* Chapman and Hall, London, 1971.
PRABHU, N. U., *Queues and Inventories,* John Wiley and Sons, New York, 1965.

Although the motivation for the earliest work in queueing theory came from the problems in telecommunications, a great deal of later work was directed toward solving problems in operations research—including inventory control, service scheduling, traffic control, equipment maintenance, etc. Thus there are many books on operations research which include a chapter or two on elementary queueing theory presented in clear and simple terms with low mathematical content and with an orientation towards application. See, for example,

HILLIER, F. S. and G. J. LIEBERMAN, *Introduction to Operations Research*, Holden-Day, San Francisco, Calif., 1967.
HOULDEN, B. T., *Some Techniques of Operations Research,* E.U.P., London, 1962.
WAGNER, H. M., *Principles of Operations Research,* Prentice-Hall of India, New Delhi, 1973 (Chapter 20).

As remarked earlier, the analysis of queues in many cases led to very complex results. In the pre-computer era there was no possibility of getting numerical results except in very simple cases. Now through simulation one can get numerical results for almost any queueing situation. Because of the importance of queues virtually every textbook on discrete system simulation contains some discussion on simulation of queues. Chapter 5 of

NAYLOR, T. H., J. L. BALINTFY, D. S. BURDICK and K. CHU, *Computer Simulation Techniques,* John Wiley and Sons, New York, 1966

contains a good treatment and flowcharts showing distinctions between the simulation of a fixed-time step model and a next-event model of queueing system. Note, however, that their flowcharts do not provide for determining the queue lengths. Chapter 7 of

CARTER, L. R. and E. HUZAN, *A Practical Approach to Computer Simulation in Business,* George Allen and Unwin Ltd., London, 1973

has a good discussion of simulation of a queueing problem. It includes examples of several real-life applications as well as a FORTRAN program for simulating a multi-server queue (without determining the queue length). The roller conveyor example in Sec. 4-1 is adopted from

PARZEN, E., 'Applications of Multichannel Queueing Results to the Analysis of Conveyor Systems,' *J. of Industrial Engineering,* XVII, January, 1966, pp. 14-21.

A FORTRAN program for simulating a realistic queueing situation can become very large and unwieldy. In such cases the program must be suitably partitioned into subprograms (SUBROUTINE and FUNCTION) as illustrated in Sections 4-2 and 4-3. In particular, the jobs of (i) data generation, (ii) statistics collection, and (iii) report generation (output formatting, etc.) can be relegated to subprograms. Preparation of these and other subroutines as well as information transfers between these modules in the main program often becomes a great programming burden. To solve this problem, higher-level, discrete-event, simulation languages have been designed which facilitate the writing of simulation programs. We will defer the discussion of simulation languages till Chapter 8. However, in the context of the queueing situation it would be instructive to observe how conveniently a complex queue can be simulated with the help of a higher-level language. See, for example,

PRITSKER, A. A. B. and P. J. KIVIAT, *Simulation with GASP II,* Prentice-Hall, Englewood Cliffs, N.J., 1969.

Chapter 4 of this book contains programs for simulating five different queueing situations—including a multi-server queue and a queueing system in which the servers are in series. The programs are in GASP II, a FORTRAN based language.

4-6. Exercises

4-1. For a 1-server queue with Poisson arrival pattern and exponential service time, plot the following two quantities as a function of the utilization factor ρ: (i) the average queue length, and (ii) the probability of queue length exceeding 5. Make sure to take enough points for higher values of ρ so that meaningful curves are obtained.

4-2. For the queueing system in Exercise 4-1, derive expressions for (i) the average length of nonempty queues, (ii) the average waiting time of a customer before he is served, (iii) the average total time spent by a customer in the system, and (iv) the average waiting time of those customers that have to wait.

4-3. Derive expression (4-19) which gives the probability P_n of having n customers in a queueing system, when the arrival is Poisson but the service time is a constant.

4-4. Write a SUBROUTINE for generation of exponentially distributed random interarrival times as well as service times to go with the flowchart of Fig. 4-4.

4-5. Using the flowchart in Fig. 4-4 write a FORTRAN program for determining the behaviour of a 1-server queueing system when both the interarrival times and the service times are exponentially distributed with average values $\alpha = 20$ and $\beta = 13$ seconds. Simulate the system for 500 arrivals. Compute the average waiting time for the customers, average idle time, and the average queue length (define the average queue length in your own way). Compare these values with those obtained analytically.

4-6. The flowchart in Fig. 4-4 uses the next-event model of a 1-server queue. Give a similar flowchart using the fixed-time step model. Implement your flowchart into a FORTRAN program. Test your program by simulating as in Exercise 4-4 for this model, for a period of 10,000 seconds. Compare the results of the two exercises.

4-7. Write a SUBROUTINE for gathering and neatly printing the following statistics for a 1-server queue to go with the flowchart of Fig. 4-4: Average interarrival time (given); Average service time (given); Average interarrival time (generated); Average service time (generated); Total simulation time; Number of customers served; Total waiting time; Average waiting time; Maximum waiting time; Total idle time; Average queue length; Maximum queue length; Server utilization ratio.

4-8. Convert the 2-server simulation program in Sec. 4-3 to a K-server simulation program. Test your program by running it for the case of a 4-server queue.

4-9. For the 2-server queue simulation in Sec. 4-3, it was assumed that in the event of both servers being free the customer goes to the server that has been idle longer. Modify the flowchart and the program so that the customer always goes to Server 1 if both servers are free.

4-10. In simulating the 2-server queue in Sec. 4-3, we assumed that both servers were equally efficient. The service time ST_i was independent of the server which the ith customer went to. This is why we were able to generate and store all ST_i's in the beginning itself. Modify the program to take into account the difference in efficiencies of the two servers.

4-11. At a college library the following situation exists. The library remains open from 7 a.m. to 9 p.m. There are two counters for issuing books to students. The students arrive for taking out books according to the Poisson distribution, but their arrival rate changes every two hours as follows:

Hours	Average interarrival time
7–9	5.7 min.
9–11	3.3 min.
11–13	1.8 min.
13–15	2.5 min.
15–17	4.8 min.
17–19	6.2 min.
19–21	10.7 min.

The check-out time (service time) varies uniformly from 1 minute to 5 minutes per student depending on the individual student and the number of books he wants to take out. Write a FORTRAN program to get the maximum queue length, average queue length and the total idle time of the counters each day. Simulate the system for 100 days and comment.

4-12. In Exercise 4-11 suppose there was a third counter for issuing books exclusively to the faculty members. The interarrival time of faculty is also distributed exponentially with the same average of 10 minutes throughout the day. The service time for faculty is the same as for the students. A new librarian takes charge and allows the faculty counter to be used for students also. However, he puts the faculty on a non-pre-emptive priority. Simulate the system now and determine if the new arrangement has improved the students' lot.

5

Simulation of a Pert Network

Before the late 1950's there was no effective formal method to aid managers in planning and scheduling large projects. The development of *CPM* (Critical Path Method) and *PERT* (Program Evaluation and Review Technique) in 1957–1959 proved to be of great help in this direction. Both *CPM* and *PERT* depict the interrelationships between various 'activities' of a project and identify critical activities which need to be paid most attention. *CPM* is used for projects in which the duration of each activity is deterministic. On the other hand, *PERT* is used when there is a good deal of uncertainty regarding the time taken by various activities in the project. For example, the project may be of research and development type and therefore be dependent on technical 'breakthroughs.' Since *CPM* is based on a single time estimate, it is, in general, much simpler than *PERT*.

Traditionally the analysis of a project through *PERT* is based on three time estimates for each activity: most optimistic time (shortest), the most pessimistic time (longest), and the most likely time for completion of each activity. More recently it has, however, been shown that this approach of using only three time estimates (instead of a probability distribution) often leads to overly optimistic results. Simulation, using an appropriate probability distribution for each activity, yields a much more realistic result. In this chapter we will show how to perform this simulation.

5-1. Network model of a project

Generally any nontrivial project can be thought of as consisting of a number of separate *activities*. For example, activities in a building construction project could be selection of the site, decision on the architecture, laying of the foundation, etc. Due to technical reasons some activities cannot be started before some others are complete (e.g., we must complete laying the foundation before erecting walls). Thus there will be precedence relationships between activities. In addition, each activity will require certain time, called its *duration*. The activities, the precedence relationships, and durations can be conveniently represented by means of an arrow diagram called an *activity network* or *activity graph*. The activities are shown as directed *lines* or *edges* (also called *branches, arcs* or *arrows*), and the *nodes* (or *vertices*) represent the beginning and completion of activities, called *events* or *milestones* in the project. An activity represented by edge (i, j) cannot be started before all activities leading to node i have been completed.

Let us take an extremely simple example. Suppose that we have a project consisting of six well-defined, nonoverlapping individual jobs, A, B, C, D, E, F with the restriction that A must precede C and D; B and D must precede E; and C must precede F. The durations of activities are 5.1, 7.2, 6.0, 4.5, 15.8, and 2.5 days. The activity network of this project is shown in Fig. 5-1.

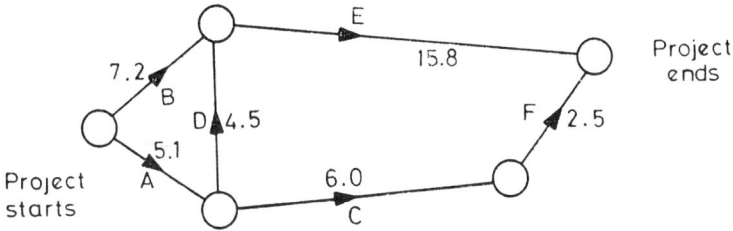

Fig. 5-1:   Activity network.

Observe that an activity network cannot have a 'cycle'; otherwise, we would have an impossible situation in which no activity lying in the cycle could be initiated.

Dummy activity: In the example of Fig. 5-1, suppose we had an additional restriction that activity F could not be initiated before B and D were completed. We can incorporate this precedence relationship by drawing an additional edge G as shown in Fig. 5-2. Such an edge, which represents only a precedence relationship and not any job in the project is called a *dummy activity*. Dummy activities become necessary when the existing activities are not enough to portray all precedence relationships accurately. All dummy activities are of zero duration and are usually shown in broken lines.

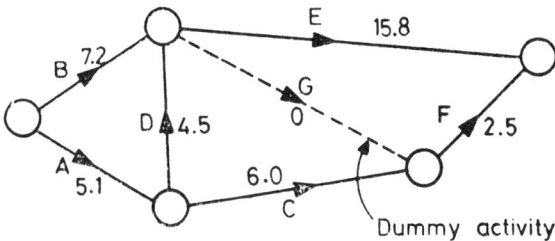

Fig. 5-2:   Dummy activity in a network.

The number of edges entering a node is called the *in-degree* of that node, and the number of edges going out of a node is called its *out-degree*. It can be seen that in an activity network there will be at least one node with zero in-degree and at least one node with zero out-degree. If the network has more than one node with zero in-degree, we can arbitrarily select one of the nodes and draw dummy edges from this node to all others. The resulting network will have exactly one node with zero in-degree. This node is called the *source* node. Likewise, by suitably adding dummy activities (if necessary) the network can be made to have exactly one node with zero *out-degree,* called the *sink* node. The source node represents the start of the project and the sink node represents the completion. From now on we will assume that every activity network has exactly one source node and exactly one sink node. It has no cycles, and there is a real number (duration) associated with every edge.

5-2. Analysis of an activity network

Activity networks are analysed by managers for studying and optimizing the execution of projects. The two most popular names in this connection are *CPM* and *PERT.* A sequence of adjacent edges from the source node to the sink node is called a *path* in a network. For example, in Fig. 5-2 *ADE* is a path, *BGF* is another path. The *length* of a path is the sum of the durations of all the activities along that path. In Fig. 5-2, for example, we have:

Length of *ADE*	$= 5.1 + 4.5 + 15.8$	$= 25.4$ days
Length of *ADGF*	$= 5.1 + 4.5 + 0 + 2.5$	$= 12.1$ days
Length of *ACF*	$= 5.1 + 6.0 + 2.5$	$= 13.6$ days
Length of *BGF*	$= 7.2 + 0 + 2.5$	$= 9.7$ days
Length of *BE*	$= 7.2 + 15.8$	$= 23$ days

The longest path is called the *critical path* in the network. The activities along a critical path are called *critical activities.* Activities *A, D,* and *E* are critical in Fig. 5-2. The length of a critical path is the time required to complete the project. An important part of analyzing a network is identification of the critical activities and determination of the project completion time. Any delay in execution of critical activities will delay the entire project, and therefore the management must pay special attention to them. In a network there may be more than one critical path. An activity in each of these is a critical activity.

In order to facilitate the analysis of a network it is helpful to sort the activities in a certain order. A list of activities from a project is said to be in *topological order* if no activity appears in the list before all of its immediate predecessors have appeared. For example in Fig. 5-2, list *A, B, C, D, E, G, F* is in topological order; but the list *A, B, C, D, E, F, G* is not because activity *F* appears before *G* in the list even though *G* is a predecessor of *F.* Usually there is more than one topological ordering possible. In Fig. 5-2, list *B, A, D, C, E, G, F* is also in topological order.

It can be shown that a topological ordering is possible if and only if there is no cycle in the network.   From now onwards we will assume that the activities are listed in a topological order.   (If not, it is simple to prepare a list which is ordered topologically: We start by taking an activity which is not preceded by any other in the network.   This is put first in the list.   Now we remove this activity from the network, and pick another activity which is not preceded by any other in the remaining network.   We place this activity as the second in the list and also remove it from the network.   This process is repeated till all activities are removed from the network and placed on the list.   The resulting list is in topological order. Standard subroutines are available for doing topological ordering.)

Let the given activity network consist of N activities and M nodes.   Let the activities be listed in topological order and be labelled 1, 2, ..., N (including the dummy activities), and the nodes be labelled as 1, 2, ..., M. Node 1 is the source node and node M is the sink node.   Let each activity be specified by its starting node, finishing node and its duration.   That is $S(k)$ is the node at which the kth activity originates, $F(k)$ is the node at which the kth activity terminates, and $T(k)$ is the duration of the kth activity; for $k = 1, 2, ..., N$.   For example, the network of Fig. 5-2 (with its activities in topological order 1, 2, ..., 7 and nodes relabelled 1, 2, ..., 5) is represented as shown in Fig. 5-3.   The activity durations are shown in parentheses.

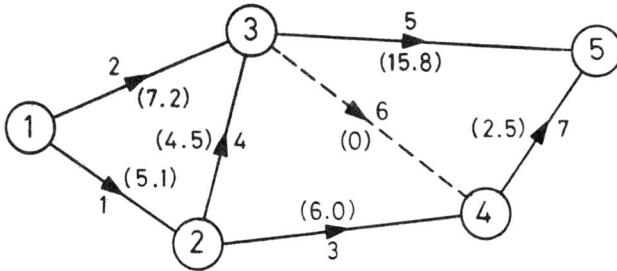

Activity No., K	S(k)	F(k)	T(k)
1	1	2	5.1
2	1	3	7.2
3	2	4	6.0
4	2	3	4.5
5	3	5	15.8
6	3	4	0
7	4	5	2.5

Fig. 5-3:   Topologically ordered activities and their representation.

5.3. Critical path computation

Once a network representation of a project has been completed, the activities labelled properly and described in appropriate form [namely, as vectors $S(k)$, $F(k)$ and $T(k)$], we are ready to determine the total time it would take to complete the entire project and to identify the critical activities. For this purpose we will first determine the earliest possible start and completion times for each of the activities.

Clearly kth activity cannot begin until all activities terminating in node $S(k)$ (i.e., start node for k) are completed. Therefore, the earliest an activity k can begin is at the completion of the last (chronologically) activity terminating in node $S(k)$. Let $EST(k)$ denote the earliest starting time for the kth activity, and $EFT(k)$ denote the earliest finish time for the kth activity. Therefore,

$$EFT(k) = EST(k) + T(k) \qquad \qquad \ldots(5\text{-}1)$$

Recall that nodes represent milestones. A milestone i is said to be *achieved* when all activities terminating in node i are completed. Let $ENT(i)$ denote the earliest time when node i is achieved. Therefore

$$ENT(i) = Max \ \{EFT \text{ (all activities terminating in } i)\} \qquad \ldots(5\text{-}2)$$

Since the earliest an activity k can begin is the time when node $S(k)$ is achieved, we have

$$EST(k) = ENT(S(k)) \qquad \qquad \ldots(5\text{-}3)$$

Forward pass: We will now traverse the network in forward direction from the source node to the sink node passing through every edge once. The purpose of this forward pass is to compute the earliest start time, earliest finish time of all activities, and the earliest time to achieve each of the nodes. We start at node 1 (the source node) and set its achievement time to 0.

$$ENT(1) = 0$$

Since activity 1 begins at node 1

$$EST(1) = 0, \text{ and}$$

$$EFT(1) = 0 + T(1)$$

Likewise, we compute EFT's of all activities originating at node 1. Now, using Eq. (5-2) we would be able to compute the ENT of the next node. Then we can compute the EST's and EFT's of some more activities; and so on, until all activities in the project have been considered. Notice that this simple approach was possible because the activities were considered in topological order. No activity was taken up until all its immediate predecessors had been. A flowchart for this forward pass procedure is given in Fig. 5-4. The notations are those of FORTRAN, and the flowchart is readily convertible into a FORTRAN program.

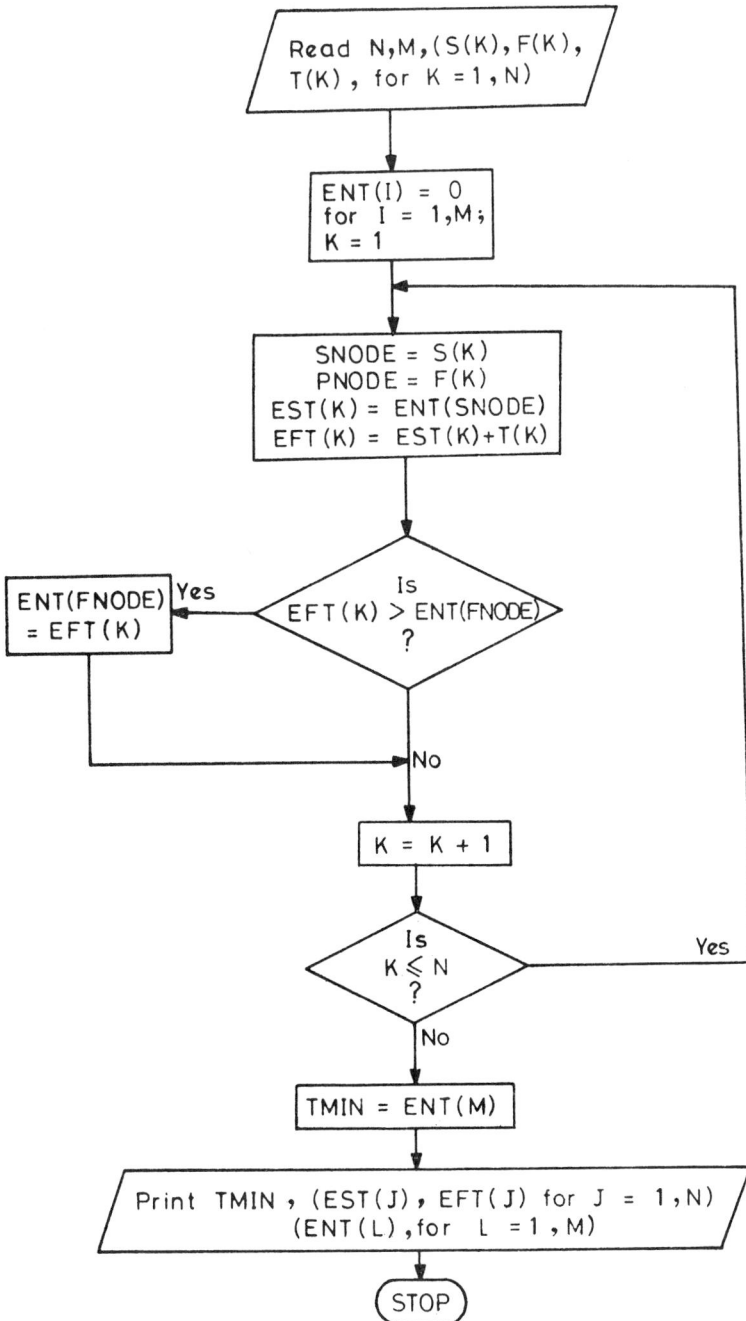

Fig. 5-4:   Flowchart for forward pass.

To illustrate this flowchart let us conduct a forward pass through the simple network of Fig. 5-3:

$N = 7$, $M = 5$, and $S(K)$, $F(K)$ and $T(K)$ are read as given in Fig. 5-3. Initially ENT of all five nodes are set to zero. $K = 1$. During the first pass through the loop we have

$SNODE = S(1) = 1$
$FNODE = F(1) = 2$
$EST(1) = ENT(1) = 0$
$EFT(1) = EST(1) + T(1) = 0 + 5.1 = 5.1$
Since $EFT(1) = 5.1 > ENT(2) = 0$, we set
$ENT(2) = 5.1$
$K = 2$

Since $2 \leqslant 7$, we enter the loop again and set

$SNODE = S(2) = 1$
$FNODE = F(2) = 3$
$EST(2) = ENT(1) = 0$
$EFT(2) = 0 + T(2) = 7.2$

Since $EFT(2) = 7.2 > ENT(3) = 0$, we set

$ENT(3) = 7.2$, (temporarily)
$K = 3$

Since $3 \leqslant 7$, we again enter the loop, and compute

$SNODE = S(3) = 2$
$FNODE = F(3) = 4$
$EST(3) = ENT(2) = 5.1$
$EFT(3) = EST(3) + T(3) = 5.1 + 6.0 = 11.1$

and so on.

When $K = 8$, we exit the loop with the following values:

Vectors $EST = (0, 0, 5.1, 5.1, 9.6, 9.6, 11.1)$
$EFT = (5.1, 7.2, 11.1, 9.6, 25.4, 9.6, 13.6)$
$ENT = (0, 5.1, 9.6, 11.1, 25.4)$, and
$TMIN = ENT(5) = 25.4$, which is the project completion time.

A forward pass through the network gives ENT's, i.e., the earliest time each of the nodes can be achieved. In particular, $ENT(M)$, the earliest time to achieve the sink node, is the time required to complete the project. This time is equal to the length of the critical path in the network. We are interested in finding out not only the completion time of the project but also the actual activities which are critical; the critical activities must be paid special attention.   Theoretically one could trace all their lengths, and then identify the critical path as the longest amongst these.   In reality, however, this approach is impractical, because a typical activity network will have too many paths from source node to sink node.   The following technique for finding a critical path by traversing the network backwards is much more efficient.

Let us consider an activity J in the network, originating in node $S(J)$ and terminating in node $F(J)$.   We have already computed the earliest possible time by which J can be initiated, which is $EST(J)$, and the earliest time $EFT(J)$ by which activity J can be completed.   We would also like to know how late can the completion of J be made without delaying the completion of the project.   Let $LFT(J)$ denote the latest time by which J must be finished without delaying the overall project completion time. Then the latest start time LST of J (without causing a delay in the project completion) is

$$LST(J) = LFT(J) - T(J), \qquad \ldots (5\text{-}4)$$

where $T(J)$ is the duration of activity J.   Moreover, the latest time by which a node i can be achieved (without lengthening the project as a whole) has to be the minimum of all the LST's of the activities originating from node i.   That is,

$$LNT(i) = Min \{LST \text{ (all activities originating in } i)\} \qquad \ldots (5\text{-}5)$$

Similarly, the completion of any activity terminating in node i can be delayed up to (but not beyond) $LNT(i)$.   In other words,

$$LFT \text{ (every activity terminating in } i) = LNT(i) \qquad \ldots (5\text{-}6)$$

Backward pass: Now we start at the sink vertex M and set its latest node time equal to the project completion time $TMIN$ (which was computed during the forward pass).   That is,

$$LNT(M) = TMIN = ENT(M)$$

Using Eq. (5-6) we set this time to be the LFT of each activity terminating in M.   From these LFT's we compute the LST's using Eq. (5-4).   Now we will have at least one node (other than M), say x, such that the LST of all activities originating from x have been computed.   This enables us to compute $LNT(x)$ using Eq. (5-5).   From this in turn we get LFT's of all activities terminating in x using Eq. (5-6).   Thus we continue moving backwards through the network using Eqs. (5-6), (5-4) and (5-5) alternately till we reach the start node 1, having calculated the LNT of all nodes and the LFT and LST of all activities in the network.

As an example, let us apply this procedure to the network of Fig. 5-3:

$LNT(5) = 25.4$ days
$LFT(7) = LFT(5) = 25.4$ days
$LST(7) = 25.4 - 2.5 = 22.9$ days
$LST(5) = 25.4 - 15.8 = 9.6$ days
$LNT(4) = 22.9$ days
$LFT(6) = LFT(3) = 22.9$ days
$LST(6) = 22.9 - 0.0 = 22.9$ days
$LST(3) = 22.9 - 6.0 = 16.9$ days
$LNT(3) = Min\{22.9, 9.6\} = 9.6$ days
$LFT(4) = LFT(2) = 9.6$ days
$LST(4) = 9.6 - 4.5 = 5.1$ days
$LST(2) = 9.6 - 7.2 = 2.4$ days
$LNT(2) = Min\{16.9, 5.1\} = 5.1$ days
$LFT(1) = 5.1$ days
$LST(1) = 5.1 - 5.1 = 0.0$ days
$LNT(1) = min\ (0.0, 2.4) = 0.0$ days

Thus a backward pass gives us $LNT(i)$ for every node i and $LST(J)$ and $LFT(J)$ for every activity J in the network. The forward pass, on the other hand, yielded $ENT(i)$'s, $EST(J)$'s and $EFT(J)$'s.

Slack: The difference between the latest time by which a node can be achieved (without causing an overall delay in the completion of the project) and the earliest time by which it is possible to achieve this node, represents the latitude available at each node. That is, $LNT(i) - ENT(i)$ is the amount of time by which achieving of node i can slip and still the project can be completed in time. This difference is called *slack* at node i. Clearly for a node that falls on the critical path this slack is zero. Similarly for an activity J the quantity

$$LST(J) - EST(J) = LFT(J) - EFT(J)$$

represents a latitude. This latitude (or slack) is zero if and only if J is a critical activity.

Thus, after making a backward pass through the network we can identify the critical activities by checking that their LST's and EST's are equal.

Implementation of a backward pass: As in the case of the forward pass, it is convenient for the computer implementation of the backward pass to have the activities listed in a topological order and begin at the bottom of the list. Instead of considering the nodes, we consider only the activities and take one activity at a time working from bottom of the list to the top. The flowchart shown in Fig. 5-5 performs a backward pass and identifies the critical activities. Note that initially we set LNT's of all nodes at $TMIN$, and then as we proceed these times are recomputed for each node except for the sink node M. Also, we have assumed that EST's of all activities (computed during the forward pass) are available during the backward pass.

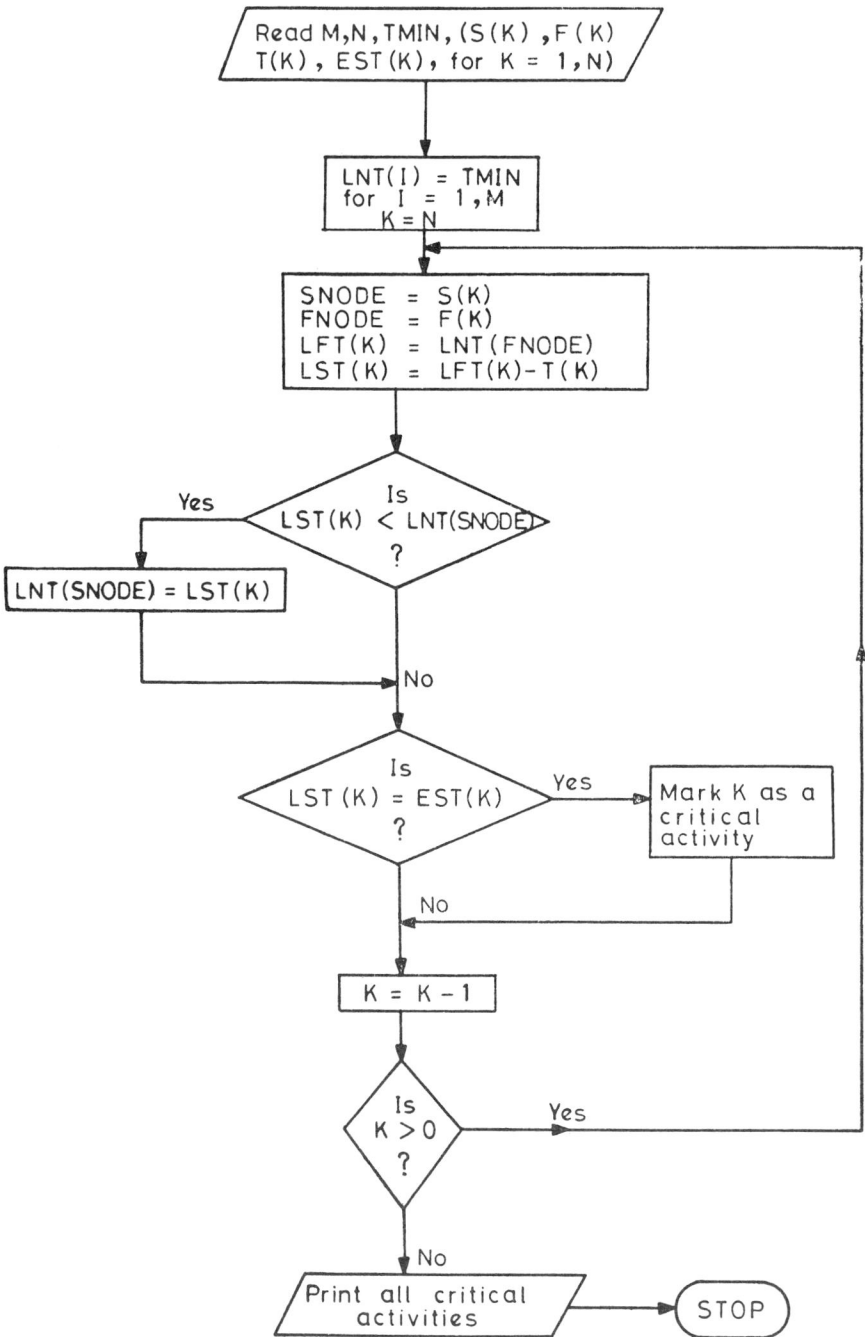

Fig. 5-5:   Flowchart for backward pass and critical path.

As we will see shortly, it is easy to combine flowcharts in Figs. 5-4 and 5-5 to produce a composite program to identify the critical activities in the network.

5-4.   Uncertainties in activity durations

So far we have assumed that each activity takes a fixed amount of time to complete and this amount is known precisely. In many projects, however, there may be a good deal of uncertainties about the durations of various activities. This is particularly true for projects involving research and development type of activities. In such cases, it is reasonable to regard the duration of each activity as a random sample from a probability distribution associated with that particular activity. If the durations of activities are random variables, then the critical path and its total length will depend on the specific samples drawn to represent the different activity durations. When calculations are repeated with different sample sets, the critical path itself may not be the same.

In face of the uncertainties in activity durations, one attempts to obtain the best possible estimate of each duration distribution. In the original *PERT* procedure (which was developed by the U.S. Navy in 1957 to plan and schedule the development of the Polaris missiles), it was assumed that the duration of every activity was given by a beta distribution. For each activity, J, an appropriate knowledgeable person could supply the most optimistic estimate $a(J)$, most pessimistic estimate $b(J)$ and the estimate of the most likely duration $m(J)$. See Fig. 5-6.

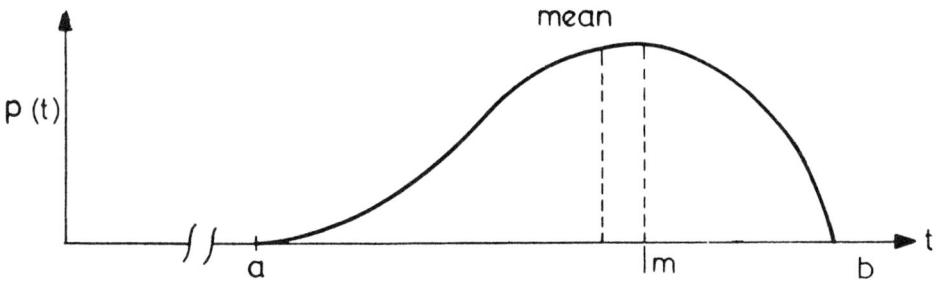

Fig. 5-6:   Beta distribution.

From these three parameters the average value of the duration T_{AV} and various VAR are estimated by means of the formulas

$$T_{AV}(J) = \frac{a(J) + 4m(J) + b(J)}{6}$$

$$VAR(J) = \left(\frac{b(J) - a(J)}{6}\right)^2$$

for $J = 1, 2, \ldots, N$.

Next, using these average values for activity durations, one computes the project completion time and the critical path. In a typical large network the critical path will consist of a large number of branches. Therefore, invoking the Central Limit Theorem,* one can conclude that (*i*) the project completion time will be normally distributed, (*ii*) whose expected value would be the sum of average durations of the activities in the critical path, and (*iii*) whose variance would be the sum of the variances of all activities on the critical path.

This technique, although very popular, is often found to yield overly optimistic results. The reason is that a network may have many paths which are not critical but slightly shorter than critical, on the basis of their average durations. Due to the randomness of durations, these paths, under some combination of activity durations, could become longer (and hence critical) than the average longest path. Such paths would be ignored if we compute only one critical path based on the T_{AV}'s.

Thus the usual *PERT* procedure that computes only a single critical path based on $T_{AV}(J)$ and $VAR(J)$ can lead to a grossly optimistic estimate of the probabilities of completing a project by a given date. This is particularly true if the network contains a number of near critical paths and if the variances of the activity durations are relatively large. In such conditions to get more realistic results we resort to simulation.

5-5. Simulation of an activity network

We are given (i) a topologically ordered list of activities 1, 2, ..., N, (ii) the start node $S(J)$ and finish node $F(J)$ for each activity J, for $J = 1, 2$, ..., N, and (iii) the probability distribution with appropriate parameters for the duration of each activity. To simulate this stochastic situation, we generate one sample for the duration of each activity randomly from the corresponding probability distribution. Let these time samples be denoted by $TS(J)$, for $J = 1, 2, ..., N$. Then based on these durations we compute the project completion time $TMIN$ and identify the critical activities as usual. Next, another sample from the duration distribution of each activity is randomly generated and, using the new value, the critical activities and project completion time $TMIN$ are determined again. This procedure is repeated many times (typically several thousand times) and a record is kept of the project completion time $TMIN$ for each sampling. A frequency plot of the project completion times will usually turn out to be normally distributed because of the Central Limit Theorem. Its average and standard deviation are easily calculated. This estimate of the probabilities of completing the project at various times is more reliable than the usual *PERT* procedure (as obtained earlier), because we are taking into account the effects of near-critical paths also, which may sometimes become

---

*Those not familiar with the Central Limit Theorem, see Chapter 7.

critical if the activities forming them take more time than their average durations.

Criticality index: Finding critical activities with simulated data yields another piece of useful information (besides providing a more realistic estimate of the project completion time). By keeping a running count of how many times an activity became critical we can determine percentage of the simulation runs in which an activity became critical. This is called the *criticality index* of that particular activity. For example, if an activity K is on a critical path 1,500 times out of 10,000 simulation runs, then the criticality index of K is 15 per cent. This activity K might not have appeared at all on the critical path if the usual *PERT* calculations based on only average durations were used. But the simulation tells us that there is a 15 per cent probability of activity K being critical. Obviously, the higher the criticality index of an activity the more carefully it would have to be watched.

The simulation procedure thus helps to extend the notion of uncertainty to the critical path itself. Instead of identifying a single critical path, it identifies activities with various degrees of criticalities, and thus reduces the chance for the near-critical activities of being ignored by the project manager.

The complete procedure for simulating an activity network is shown in the flowchart of Fig. 5-7.

In the flowchart in Fig. 5-7 we show that all *TMIN*'s are stored and then printed at the end of the simulation. In practice, however, such an output of, say, 10,000 different values of *TMIN* is not very useful. What we would like is a frequency distribution (or a histogram) of the project completion times *TMIN*'s. This can be achieved by dividing the project completion times into K different ranges each of a specified width and by counting how many times *TMIN* falls in each range. In a particular run, if *TMIN* falls in the Jth range then the count of that range $COUNT(J)$ is incremented by 1. Initially, of course, the $COUNT$ array is set to zero. This division of *TMIN*'s into different ranges for the purpose of a histogram can be accomplished by means of a separate subprogram. The input to this subprogram would be *TMIN*; the width of each range ($WIDTH$); the lowest value of the X-axis where histogram starts ($TLOW$); and the number of ranges, K. The output is an array $COUNT$ of size K. Although we would choose $TLOW$ so that no *TMIN* would be less than $TLOW$, but just to be on the safe side we should make sure that any value of *TMIN* falling below $TLOW$ is taken account of by increasing $COUNT(1)$. The subroutine *HSTGRM* is given as part of the complete simulation program in the next section.

5-6. Computer program for simulation

Now we are ready to write down the complete computer program for simulating an activity network. We will use four subroutines—one for

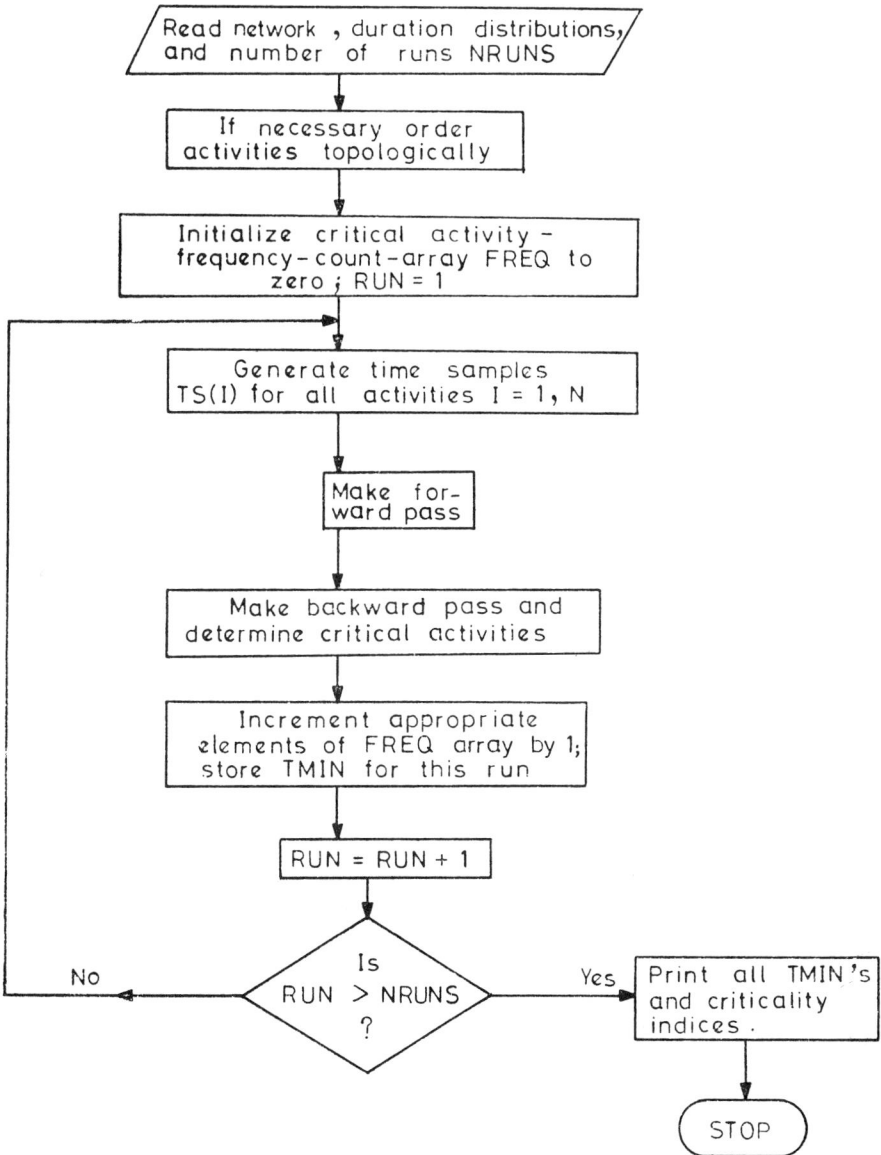

Fig. 5-7: Simulation of activity network.

generating random samples of activity durations, *GENRAT*; one for conducting a forward pass, *FWDPAS*; one for a backward pass and identification of critical activities, *BWDPAS;* and the fourth one, *HSTGRM*, for putting *TMIN*'s into various ranges for the purpose of a histogram. For subroutine *GENRAT* it is assumed that the duration of every activity is distributed normally with a specified mean *MU* and a standard deviation *SIGMA*. The subroutine uses the Box-Muller transformation for generating random sample. as discussed in Sec. 3-4. The other three subroutines have already been explained earlier in this chapter.

Calling of these four subroutines as well as computation of the criticality index of each activity is done by the main program. The latter is accomplished by keeping a frequency array *FREQ* of size *N*, whose *I*th component indicates the number of times activity *I* has been critical, for $I = 1, 2, ..., N$. At the end of the simulation we divide *FREQ(I)* with the number of runs made, *NRUN*, to get criticality index *CRIT(I)*, for $I = 1$ to *N*.

The *LST*'s and *EST*'s are *REAL* numbers. Theoretically the absolute value of their difference *ABS (LST(I) − EST(I))* should be zero if activity *I* is critical. However, to take into account the computational errors in adding *REAL* numbers, we will let the difference be treated as zero when it is less than some small value, *ERR*. In our example, we will set this permissible error, $ERR = 0.001$ units of time.

The following is a complete format free *FORTRAN* program to simulate an activity network. It is dimensioned to handle networks of up to 300 activities and 300 nodes. The number of ranges for the histogram could be up to 50. The number of runs made during a simulation is 1,000. The activities are assumed to be ordered topologically and their durations are assumed to be distributed normally.

```
        INTEGER RUN, S(300), F(300), COUNT(50)
        REAL T(300), MU(300), SIGMA(300), EST(300), EFT(300)
        REAL LST(300), LFT(300), FREQ(300), CRIT(300)
C       INITIALISATION AND INPUT
        ERR = 0.001
        RUN = 1
        READ, TLOW, WIDTH, K
        READ, NRUNS, N, M
        READ, (S(I), F(I), MU(I), SIGMA(I), I = 1, N)
        DO 10 I = 1, N
10      FREQ(I) = 0
        DO 15 I = 1, K
15      COUNT(I) = 0
20      CALL GENRAT(MU, SIGMA, T, N)
        CALL FWDPAS (S, F, T, EST, EFT, TMIN, N, M)
        CALL BWDPAS (S, F, T, EST, LST, LFT, TMIN, N, M)
        CALL HSTGRM (TMIN, TLOW, WIDTH, K, COUNT)
        J = 0
```

```
C       FIND CRITICAL ACTIVITIES AND UPDATE FREQUENCIES
        DO 30 I = 1, N
        IF (ABS(LST (I) − EST (I)) . LT . ERR) FREQ (I) = FREQ (I) + 1
   30   CONTINUE
        RUN = RUN + 1
        IF (RUN . LE . NRUNS) GO TO 20
C       CALCULATION OF CRITICALITY INDEX
        RUNS = NRUNS
        DO 40 I = 1, N
        CRIT(I) = FREQ(I)/RUNS
        PRINT, (CRIT(I), I = 1, N)
        PRINT, (COUNT(J), J = 1, N)
        STOP
        END

        SUBROUTINE GENRAT(MU, SIGMA, T, N)
        REAL MU(300), SIGMA(300), T(300)
        DO 50 I = 1, N
        R1 = RNDY1(I)
        R2 = RNDY2(I)
        V = ((−2.*ALOG(R1))** 0.5)*COS(6.283*R2)
   50   T(I) = SIGMA(I)*V + MU(I)
        RETURN
        END

        SUBROUTINE FWDPAS(S, F, T, EST, EFT, TMIN, N, M)
        INTEGER S(300), F(300), SNODE, FNODE
        REAL T(300), EST(300), EFT(300), ENT(300)
C       INITIALISATION
        DO 60 I = 1,M
   60   ENT(I) = 0.
C       CALCULATION OF NODE AND ACTIVITY EARLIEST TIMES
        K = 1
   70   SNODE = S(K)
        FNODE = F(K)
        EST(K) = ENT(SNODE)
        EFT(K) = EST(K) + T(K)
        IF (EFT(K) . GT . ENT(FNODE)) ENT(FNODE) = EFT(K)
        K = K + 1
        IF (K . LE . N) GO TO 70
        TMIN = ENT(M)
        RETURN
        END

        SUBROUTINE BWDPAS S, F, T, EST, LST, LFT, TMIN, N, M)
        INTEGER S(300), F(300), MARK(300), SNODE, FNODE
        REAL T(300), LST(300), LFT(300), LNT(200), EST(300)
C       INITIALISATION
        ERR = 0.001
        DO 80 I = 1,M
   80   LNT(I) = TMIN
C       CALCULATION OF NODE AND ACTIVITY LATEST TIMES
        K = N
```

```
 90  SNODE = S(K)
     FNODE = F(K)
     LFT(K) = LNT(FNODE)
     LST(K) = LFT(K) − T(K)
     MARK(K) = 0
     IF (LST(K) . LT . LNT(SNODE)) LNT(SNODE) = LST(K)
     K = K − 1
     IF (K . GT . O) GO TO 90
     DO 100 I = 1, N
     IF (ABS(LST(I) − EST(I)) . LT . ERR) MARK(I) = 1
100  CONTINUE
     RETURN
     END

     SUBROUTINE HSTGRM(TMIN, TLOW, WIDTH, K, COUNT)
     INTEGER COUNT(50)
     T1 = TMIN−TLOW
     IF (T1) 110, 120, 120
110  IC= 1
     GO TO 140
120  IC = T1/WIDTH + 1.
     IF (IC − K) 140, 140, 130
130  IC = K
140  COUNT(IC) = COUNT(IC) + 1
     RETURN
     END
```

5-7. An example

A network of 25 activities and 13 nodes, shown in Fig. 5-8, was simulated using the preceding program. The activity durations are normally distributed. The average duration MU and standard deviation, SIGMA are given in Table 5-1, in weeks. The activities are already in topological order.

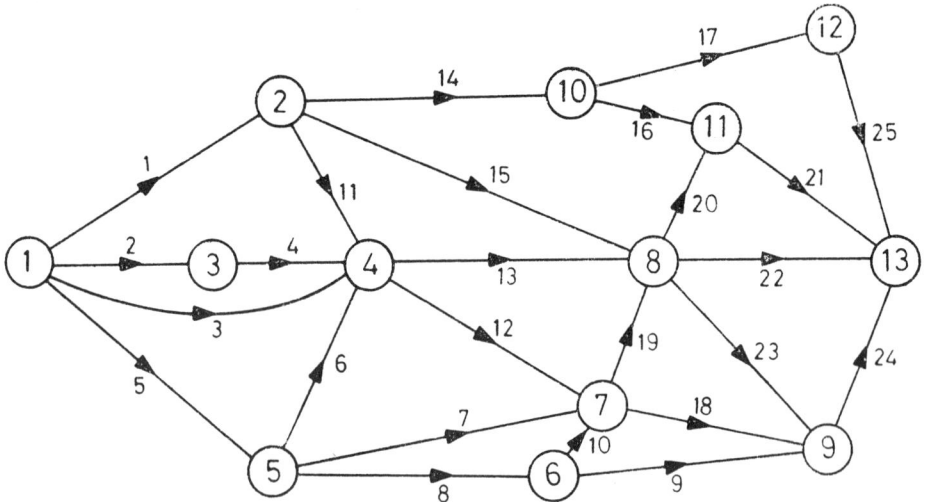

Fig. 5-8: Activity network.

Activity No. K	Node S(K)	Node F(K)	MU	SIGMA
1	1	2	5.00	1.17
2	1	3	10.00	2.53
3	1	4	6.00	1.24
4	3	4	9.00	1.99
5	1	5	8.00	1.52
6	5	4	15.00	3.36
7	5	7	19.00	3.68
8	5	6	6.00	1.05
9	6	9	8.00	0.98
10	6	7	11.00	2.39
11	2	4	7.00	0.05
12	4	7	9.00	0.32
13	4	8	3.00	0.67
14	2	10	2.00	0.43
15	2	8	8.00	1.64
16	10	11	6.00	0.09
17	10	12	1.00	0.20
18	7	9	10.00	1.09
19	7	8	3.00	0.70
20	8	11	1.00	0.25
21	11	13	4.00	0.69
22	8	13	5.00	0.11
23	8	9	9.00	0.53
24	9	13	14.00	3.67
25	12	13	10.00	2.08

Table 5-1.

This network was simulated for 1,000 sample runs, i.e., $NRUNS = 1,000$. For the histogram data, the lowest value, $TLOW$, that the $TMIN$ could go was assumed to be 38 weeks and the width of each range was made 2 weeks. The output (i.e., the criticality index of each activity and the frequencies of occurrence of $TMIN$ in different ranges) is shown in Tables 5-2 and 5-3.

Activity No.	Criticality Index
1	0.000
2	0.176
3	0.000
4	0.176
5	0.824
6	0.688
7	0.118
8	0.118
9	0.000
10	0.018
11	0.000
12	0.864
13	0.000
14	0.000
15	0.000
16	0.000
17	0.000
18	0.074
19	0.927
20	0.000
21	0.000
22	0.000
23	0.927
24	1.000
25	0.000

Table 5-2:   Criticality index of different activities.

I	TMIN Range	Count (I)
1	38 – 40	0
2	40 – 42	0
3	42 – 44	1
4	44 – 46	2
5	46 – 48	8
6	48 – 50	9
7	50 – 52	48
8	52 – 54	64
9	54 – 56	120
10	56 – 58	135
11	58 – 60	168
12	60 – 62	147
13	62 – 64	130
14	64 – 66	80
15	66 – 68	58
16	68 – 70	13
17	70 – 72	12
18	72 – 74	4
19	74 – 76	1
20	76 – 78	0

Table 5-3:   Output data for histogram.

For the sake of a pictorial representation we now plot a histogram of the output data given in Table 5-3. The plot is shown in Fig. 5-9. It appears reasonably close to a normal distribution. We can use this histogram as it is to estimate the probability of completing the project in a given time. Or we can approximate it to a normal distribution, whose expected value and standard deviation can be determined from the data in Table 5-3. In case we feel that Fig. 5-9 is not smooth enough, we could divide *TMIN* into finer intervals by reducing *WIDTH* to, say, 1 week or even less. We could also increase the number of trials from 1,000 to, say, 5,000 to enhance the confidence in the histogram.

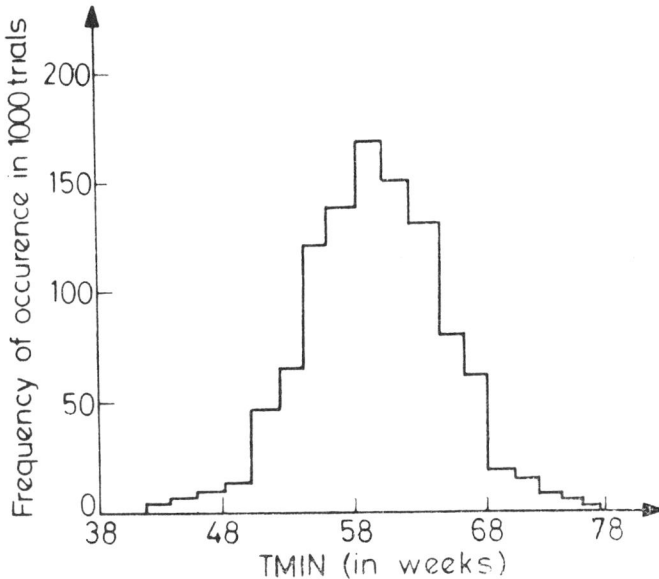

Fig. 5-9: Frequency distribution of the project comlpetion time, TMIN, in 1,000 trials.

5-8. Resource allocation and cost considerations

In studying the *PERT* network the only factor that we have considered so far is time. It was assumed that there was no limitation on resources (manpower, workspace, equipment, etc.), needed for starting any number of activities simultaneously. In reality, however, resources are often limited. Given that only a fixed quantity of resource of each type is available for the project, and given the quantity of each of these resources required by each of the activities, one would like to determine the sequence of performing these activities so that the project is completed in the shortest time possible. (Assume, for simplicity, that the activity-durations are deterministic.)

When there is a limitation on only one resource (other resources being unlimited), the classical resource allocation approach is as follows: The network is first analyzed to determine the critical activities, assuming no resource limitations. Then the resource requirement along the critical path is tabulated and made available to critical activities; for otherwise, the project would be delayed. The rest of the resource is assigned to non-critical activities on the basis of slack (i.e., their criticalities). The assignment of a resource to noncritical activities, in general, allows a good deal of flexibility. In allocating a resource, an attempt is made to keep the resource requirement as uniform as possible throughout the project period. Numerous computer algorithms have been proposed and implemented for this type of *resource levelling*. None of the resource levelling programs, however, provide an exact optimal solution. Each uses certain heuristics to obtain a near-optimal allocation.

The situation is further complicated if several resources are to be considered simultaneously. In such a case, the approach has been to use one of many rules proposed in the literature and hope to come fairly close to an optimal solution. For example, one such rule is to take up the activity with the shortest duration first. Another will be to take up the activity with the longest duration first. And so on. There is no analytic tool available to determine which rule would lead to a better solution, let alone be the optimal solution. It has therefore been suggested that before deciding on one specific rule, the network should be simulated using different rules and then pick the one which completes the project in the shortest time. Note that this simulation would be deterministic, and no random numbers would be required.

Cash-flow: In addition to the time duration and resource requirement, each activity may also have some cost associated with it. It is often important to know the amount of cash-flow at different times while the project is in progress. Once the cost of each activity has been determined, it is not difficult to obtain a curve of time versus the total money spent for various points in the project. There are several standard computer programs that generate such curves.

Expediting: There is yet another dimension to an activity network. Most activities can be expedited if more money is spent on them. In general, one can determine a cost versus completion time curve for each activity. Most often it is a straight line based on two points, a normal time—normal cost point and a crash time—crash cost point. The total project can be expedited by shortening the times of the critical and near-critical activities. By repeated calculations one can determine the completion time versus the cost curve for the entire project. On this curve one may then pick a satisfactory point for which cost and time requirements are both met.

5-9. Remarks and references

Since their first application in 1958, network techniques such as *PERT* and *CPM*, are being put to increasing use in studying and scheduling of large projects. There are numerous textbooks that deal with *CPM* and *PERT* analysis. For example,

WIEST, J. D. and F. K. LEVY, *A Management Guide to PERT/CPM*, 2nd Ed., Prentice-Hall of India, New Delhi, 1978.

MODER, J. J. and C. R. PHILLIPS, *Project Management with CPM and PERT*, Reinhold Publishing Corp., New York, 1964.

WHITEHOUSE, G. E., *Systems Analysis and Design Using Network Techniques*, Prentice-Hall, Englewood Cliffs, N.J., 1973.

After a few years of its use in the early 1960's, it was realized that the assumptions made by the original users of *PERT* (that the activity durations were β-distributed and that a single critical path identified on the basis of average durations would suffice) often led to erroneous estimates. In 1963 R. M. Van Slyke showed, in the following paper, how simulation can be used to obtain more realistic estimates of project-completion time.

VAN SLYKE, R. M., "Monte Carlo Methods and the PERT Problem," *Oper. Res.*, Vol. XI, 1963, pp. 839–60.

The simulation of an activity network performed in this chapter basically follows the method used by Van Slyke. It was the next-event simulation approach. An event takes place each time an activity is completed during the forward pass. Time moves forward from 0 to *TMIN* as we move from event to event.

A good treatment of simulation using *PERT* can be found in Chapter 6 of

PRITSKER, A. A. B. and P. J. KIVIAT, *Simulation With GASP II*, Prentice-Hall, Englewood Cliffs, N.J., 1969

which gives a *PERT* simulation program written in *GASP* II. A similar treatment is also given in Chapter 4 of

PRITSKER, A. A. B, *The GASP IV Simulation Language*, John Wiley and Sons, New York, 1974.

These two textbooks also give an example showing how various decision rules for scheduling activities can be simulated when there are multiple resources to be allocated.

Another example of simulation of a stochastic network can be found in

BURT, J. M., Jr., D. P. GRAVER, and M. PERLAS, "Simple Stochastic Networks: Some Problems and Procedures," *New. Res. Logistics Quart*, Vol. 17, No. 4, Dec. 1970, pp. 439–460.

The technique of simulating a stochastic *PERT* process is incorporated into another procedure called *GERT* (Graphical Evaluation and Review Technique), described in the textbook by Whitehouse cited above. It has even led to two special network simulation languages *GERT* and *SMOOTH*. The latter is described in

SIGAL, C. E. and A. A. B. PRITSKER, 'SMOOTH: A Combined Continuous Discrete Nework Simulation Language," *SIMULATION*, Vol. 21, March 1974.

Simulation plays an extremely valuable role in planning large construction projects. Even the effect of weather can be simulated in optimizing the cost and duration of a project, as illustrated in

BENJAMIN, N. B. H. and T. W. GREENWOLD, "Simulating Effects of Weather on Construction," *Proc. ASEE, Journal Const. Divn.*, Vol. 99, July 1973, pp. 175–190.

5-10. Exercises

5-1. Think of two different projects on your own. Partition each project into distinct, nontrivial, nonoverlapping jobs. Determine the precedence relationships that these jobs must satisfy. Draw an activity network for each project.

5-2. Show that the activities in a project network can be ordered topologically if and only if the network contains no cycles.

5-3. In Sec. 5-2 a method was outlined for ordering the activities of a network topologically. Write a *FORTRAN* program (using this method or any other which renumbers the activities 1, 2, ..., N such that they are in a topological order. The input consists of N, M and M pairs of integers (i, j) denoting that activity i must precede activity j. (Note that N is the number of branches and M the number of nodes in the network.) Give the output in the form of a linear array A of size N, whose kth element $A(k)$, the new label of the activity whose original name was k.

5-4. A project network with nine activities is given in Fig. 5-10. All activity durations are uniformly distributed, ranging $\pm$ 20 per cent from the mean. The mean values for the durations of activities A, B, C, D, E, F, G, H, I are 7, 8, 2, 8, 5, 7, 13, 2, 12, respectively. Simulate the network, with 500 runs, to obtain a histogram as in Sec. 5-7. Compare the simulation results with those obtained by a deterministic analysis using the mean values only.

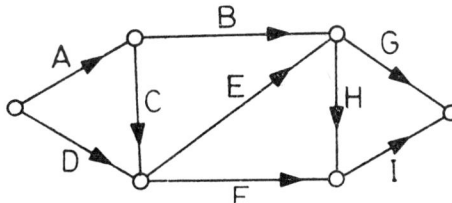

Fig. 5-10.

5-5. Repeat Exercise 5-4 assuming that duration distributions of activities A, C, F, and I are Lognormal and those of the remaining five are exponential. The mean values are as given in Exercise 5-4 and the standard deviations are 10 per cent of the mean.

5-6. Write a FORTRAN SUBROUTINE to evaluate the mean and standard deviations of a normal distribution which approximates a histogram such as in Fig. 5-9 (or Table 5-3), produced by a simulation experiment.

5-7. For the network given in Fig. 5-8, compute and plot on a common sheet the two normal curves for the project duration: (i) obtained as a result of the simulation, (ii) obtained using a single mean value for each activity and the relationship that the variance of sum is the sum of variances.

5-8. Simulate the network in Fig. 5-8, assuming that all activity distributions are exponential. Use the same mean and standard deviations as in Table 5-1. Keep the number of simulation runs $NRUNS = 1,000$.

5-9. The histogram in Fig. 5-9 gives the histogram of time for realizing node 13 (corresponding to the project completion). Obtain a similar histogram for the intermediate node 8.

5-10. Repeat the simulation experiment in Sec. 5-7 with the number of runs $NRUNS$ (i) 500, (ii) 5,000. Then compare the three results.

5-11. Determining the number of runs in a simulation experiment, in order to achieve a specified level of confidence in its results, is extremely important and will be dealt with in Chapter 7 in a greater detail. For now, determine the number of simulations of a network that are required so that there is a 97 per cent probability that (i) the estimated project duration does not differ from the true project duration by more than one-tenth of the standard deviation, (ii) the estimated criticality indices do not differ from the true values by more than 0.05. (See Van Slyke's paper.)

6

Inventory Control and Forecasting

Like queueing systems, inventory systems have also been studied, modelled, analyzed and simulated very extensively. As in the case of the waiting lines, the study of inventories is mathematically interesting as well as economically rewarding. Both queueing theory and inventory theory are well-developed areas of operations research and management science. Because of their cost saving potentials both evoke very widespread interest.

Broadly speaking, the inventory management problem is one of maintaining an adequate supply of some item to meet an expected pattern of demand, while striking a reasonable balance between the cost of holding the items in inventory and the penalty (loss of sales and goodwill, say) of running out. The item may be a commodity sold by a store; it may be spare machine parts in a factory; it may be railway wagons; it may be cash in the bank to meet the customers' demand; it may even be the engineering graduates in a country to meet their projected demand. It is indeed surprising to find that a very wide variety of seemingly different problems can be mathematically formulated as an inventory-control problem. There are, of course, several different models of inventory systems. As we did for queueing systems, we will first consider a very simple inventory system and derive an analytic expression to get a flavour of the basic inventory theory.

6-1. Elements of inventory theory

There are three types of expenses associated with an inventory system. The relative importance of these will depend on the specific system. They are: (i) administrative cost of placing an order, called *reorder cost* or *set up cost*; (ii) cost of maintaining an inventory, called *inventory holding cost* or *carrying cost,* which includes storage charge, interest, insurance, etc., and (iii) *shortage cost* is a loss of profit, goodwill, etc., when we run out of stock. Given these three costs and a demand pattern, we are usually interested in determining (a) when to reorder and (b) how much to reorder so that the total inventory cost is minimized. Frequently, there is another parameter of the system, called the *delivery lag* or *lead time*. This is the time that elapses after a reorder is initiated and before the items are received.

The simplest inventory model for a single item is shown in Fig. 6-1. In the model the daily demand for the item is a known constant. When the stock goes down to zero, Q items are ordered and are delivered immediately without any delivery lag. The inventory level starts at Q, goes down to zero at a constant rate, and then jumps back to a level Q. The average inventory level throughout the year is $Q/2$ items. Since in this particular

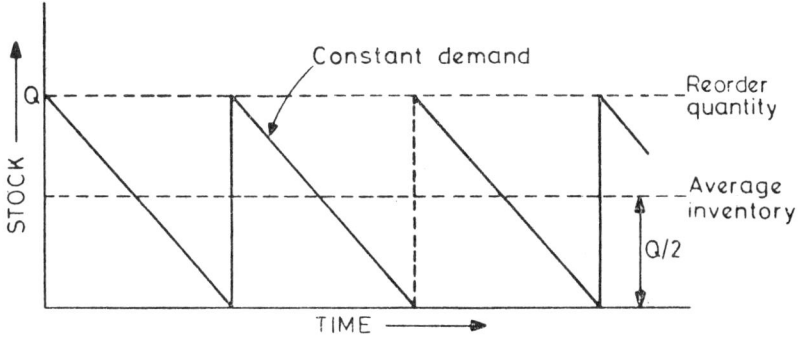

Fig. 6-1:   Constant demand inventory model.

model, we need never run out of stock, there is no shortage cost involved. The total inventory cost per day (or any unit of time) is

$$C = \text{holding cost} + \text{reorder cost}$$

$$= \frac{Q}{2} \cdot k + \frac{D}{Q} \cdot r,$$

where k is the carrying cost per item per day, D is the volume of the daily sale, and r is the order cost of one delivery. (Q/D is the number of days between two consecutive deliveries). On differentiating C with respect to Q and setting $\frac{dC}{dQ}$ to zero we get

$$Q = \sqrt{\frac{2Dr}{k}} \qquad \ldots(6\text{-}1)$$

The value of Q in Eq. (6-1) gives the size of reorder which will minimize the total inventory cost C. This optimal reorder quantity Q is referred to as the *EOQ* (*Economical Order Quantity*). The question *when* to place an order is also answered by Eq. (6-1). We place an order of $Q = \sqrt{\frac{2Dr}{k}}$ items, at fixed regular intervals of $\frac{Q}{D} = \sqrt{\frac{2r}{Dk}}$ days. The average inventory is $\frac{Q}{2} = \sqrt{\frac{Dr}{2k}}$. Observe that this average stock level increases only in pro-portion to the square root of the daily demand D. Equation (6-1), known as the Wilson Formula (named after R. H. Wilson), or the *lot size formula* has been in use for more than 50 years. It is the best known formula in inventory theory.

Constant delivery lag: In the simplest inventory system, for which Eq. (6-1) was derived, we assumed there was no delivery lag. Suppose we make the model a bit more realistic by adding that there is a nonzero delivery lag of d days, a constant value. Since we know the delivery lag d, and we also know exactly the time when the order should arrive, all we need to do is to place the order d days earlier. This implies no added complication to the basic model, as long as the delivery lag time d remains constant. However, the problem would get complicated if d is made a random variable.

EOQ with shortage cost: The economic order quantity (EOQ) given by Eq. (6-1) was derived for an inventory system in which the demand was constant and we never ran out of stock. A similar expression can be derived for a system in which we run out of stock for a certain fraction of the time. Usually, two types of situations occur when the dealer runs out of stock: (i) The customer goes somewhere else, and therefore any sale that would have resulted is *lost* for ever;   (ii) The customer leaves his order with the dealer and this *backlog* or *back order* is filled as soon as the stock is replenished. There is, however, a penalty associated per item per unit of time for which the back orders are outstanding (cost of keeping backlog reorders, cost of shipping the items to the customer, loss in some goodwill, etc.). Let us first consider the back order type of situation.

Consider a system with a constant daily demand D, a reorder quantity Q, and a constant nonzero lead time d, as shown in Fig. 6-2. For a fraction α of the time, we have a non-zero inventory and for the remaining $(1 - \alpha)$ of the period we keep a backlog of orders (shown in shaded area below the x-axis). The backlog is filled as soon as the next delivery (of Q items) is made.

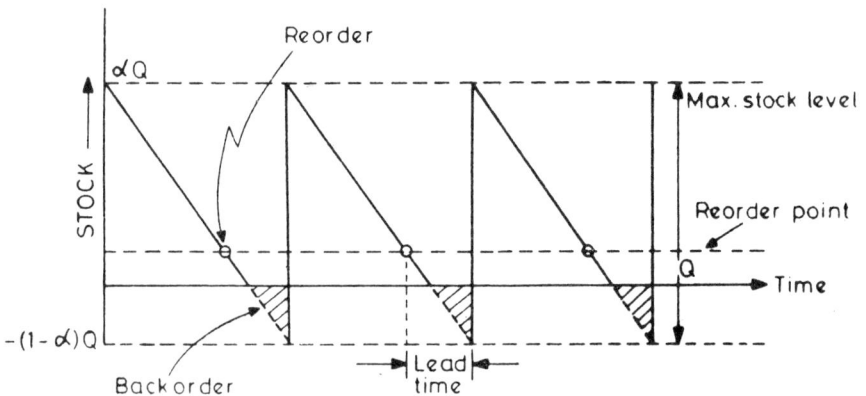

Fig. 6-2:   Constant demand with shortages.

For such an inventory system the following hold:

Average inventory during the days when there is a positive inventory $= \dfrac{Q\alpha}{2}$.

Average daily inventory, averaged over all days $= \dfrac{Q\alpha^2}{2}$

Therefore, the average daily holding cost $= k \cdot \dfrac{Q\alpha^2}{2}$,

where k is the holding cost per item per day.
Likewise,
Average shortage during the days when there is a shortage

$$= \dfrac{(1-\alpha)\,Q}{2}$$

Average shortage, averaged over all days $= \dfrac{(1-\alpha)^2\,Q}{2}$

Therefore, the average daily shortage cost $= b \cdot \dfrac{(1-\alpha)^2\,Q}{2}$,

where b is the shortage cost of backlog per item per day.

Since the daily demand is D, a reorder is placed every Q/D days. Therefore, the average reorder cost per day $= r \cdot D/Q$, where r is the reorder cost. Adding these three costs we get

Total average inventory cost per day,

$$C = \frac{kQ\alpha^2}{2} + \frac{b\,(1-\alpha)^2\,Q}{2} + \frac{Dr}{Q} = \frac{Q}{2}\Big[k\alpha^2 + b\,(1-\alpha)^2\Big] + \frac{Dr}{Q} \quad ...(6\text{-}2)$$

To determine an optimal value of the fraction α, we differentiate Eq. (6-2) with respect to α and set the derivative to zero. Thus

$$\frac{dC}{d\alpha} = \frac{Q}{2}\,[2k\alpha - 2b\,(1-\alpha)] = 0,$$

which yields

$$\alpha = \frac{b}{k+b} \qquad\qquad ...(6\text{-}3)$$

Substituting this value of α in Eq. (6-2), we get the total cost

$$C = \frac{Q}{2}\,\frac{bk}{k+b} + \frac{Dr}{Q} \qquad\qquad ...(6\text{-}4)$$

In order to determine the optimal value of the reorder quantity Q, we differentiate Eq. (6-4) with respect to Q and set it to zero.

$$\frac{dC}{dQ} = \frac{bk}{2\,(k+b)} - \frac{Dr}{Q^2} = 0$$

which gives the economic reorder quantity (EOQ) for this system as

$$\text{Optimal } Q = \sqrt{\frac{2Dr}{k}} \cdot \sqrt{\frac{k+b}{b}} \qquad\qquad ...(6\text{-}5)$$

The first factor in this expression is the EOQ given by Eq. (6-1), when no shortages were allowed. The second factor is greater than 1, and it arises due to the finite value of the backlog cost b. If this cost b is much larger than k (which in effect amounts to allowing no shortages), Eq. (6-5) reduces to Eq. (6-1). Notice that due to finite value of shortage cost b the optimal order size Q increases, but the maximum inventory αQ decreases. The average daily cost under optimal conditions is obtained by substituting Eq. (6-5) into Eq. (6-4), as

$$\text{minimum } C = \sqrt{\frac{2Drbk}{k+b}} \qquad \qquad ...(6\text{-}6)$$

which is less by a factor of $\sqrt{\dfrac{b}{k+b}}$ than the corresponding cost if shortages were not allowed.

To illustrate the use of these formulas, let us consider the following numerical example:

$D = 50$ units per day
$r = $ Rs. 200 per reorder
$k = $ Re. 0.005 per unit per day
$b = $ Re. 0.02 per day per unit back ordered.

Substituting these values in Eq. (6-1), we get the economical reorder quantity with no shortage allowed as

$$\sqrt{\frac{2Dr}{k}} = 2,000 \text{ units}$$

If shortages are allowed, we use Eq. (6-5) and get the optimal reorder quantity as

$$2,000 \times \sqrt{\frac{k+b}{b}} = 2,236 \text{ units}$$

Likewise, the minimum total inventory cost C, when shortages are not allowed is

$$\sqrt{2Drk} = \text{Rs. 10 per day.}$$

If shortages are allowed the minimum total cost of maintaining the inventory is

$$10 \times \sqrt{\frac{b}{k+b}} = \text{Rs. 8.94 per day,}$$

showing a reduction of Rs. 1.06 per day if shortages are allowed.

The quantity α, the fraction of time for which we have a nonzero stock, is an indicator of the 'service level' of an inventory system. The most economical value of α given by Eq. (6-3)

$$\alpha = \frac{b}{k+b} = \frac{.02}{.005 + .02} = 0.8$$

for this particular numerical example. Whether or not a service level of

80 per cent is tolerable is a different issue, but under the assumption made, it is the most economical level. A 100 per cent service level (no shortages) cost is Rs. 10 per day, whereas an 80 per cent level affects a saving of Rs. 1.06 per day.

6-2. More complex inventory models

The analytic expressions derived so far, for the two different inventory models, are extremely simple. These were included just to give a flavour for the type of analytic expressions available in inventory theory. There are more complicated formulas available in mathematical inventory theory dealing with different types of inventory models. The following are some of the complicating factors.

Gradual replenishment: In deriving Eq. (6-1) we assumed that the stock was replenished abruptly and instantaneously, as soon as the ordered lot was received (from, say, the wholesaler). In many cases, particularly in a production environment, the replenishment occurs gradually. The demand is met from the stock as well as from the production. If during the production period p units are being produced per day and D units are sold, inventory increases at the rate of $(p-D)$ units per day during this period. It is left as an exercise (Exercise 6-4) to show that under such a production environment, Eq. (6-7)

$$Q = \sqrt{\frac{2Dr}{k(1 - D/p)}} \qquad \qquad ...(6\text{-}7)$$

would give the economic batch quantity for production.

Multi-item production: Formula (6-7) holds when only one item is being produced; or if different products are manufactured they are totally independent of each other. Often a manufacturer produces several different items, one after another, using the same plant facilities. He must produce these items in large enough batches so that a batch will last while all other batches of different products are being produced. In such a case, a "production cycle" is established such that one batch of every product is produced in one cycle. It can be shown that under this situation, the optimal number of such production cycles per unit of time is given by

$$\sqrt{\frac{\Sigma D_j k_j (1 - D_j/p_j)}{2 \Sigma r_i}} \qquad \qquad ...(6\text{-}8)$$

where D_j = demand for the jth product per unit of time
k_j = carrying cost for the jth product per unit of time
r_j = set up cost for the jth product, and
p_j = production rate for the jth product.

Capital restriction: In deriving formula, such as Eq. (6-8), it was assumed that there was no capital shortage, and we could stock up as many units as given by an EOQ formula. This may not always hold. A restriction is often imposed that the value of the total inventory should not exceed x rupees. Equation (6-8) can be suitably modified to handle this restriction.

Quantity discounts: In most purchasing situations price advantages are available with larger orders. This price break may occur at discrete points or it may be continuous. In the first case, the price changes abruptly when the order size reaches or exceeds certain numbers, say, 100, 5,000, etc. The effect of a quantity discount or price break is threefold: (1) There is a direct saving due to the reduced price; (2) Due to the reduced cost of the items, the interest is reduced and hence the carrying cost per unit is decreased; (3) However, to take advantage of discount, larger orders are placed, which means increased average stock and hence increased carrying cost.

Taking these into account, for each price range an equation is set up giving the total inventory cost per unit time. By differentiating these equations the *EOQ* is determined for each price range. These in turn are used to find the optimal cost of inventory for purchased quantities in each discount range. Then the least expensive amongst these will be taken as the optimal lot size.

In the second case the price reduction varies continuously with the size of the lot. Then the reorder cost r can be replaced with

$$r - Q \cdot a,$$

where a represents the discount available, which increases linearly with reorder quantity Q. It can be easily seen that such a discount does not alter the expression for *EOQ* given by Eq. (6-1). There are, however, situations where the pricing structure is more complex and cannot be handled analytically.

Varying demand: The pattern of the demand is probably the most important consideration in an inventory system. The demand will be a stochastic variable in all but trivial systems. By using historical data and forecasting techniques the probability distribution of the demand must be established. Over the basic distribution one may have to superimpose the long-term trend, seasonal variations, etc. In the simple example of the inventory system in Chapter 1, we assumed the daily demand to be uniformly distributed, from 0 to 99 units. A Poisson-distributed daily demand is more realistic, because it results from the stochastic independence of the arrivals of the customers, as discussed in Sec. 4-1. In other words, if the customers arrive independently, their interarrival time is exponential distributed; and if each customer orders only one unit, the total demand in any period will be Poisson distributed.

However, if the number of units requested varies randomly from customer to customer, we would get a different distribution for total demand during a given period, depending how the units requested vary amongst customers. For example, if the units ordered by each customer are geometrically distributed and the interarrival time between customers is exponentially distributed, the total demand in any period will have a hypergeometric distribution. The normal distribution approximates well many of the distributions such as binomial, Poisson, gamma, and hypergeometric, when their mean increases. Thus, it is often found that the demand follows a normal distribution for most time periods encountered in practice. For example, if the average number of units demanded in a period exceeds six or so, the demand can be approximated by a normal distribution.

Variations in demand can be handled by adopting either of the following two policies : (1) We make periodic reviews, say, once a month, and then place orders of a varying amount, such that the inventory position reaches a specified level. Such a system, depicted in Fig. 6-3, is called a *periodic review system.* (2) Instead of fixing the review period and varying the reorder

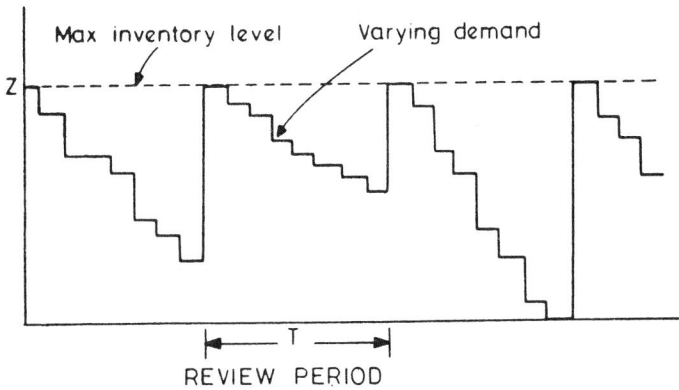

Fig. 6-3:   Periodic review system.

quantity, we may do the opposite; namely, keep the reorder quantity constant Q but vary the reorder time according to the need. Whenever the inventory position goes to or below a specified level P we order a specified quantity Q. Such a system, shown in Fig. 6-4, is called a *continuous review system* or *transaction reporting system.* It requires that a running log of the inventory position be maintained for every transaction. It is evident that if the demand varies statistically, no reasonable amount of buffer stock can guarantee that we would never run out of stock. Therefore we must always consider the *shortage cost,* when dealing with randomly varying demands. For certain simple types of stochastic systems (such as a system with Poisson distributed demand, constant procurement lead time and backorders case) it has been possible to obtain exact analytic expressions for determining the average annual cost of a specified inventory policy. An analytic expression for a general inventory system with stochastic demands, however, is not available.

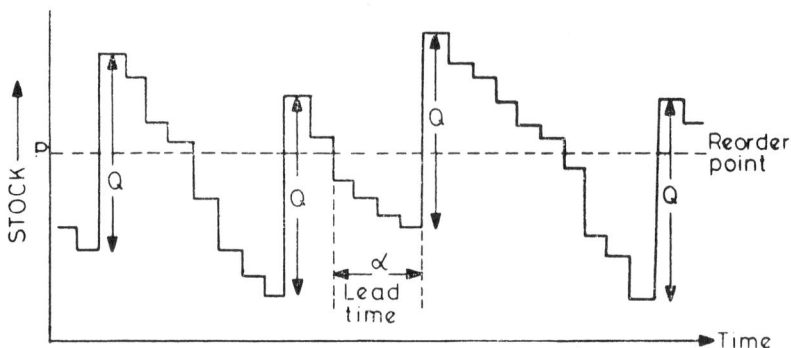

Fig. 6-4:   Variable-review-time constant-order-quantity.

Lead time variability: Although for simplicity one sometimes assumes that the procurement lead time is a fixed number of days, in reality this will rarely be the case.   The lead time will usually vary randomly, whose distribution, mean, and standard duration would have to be determined using historic data and forecasting techniques.   Using the average value and regarding it as the constant lead time can result in serious underestimation of the fraction that the system is out of stock.

It has been found that the lead time often follows as Erlang distribution (i.e., a gamma distribution with integral values of parameter k; which becomes exponential when $k = 1$, and normal when k becomes large).

Multiple orders outstanding: In the simple inventory system simulated in Chapter 1, it was stipulated that at any given time there can be at most one reorder outstanding.   Frequently we encounter systems where two or more reorders could be outstanding.   A model that allows more than a single reorder to be outstanding at any point in time and has a random lead time presents a formidable problem for an analytic handling.   For, if the lead time of two consecutive reorders are independent it is possible that the second reorder arrives before the first.   On the other hand, if reorders must always arrive in the same sequence in which they were placed, then their lead times cannot be considered independent random variables.   Because of this complex interaction between outstanding reorders, the models with multiple reorders, stochastic lead time and, of course, stochastic demand may be studied only through simulation.

Thus one can easily see that, like the queueing situations, the real-life inventory situations are so complex that without simulation it is almost impossible to determine the over-all effect of operating rules.   The mathematical analysis, using average demand figures, average lead time, etc., along with formulas, such as those obtained in Sec. 6-2, are useful only as approximate guidelines.   Since inventory control is of central importance in most business and industrial operations, the management would want to be thoroughly satisfied with the workings of a proposed set of rules before putting them into use.   A simulation experiment makes it possible to study the effects of different policies before actually implementing them.   Thus the operation of the proposed system for months, or even years, can be simulated in minutes.   The results in terms of the total inventory cost, shortages, number of reorders, average inventory level, etc., for different inventory policies can be compared and a choice amongst them can be made.

6-3.   Simulation Example—1

The *service level* for an inventory system may be defined as the ratio of the units furnished (to customers, when requested) to the total number of units requested.   The service level, usually expressed as a percentage, is a very important consideration in deciding on an inventory policy.   The management will often reject an inventory policy if the service level is too low, even if it is the most economical operating point.   For, a low service ratio indicates the inability of the system to satisfy customers, and may lead to a total loss of business in the long run.

As the desired service level is raised the average stock that has to be maintained will naturally go up.   However, for a given value of service level, there may be many different values of the average stock, depending on the reorder combination (P, Q).   We wish to experiment with a large range of inventory policies to determine which reorder combination (P, Q) yields the highest service level for a given value of the average stock.   Let our inventory system be characterized by the following parameters:

(i) The demand arrives in single units and the interdemand time follows a negative exponential distribution with an average value of 0.25 day (i.e., the average daily demand is for 4 units).

(ii) The shortages are not made good subsequently.   The lost sales are lost forever.

(iii) The procurement lead time varies between 3 and 4 days, depending on the time of the day the reorders are placed.   A reorder placed at any time during the kth day arrives at the beginning of $(k+4)$th day.

(iv) At any given time there can be at most three reorders outstanding; and on any given day at most one reorder can be placed.

(v) The total reorder cost here is insignificant in comparison with the carrying cost.   Therefore, the number of reorders in a given period is of no interest to us.   We are interested only in the value of the average stock and in the number of lost sales.

(vi) Initially there is a stock of 10 units and no reorders are outstanding. We wish to find the list of policies (P, Q)'s which give us the lowest average values of stock for various service levels.

We will write a program to simulate all combinations of the reorder point, P, from 5 to 25 in steps of 2 and reorder quantity, Q, from 5 to 15 in steps of 2.   For each of these $11 \times 6 = 66$ different (P, Q) combinations the average stock level and the service level will be computed and printed.

The length of each simulation run will be made $NDAYS = 500$ days. We will assume the initial stock to be 10 units, and no reorders outstanding at the beginning of the simulation period.

Since the simulation is to be repeated for various values of (P, Q) two main loops are set up with reorder point P-loop within the reorder quantity Q-loop. For each run we must use the same set of random numbers. Within each run, for a period of 500 days, certain data have to be initialized. These are: the cumulative total demand (CTD), total units supplied (TUS), and the cumulative stock held (CSH) are set to zero; the actual current stock ($STOCK$) is set to 10, and since there is no order outstanding, the inventory position ($INVPOS$) is also set to 10. (Note that $INVPOS$ is the sum of the actual current stock and the number of units on various reorders.) The current time (T) is set to zero.

In simulating the inventory system in Chapter 1 we used the fixed time-step method—advancing time by one day, for 180 days. Here we will use the next-event simulation philosophy. Two types of events occur during the simulation: (a) the next demand event, and (b) the next delivery-of-reorder event.

Since at any time there can be as many as three reorders outstanding, we need to maintain two pieces of information: the number of outstanding reorders and the due date of each. We will use a single linear array DD (for due dates) of size three to indicate both pieces of information. When a reorder is outstanding the corresponding $DD(I)$ gives the actual time the order is to be received at the store. When a reorder is not outstanding the corresponding $DD(I)$ is set to a large value, $INFNTY$ (set to 999 in this case because the simulated time T goes only up to 500). As there are no reorders outstanding at the beginning of each run, we initialize $DD(I) = INFNTY$, for $I = 1$ to 3.

Another decision to be made is the way in which we define the cumulative average stock, and this in turn would depend on the method of charging the carrying cost. For example, one may be paying carrying charges only on the basis of the actual stock left over each night. In another situation one may be paying on the basis of the maximum stock level each day. In this simulation, we will use the exact mathematical definition of the cumulative average stock, that is, we will multiply the actual stock $STOCK$ between two consecutive events by the time gap between the two, sum all such products and divide the sum by 500, the duration of the simulation. This would give us the exact daily cumulative average over the entire simulation period. Thus the daily cumulative average stock up to any time t is given by

$$\frac{1}{t} \sum_i (t_{i+1} - t_i) . s_i \qquad \qquad ...(6\text{-}9)$$

when t_i is the time of the ith event occurring (in days); t_{i+1} is the $(i+1)$th event occurring; s_i is the stock immediately after instant t_i.

The division by the total simulated time $NDAYS$ need be performed only at the end of a run.   During the run, as each event occurs the quantity

$$(t_{i+1} - t_i) \cdot s_i \qquad \ldots (6\text{-}10)$$

will be added to the running sum (called cumulative stock held, *CHS*).

In the actual program, for convenience, we will split this quantity into two parts.   First part is due to demand events only.   The second part is due to delivery-of-reorders, occurring between two cumulative demands.

The flowchart in Fig. 6-5 gives the logic of the program for this simulation.   The flowchart is only for a single (P, Q) combination, the two outer

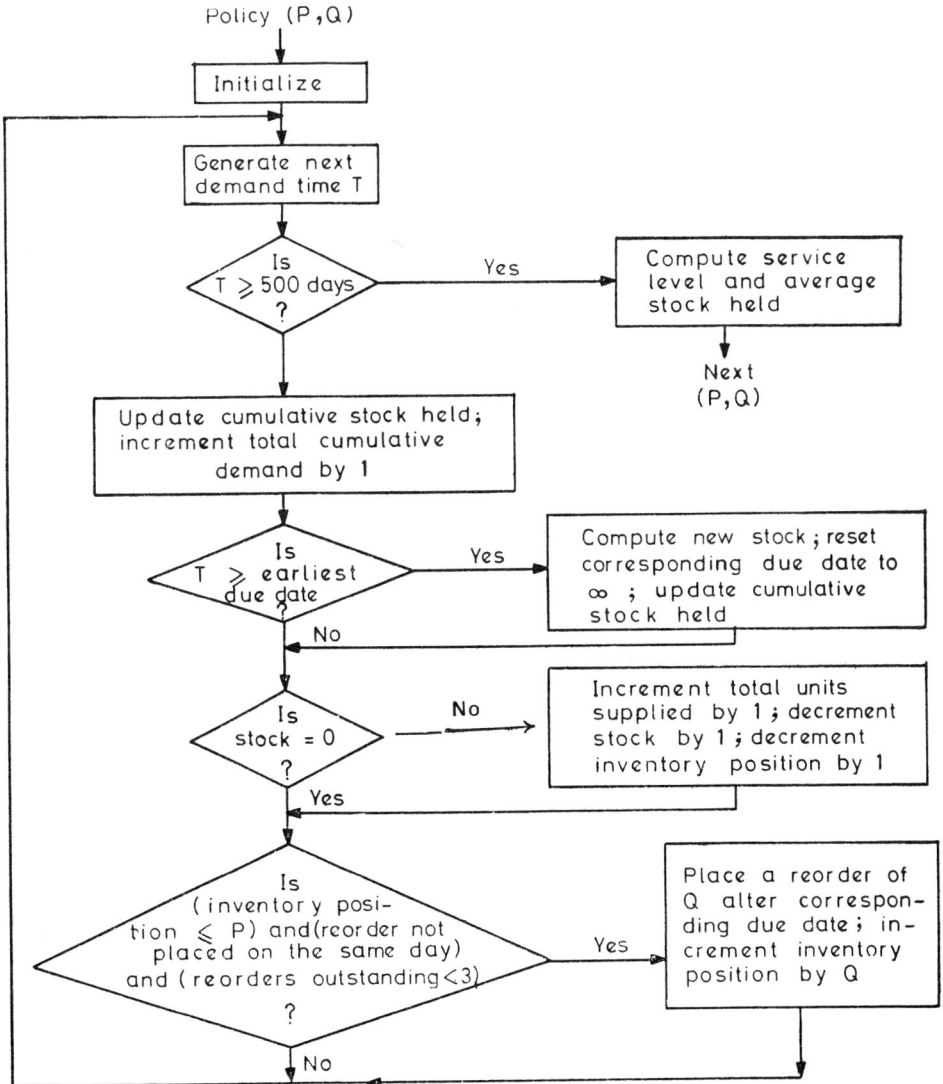

Fig. 6-5:   **Simulation of an Inventory Policy (P, Q).**

loops for varying P and Q have been omitted to avoid cluttering the figure.

After initialization, the next demand time T (arrival time of the next customer) is generated using a negative-exponential variate generator. If this time T exceeds the total simulation period of 500 days, this simulation run is finished; otherwise, we add 1 to the total cumulative demand and add an appropriate term to the cumulative stock held (*CSH*). Next, we check to see if any of the outstanding reorders has arrived between the current demand-event and the previous demand-event. This is accomplished by comparing the three due dates $DD(I)$ with integral part of T (because an order can arrive only in the morning). In case one or more reorders did arrive the stock is increased appropriately, and the corresponding $DD(I)$'s are set to *INFNTY*, for subsequent use. The effect of reorder arrivals on cumulative stock held is also taken into account.

The next step is to check if we can supply a unit to the current customer (i.e., if the stock is nonzero). If we can, we supply a unit and note its effect on statistics. Finally, we test if a reorder is to be placed at T. Three conditions must simultaneously be supplied for placing a reorder, namely, (i) the inventory position must be P units or less, and (ii) we must not have placed another reorder earlier in the day, and (iii) the number of orders outstanding must be less than 3. If all three conditions are satisfied a reorder is placed for Q units, inventory position is increased by Q and one of the $DD(I)$ which was ∞ is set to the delivery date, which is the integral part of T plus 4 days.

Since this completes all possible actions to be taken at time T, we go back to the beginning of the loop and generate the arrival of the next customer. When T exceeds 500 days (we have gone through the inner loop about 5,000 times) the service level and the average stock for this particular combination (P, Q) are computed and printed out.

The following is a (Format-free) *FORTRAN* program which simulates the 66 different inventory policies and prints out the service level and average stock values for each.

```
      INTEGER P, Q, TUS, CTD, STOCK, INFNTY, NDAYS, INVPOS, ISEED,
     LRD, DD(3)
      READ, NDAYS, INFNTY, ISEED
      DO 160 Q = 5, 15, 2
      DO 160 P = 5, 25, 2
C     INITIALISATION
      STOCK = 10
      INVPOS = STOCK
      CSH = 0.0
      TUS = 0
      CTD = 0
      T = 0.0
      LRD = INFNTY
      ISED = ISEED
      DO 100 I = 1, 3
```

```
100  DD(I) = INFNTY
C    GENERATION OF NEXT DEMAND TIME
110  RN = SNDY(ISED)
     T1 = T
     T = T − 0.25*ALOG(RN)
     IF(T . GE . FLOAT(NDAYS)) GO TO 150
     CTD = CTD + 1
     CSH = CSH + FLOAT(STOCK) * (T − T1)
C    CHECKING ARRIVAL OF REORDERS BETWEEN T1 AND T
     DO 120 I = 1, 3
     IF(FLOAT(DD(I)) . GT . T) GO TO 120
     STOCK = STOCK + Q
     CSH = CSH + FLOAT(Q)* (T − FLOAT(DD(I)))
     DD(I) = INFNTY
120  CONTINUE
     IF(STOCK . LT . 1) GO TO 130
     STOCK = STOCK − 1
     INVPOS = INVPOS − 1
     TUS = TUS + 1
C    CHECK AND PLACE A REORDER
130  IF(INVPOS . GT . P) GO TO 110
     IF(INT(T) . EQ . LRD) GO TO 110
     DO 140 I = 1, 3
     IF(DD(I) . LT . INFNTY) GO TO 140
     LRD = INT(T)
     DD(I) = INT(T) + 4
     INVPOS = INVPOS + Q
     GO TO 110
140  CONTINUE
     GO TO 110
C    COMPUTE SERVICE LEVEL AND AVERAGE DAILY STOCK
150  SL = FLOAT(TUS)/FLOAT(CTD)*100.0
     AVSTOK = CSH/FLOAT(NDAYS)
     PRINT, P, Q, SL, AVSTOCK
160  CONTINUE
     STOP
     END
```

The function $SNDY(X)$ for generating pseudorandom numbers is

```
FUNCTION SNDY(X)
INTEGER A, X
DATA A/189277/
X = A * X
SNDY = FLOAT(X)/34359738368.0
RETURN
END
```

Observe that this generator (for a 36-bit binary machine) is the same as *RNDY*1, discussed in Sec. 3-3, except that in *RNDY*1 the seed was specified in the subroutine itself, and the user had no control over it. In *SNDY* the seed must be supplied by the calling program—either read in as data or included as part of the main program. Here we are reading the seed

(*ISEED*) as data, but keeping its value 11, 750, 920, 161, identical to the seed in *RNDY*1. By inserting the same seed at the beginning of the simulation run for each (*P*, *Q*) policy, we are ensuring that all policies are tested with identical interdemand-time sequence.

Output: The output of the program gave the service level and average stock for each policy (*P*, *Q*). From this output, a plot of service level vs. average stock was made. The lowest points in this plot were joined by straight line segments, as shown in Fig. 6-6. This curve represents the lowest average stock for a given service level. Note that in Fig. 6-6 we have shown only 20 points, the remaining points were omitted in order to avoid cluttering the figure. The policies lying on the curve represent the best policies (amongst those that were tried). Those lying above are inefficient ones, because they result in keeping higher average daily stock for the same service level. For example, the (9, 5) policy yields a service level of 61.2 per cent and requires an average daily stock of 2.1 units, whereas the (7, 11) policy also gives the same service level (61.2 per cent) but requires a much larger average daily stock, of 3.8 units. Obviously the latter would be poorer inventory policy to use. Table 6-1 gives the 20 policies (out of

Service Level	Average Stock	P	Q
42.6	1.7	5	7
49.7	2.6	5	9
51.2	1.7	5	5
57.2	2.0	7	5
61.2	2.1	9	5
61.2	3.8	7	11
70.5	3.5	9	7
76.8	3.3	11	5
80.3	7.0	11	15
82.5	4.1	13	5
86.3	4.6	15	5
86.6	8.0	13	15
90.5	6.0	21	5
94.0	7.6	17	7
93.7	10.2	15	15
94.7	8.2	17	9
97.3	9.2	19	7
99.2	12.1	21	9
99.8	14.0	23	9
99.8	19.0	25	15

Table 6-1:   Average stock for a given service level.

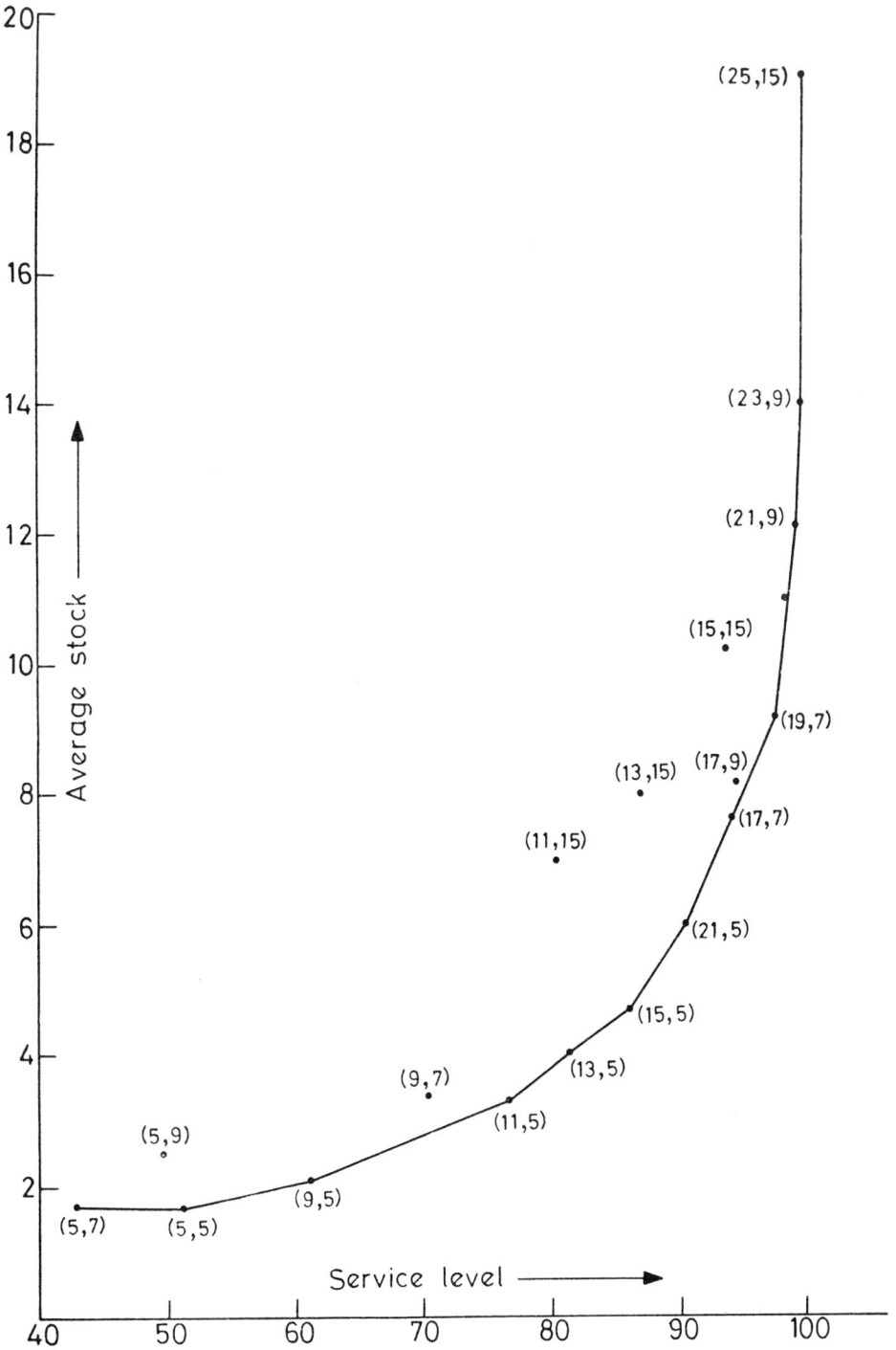

Fig. 6-6.   Average stock vs. service level.

66 simulated) sorted in order of increasing of service level. (These are the same policies that were shown in Fig. 6-6.)

It is particularly interesting to observe from Table 6-1 (or Fig. 6-6) that the best policies are not entirely based on the best reorder point P or the best reorder quantity Q alone, but on a combination of the two. This simulation also demonstrates that it would be unwise to establish a reorder quantity Q without considering its effect on the service level, even if this Q is the EOQ. Thus a curve such as the one shown in Fig. 6-6 is a very useful tool for the management in deciding on an inventory policy.

6-4.   Generation of Poisson and Erlang variates

In Sec. 4-1 we showed that if the interarrival time of customers is exponentially distributed [in accordance with Eq. (4-3)] then the number of customers arriving in a specified period is governed by a Poisson distribution [in accordance with Eq. (4-5)]. Thus if the average value of the interrarival time (exponentially distributed) is 0.25 day, then equivalently, the average number of customers arriving per day (Poisson distributed) is 4. There is, however, a subtle difference between the two demands. In the exponential case the customers are assumed to arrive one at a time. In the Poisson case it is implied that all customers for the day arrive simultaneously.

In simulating the inventory situation in Example 1, we assumed that one unit is demanded at a time, with demands occurring four times a day, on the average. It is left as an exercise to repeat the same example under the condition that the demand occurs only once a day with an average of four units per demand. It may be observed that the carrying cost will be slightly less if entire demand for the day occurs once. (What about the service level?)

In the next example of an inventory system simulation we will assume that the demand occurs only once a day with the number of units demanded varying according to a Poisson distribution. But let us first see how to generate random samples from a Poisson distribution.

Generation of Poisson variates: Let us recall that a Poisson distribution is a discrete distribution in which the probability of an event occurring exactly k times during a time interval t is given by the probability mass function

$$g_k(t) = (t\lambda)^k \frac{1}{k!} e^{-t\lambda},$$

where λ is the average number of times the event occurs in a unit period (say, a day). Putting $t = 1$ we get

$$g_k = (\lambda)^k \frac{1}{k!} e^{-\lambda} \qquad \dots(6.11)$$

Our goal is to find random values of k (the number of arrivals per unit of time) drawn from the probability mass function (6-11). To generate this we will use the relationship just discussed between exponential and Poisson distributions.

Suppose we generate exponentially distributed time intervals $t_1, t_2, t_3, \ldots$ with expected value equal to $1/\lambda$ (say, 0.25 day), and then add these intervals

$$t = t_1 + t_2 + t_3 + \ldots$$

till their sum t exceeds 1. Then we stop and count how many t_i's were added just before their sum exceeded 1 (e.g., one day). This count k then is precisely the random sample from the Poisson distribution. Expressing more compactly,

$$t_1 + t_2 + \ldots + t_k \leqslant 1 < t_1 + t_2 + \ldots + t_{k+1} \qquad \ldots(6\text{-}12)$$

where $k = 0, 1, 2, \ldots$

(Note that $k = 0$ implies that the first term t_1 itself exceeded 1.) Now these exponentially distributed variates $t_1, t_2, \ldots$ with average value $1/\lambda$, can themselves be generated by means of the relationship (as shown in Sec. 3-4)

$$t_i = -\frac{1}{\lambda} \log u_i \qquad \ldots(6\text{-}13)$$

where u_i's are uniformly distributed random numbers between 0 and 1.

Thus, by generating t_i's according to Eq. (6-13) and counting how many of them occurred within one time unit, in accordance with Eq. (6-12), we get random values of k. However, a faster method of accomplishing the same task would be to substitute Eq. (6-13) into Eq. (6-12) and get

$$-\frac{1}{\lambda} (\log u_1 + \log u_2 + \ldots + \log u_k) \leqslant 1 < -\frac{1}{\lambda} (\log u_1 +$$

$$\log u_2 + \ldots + \log u_{k+1}),$$

which gives $\qquad u_1 . u_2 \ldots u_k \geqslant e^{-\lambda} > u_1 . u_2 \ldots u_{k+1} \qquad \ldots(6\text{-}14)$

In other words, we generate uniformly distributed random numbers (between 0 and 1) and continue to take their product till it becomes less than $e^{-\lambda}$. The number of terms minus one gives the random variable k. The following **FORTRAN** function subprogram will generate the Poisson variates for any specified λ.

```
      INTEGER FUNCTION POISN (LAMDA)
      REAL LAMDA
      Z = EXP (−LAMDA)
      K = 0
      PROD = 1.0
   15 RN = RNDY (DUM)
      PROD = PROD*RN
      IF (PROD . LT . Z) GO TO 25
      K = K + 1
      GO TO 15
   25 POISN = K
      RETURN
      END
```

When λ is large, $e^{-\lambda}$ could become so small that the number of u_i's required to satisfy Eq. (6-14) is inordinately large. To save computer time a test is usually made for such a condition. Another test often incorporated is to ensure that inadvertently a negative value has not been given for λ.

Erlang distribution: Quite often the procurement lead time (i.e., the delay in delivery of a reorder) can be expressed as the sum of several independent random variables. For example, the sum of (i) the time spent in preparing reorder papers and getting them to the factory, (ii) the time taken at the factory in manufacturing, selecting, packing, etc., and (iii) the transportation time from factory to the store, equals the total lead time. Each of these times may reasonably be assumed to follow a negative exponential distribution and be mutually independent. Furthermore, if the average of each of these three times is the same, the sum is said to be Erlang-3 distributed. Thus an Erlang-m distributed random variable is the sum of m independent and identically distributed exponential distributions. Its density function can be shown to be

$$h_m(t) = \frac{1}{(m-1)!} \cdot \left(\frac{1}{\beta}\right)^m \cdot t^{m-1} \cdot e^{-t/\beta} \qquad \ldots(6\text{-}15)$$

where β is the average value (say, of time delay) of each of the m constituent exponential distributions, and therefore $m\beta$ is the average value of the (composite) Erlang distribution.

When $m = 1$ Eq. (6-15) becomes

$$h_1(t) = \frac{1}{\beta} e^{-t/\beta} \qquad \ldots(6\text{-}16)$$

the exponential distribution, which is as it should be.

Erlang distribution also arises in queues. When each customer needs m different jobs performed (at the single service counter) in a sequence, each taking an average of β units of time all exponentially distributed, then the total service time of the customers will be Erlang distributed with the mean value of $m\beta$ units of time.

This distribution is called Erlang after A. K. Erlang, who first formulated it during his investigation of telephone traffic. The Erlang distribution is a specific case of a more general distribution called *gamma*, where parameter m can take any positive value—not necessarily an integer. It can also be shown that the *chi-square* distribution is a special case of Erlang distribution.

Generation of Erlang variates: To generate a sample from an Erlang-m distribution with a mean time of $m\beta$ units, all we have to do is to generate m random samples from an exponential distribution, with a mean time of β, and add them. The following five FORTRAN statements will do the job:

```
      PROD = 1.0
      DO 15 I = 1, M
      RN = RNDY 1 (DUM)
   15 PROD = PROD*RN
      ERLNG = −BETA*ALOG (PROD)
```

where ERLNG is the desired variate; and BETA $= \beta$ and $M = m$ have been specified.

Let us now simulate an inventory system using Erlang and Poisson distributions:

6-5. Simulation Example—2

In this second example, we will simulate an inventory system with various costs as discussed in Sec. 6-1. The purpose is to simulate a wide range of inventory policies with a view to determining an optimal one. The system is characterized by the following parameters: (i) The number of units demanded is Poisson distributed with an average demand of 5 units per day. (ii) Procurement lead time is Erlang distributed with parameter $m = 3$, and the average lead time is 21 days, i.e., $\beta = 7$. (iii) Any demand that cannot be fulfilled is backordered and satisfied when a shipment is received from the factory. (iv) At any given time there may be at most 3 orders outstanding. (v) The costs associated are: the reorder cost of Rs. 200 per order, carrying cost of Re. 0.2 per day per unit, and a backorder cost of Rs. 2 per day per unit for carrying backorders.

We will simulate for all combinations of the reorder point P from 100 to 150 and the reorder quantity Q from 50 to 140, both in steps of 10. For each combination we wish to calculate and print out (1) average daily sale, ADSALE, (2) average number of backorders per day, ADBO, (3) average daily stock, AVSTOK, (4) average buffer stock, ABSTOK, (5) average daily cost under each of the three headings, i.e., carrying cost (CCOST), reorder cost (RCOST), and shortage cost (SCOST).

This problem is similar to (but a bit more involved than) the one simulated in Chapter 1 (Sec. 1-3). The fact that the lead time here is an Erlang-distributed random variable (rather than a constant) need not cause any added complication. We have only to tack on a FUNCTION subprogram for generating Erlang variates. In the example simulated in Chapter 1 there was at most one reorder outstanding. Here we can have as many as three. The multiple-reorder case can be handled by maintaining a linear array (DD) of size three, as was done for the example of inventory simulation in Sec. 6-3. Here, there are no lost sales. Every unsatisfied demand is backordered and eventually made good. Our shortage cost is therefore only the backorder cost. Regarding the output in this problem, we are collecting many more statistics than we did in either of the earlier two examples (in Sec. 1-3 and Sec. 6-3). Except for the buffer stock, the other statistics have already been defined and explained earlier.

Buffer stock: The stock on hand at the time of the arrival of a reorder is called the *buffer stock* or the *safety stock*. As the name suggests, the

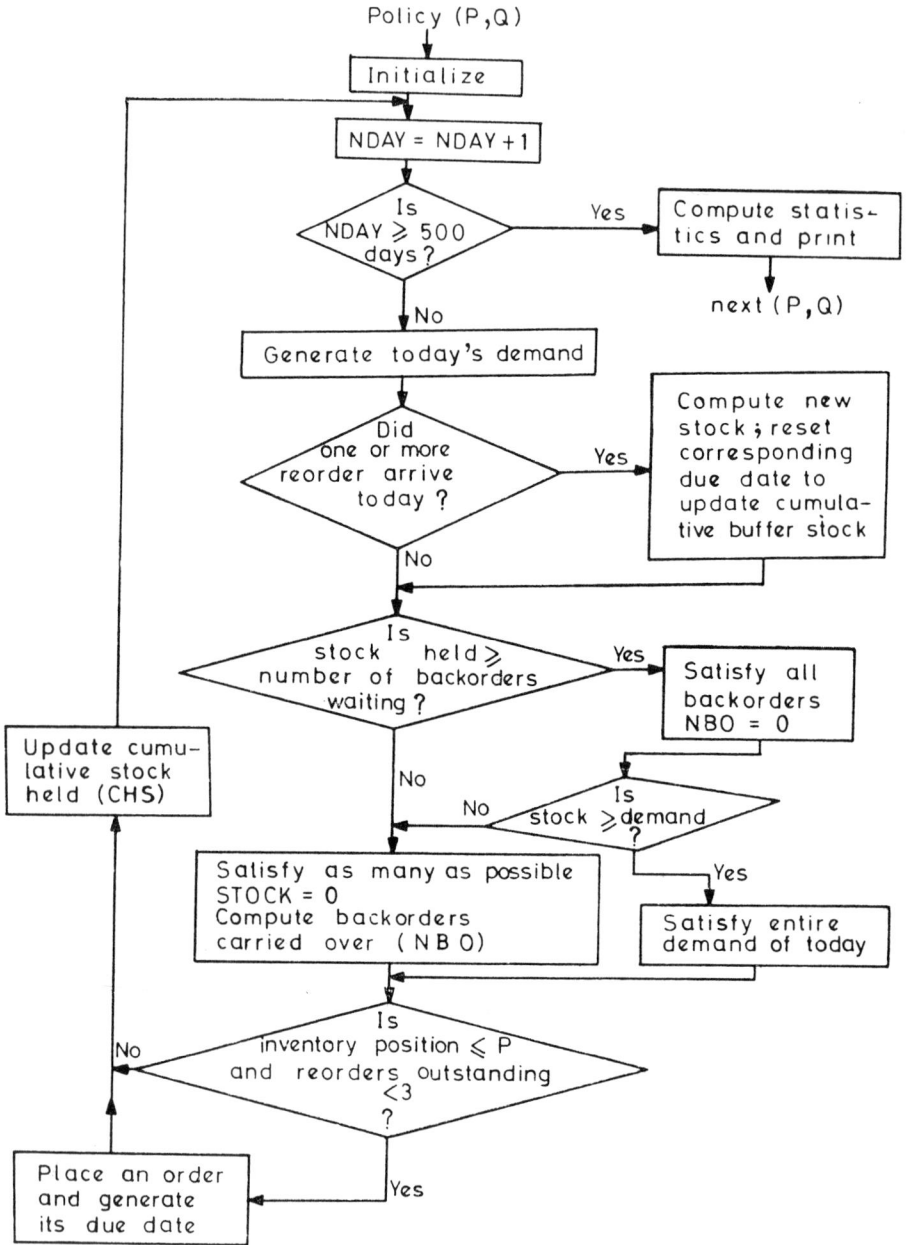

Fig. 6-7: Flowchart for Inventory Simulation Example 2.

purpose of the buffer stock is to satisfy the demand during the lead time whenever the lead-time-demand is heavier than expected. In a deterministic system we need not keep any buffer stock. We could set the reorder point P such that the stock on hand hits the zero level exactly at the time when new reorder arrives, thereby making both the stockouts and the buffer stock zero. In case of a probabilistic system, however, in order to avoid excessive stockouts, the reorder point P is usually set at a level higher than the average lead-time-demand. We can express the buffer stock at the arrival of ith reorder as

$$B_i = P - L_i,$$

where L_i is the total demand occurring between the period the ith order was placed and it arrived.

To obtain the average buffer stock, we will observe the values of stock each time a reorder arrives and take the average over all arrivals of reorders. Thus the average buffer stock is

$$ABSTOK = \frac{1}{NORD} \sum B_i,$$

where $NORD$ is total number of reorders received during the simulation. In case one is interested in the value of the average lead-time demand $\bar{L}$, it is nothing but the difference between the reorder point and the average buffer stock. That is

$$\bar{L} = P - ABSTOK$$

The flowchart in Fig. 6-7 describes the logic of this simulation. A FORTRAN program for implementing this flowchart follows.

```
      INTEGER STOCK, TUS, CSH, CBFSTK, P, Q, DEM, CNBO, DD(3), POISN,
    1    ERLANG
      REAL LAMDA
      DATA INFNTY, LAMBDA, M, BETA/999, 5.0, 3, 7.0/
      DO 800 P = 100, 150, 10
      DO 800 Q = 50, 140, 10
C     INITIALISE
      CALL INIT (NDAY, NBO, STOCK, INVPOS, TUS, CSH, CBFSTK, CNBO,
    1    NORD, DD)
100   NDAY = NDAY + 1
      IF (NDAY . GT . 500) GO TO 700
      DEM = POISN (LAMBDA)
C     CHECK ARRIVAL OF SUPPLY
      DO 200 I = 1, 3
      IF (DD(I) . NE . NDAY) GO TO 200
      CBFSTK = CBFSTK + STOCK
      STOCK  = STOCK + Q
      DD (I) = INFNTY
200   CONTINUE
      IF (STOCK.LT.NBO) GO TO 300
```

```
C       SATISFY ALL BACKORDERS
        TUS = TUS + NBO
        STOCK = STOCK - NBO
        INVPOS = INVPOS - NBO
        NBO = 0
        IF (STOCK . LT . DEM) GO TO 300
C       SATISFY ALL OF TODAY'S DEMAND
        TUS = TUS + DEM
        STOCK = STOCK - DEM
        INVPOS = INVPOS - DEM
        GO TO 400
C       COMPUTE CURRENT BACKORDER
  300   NBO = NBO + DEM - STOCK
        CNBO = CNBO + NBO
        TUS = TUS + STOCK
        INVPOS = INVPOS - STOCK
        STOCK = 0
C       CHECK INVENTORY POSITION AND REORDER
  400   IF (INVPOS . GT . P) GO TO 600
        DO 500 I = 1, 3
        IF (DD (I).LT.INFNTY) GO TO 500
        INVPOS = INVPOS + Q
        DD (I) = NDAY + ERLANG (M, BETA)
        NORD = NORD + 1
        GO TO 600
  500   CONTINUE
  600   CSH = CSH + STOCK
        GO TO 100
C       COMPUTE STATISTICS
  700   CALL STAT (P, Q, TUS, CNBO, CSH, CBFSTK, NORD)
  800   CONTINUE
        STOP
        END
```

The following program variables have the same meaning as they did in Example 1.

STOCK   = actual current stock
TUS   = total units supplied
CSH   = cumulative stock held
P   = reorder point
Q   = reorder quantity
DD   = due dates of reorders
INVPOS = inventory position (STOCK + quantity on order)
NDAY   = today
INFNTY = infinity (in our case integer 999 is sufficient).

Other variables, used in the program are:

DEM   = today's demand
NBO   = number of backorders currently waiting to be served
CNBO   = cumulative number of backorders so far

NORD   = number of reorders placed so far
CBFSTK = cumulative buffer stock so far.

The subroutine INIT for initialization is:

```
      SUBROUTINE INIT (NDAY, NBO, STOCK, INVPOS, TUS, CSH, CBFSTK,
    1   CNBO, NORD, DD)
      INTEGER STOCK, TUS, CSH, CBFSTK, CNBO, DD (3)
      DATA INFNTY, ISEED/999, 11750920161/
      NDAY = 0
      NBO = 0
      STOCK = 10
      INVPOS = 10
      TUS = 0
      CSH = 0
      CBFSTK = 0
      CNBO = 0
      NORD = 0
      DO 100 I = 1, 3
  100 DD (I) = INFNTY
      DUM = SNDY1 (ISEED)
      RETURN
      END
```

The subroutine STAT for gathering, computing, and printing required statistics is as follows:

```
      SUBROUTINE STAT (P, Q, TUS, CNBO, CSH, CBFSTK, NORD)
      INTEGER P, Q, TUS, CSH, CBFSTK, CNBO
      ADSALE = FLOAT (TUS)/500.0
      ADBO  = FLOAT (CNBO)/500.0
      AVSTOK = FLOAT (CSH)/500.0
      ABSTOK = FLOAT (CBFSTK)/FLOAT (NORD)
      CCOST = 0.2*FLOAT (CSH)/500.0
      RCOST = 200.0*FLOAT (NORD)/500.0
      SCOST = 2.0*FLOAT (CNBO)/500.0
      TOTCST = CCOST + RCOST + SCOST
      PRINT, P, Q, ADSALE, ADBO, AVSTOK, ABSTOK, CCOST, RCOST, SCOST,
    1   SCOST, TOTCST
      RETURN
      END
```

6-6. Forecasting and regression analysis

So far we have assumed that the demand and the lead time for an inventory system are specified to us in the form of some well-known probability functions. (Similar assumption was made in Chapter 4 while considering arrival and service patterns. Likewise, in Chapter 5 we assumed that the activity durations follow some well-known probability distribution.) In reality, however, one usually encounters situations where the demand is given only in the form of historical data collected through observations in the past. A major problem then is to forecast or predict the future demand before simulating the performance of the given inventory system.

The problem of prediction of a quantity based on available data is important not only in statistics and stochastic simulation but also in numerical analysis. In numerical analysis, however, the data is usually assumed to be exact and the randomness, if any, is ignored. Prediction of future values is then called *extrapolation*. In statistics and stochastic simulation the data are random samkles. The purpose is to fit an appropriate curve which can be extended into the future. Such fitting of a curve in the presence of randomness is usually called *regression* analysis.

Least squares regression: The simplest case to consider is that of linear regression, where the curve to be fitted is a straight line. Let X and Y be two variables, which seem to be linearly related. Suppose we have collected n historical observations which can be viewed as pairs (x_i, y_i), $i = 1, 2, ..., n$. We wish to determine conrtants a and b such that

$$Y = aX + b$$

is the line of best fit through the n pairs of data. The criterion chosen most often is the minimization of the sum of squares of errors, which is

$$S = \sum_{i=1}^{n} (y_i - ax_i - b)^2 \qquad \qquad ...(6\text{-}17)$$

Now the error S is a function of a and b only, because x_i's and y_i's are the observed data. In order to minimize S we differentiate Eq. (6-17) with respect to a and b, and set the partial derivatives to 0.

$$\frac{\partial S}{\partial a} = -\sum_{i=1}^{n} 2(y_i - ax_i - b)x_i = 0$$

$$\frac{\partial S}{\partial b} = -\sum_{i=1}^{n} 2(y_i - ax_i - b) = 0$$

Solving these two equations simultaneously, yields an estimate of a and b, as

$$b = \frac{\sum y_i \sum x_i^2 - \sum x_i y_i \sum x_i}{n \sum x_i^2 - (\sum x_i)^2}$$

and

$$a = \frac{\sum x_i y_i - \sum x_i \sum y_i / n}{\sum x_i^2 - \sum x_i^2 / n}$$

where the summation symbols extend from $i = 1$ to n. The line just obtained is called the *regression line of Y upon X*. Note that we have tacitly assumed that the errors are predominantly in reading y_i's, and x_i's determined accurately. For we have minimized the sum of squares in errors in y_i's. Had the y_i's been more accurate than x_i's, we would have evaluated the regression line of X upon Y, which would be somewhat different. It is straightforward to write a FORTRAN program that reads n values of x_i, y_i and computes a and b as above. The linear regression line is often used in predicting the long term trend of demand over seasonal variations.

We have considered the dependent variable Y to be a linear function of just one independent variable. Its natural extension is to consider the regression of a variable Y, on several independent variables, U, V, W, X, etc. For example, the strength of timber depends on its density and moisture content. Likewise, we may wish to fit a general polynomial curve in place of the linear curve. Naturally, multiple and polynomial regression computations get very complex, because of evaluation of many coefficients and many equations.

Simple moving average: In the least-square linear fit just discussed, all n pairs of data received equal importance. In many physical situations, however, the latest data would have more relevance to what is to happen next than the earlier ones. Therefore several methods of forecasting have been developed which place more weight on the latest figures. The simplest of these is to use a moving average of a certain period, say, 12 months. As the latest figure is incorporated into the average the oldest figure is dropped.

Clearly, the simple moving average of the data over the previous m periods to predict its value for the next period, smooths out the local irregularities and shows only the long-term trends. The higher the value of the averaging period m, the greater the smoothing or filtering. We must therefore choose m carefully, so that the forecasts predict only the bona fide movements in the trend. If m is too large, the moving average may be too slow to react to the true trend movements. If m is too small we may find spurious trend movements due to random local fluctuations.

Exponential smoothing: A more reliable forecasting technique (than simple moving average) which is widely used now is called *exponential smoothing*. It places most emphasis on the latest figure and a gradual decreasing emphasis on the older figures. The calculations are relatively simple and can be adapted to take account of any trend and seasonal pattern.

In order to forecast F_{j+1} the value of the variable for the period $(j+1)$, a weight α is chosen between 0 and 1 to give to the latest observed data x_j (for the period j). A weight of $(1-\alpha)$ is given to the old forecast F_j (for the period j). Thus

$$F_{j+1} = \alpha x_j + (1 - \alpha) F_j \qquad \ldots (6\text{-}18)$$

In turn F_j can be written as

$$F_j = \alpha x_{j-1} + (1 - \alpha) F_{j-1}$$

and therefore on substituting this in (6-18) we get

$$F_{j+1} = \alpha x_j + \alpha (1 - \alpha) x_{j-1} + (1 - \alpha)^2 F_{j-1}$$

Continuing successive substitutions for F_{j-1}, F_{j-2}, ..., we get

$$F_{j+1} = \alpha x_j + \alpha(1 - \alpha) x_{j-1} + \alpha(1 - \alpha)^2 x_{j-2} + \alpha(1 - \alpha)^3 x_{j-3} + \ldots +$$
$$\alpha(1 - \alpha)^k F_{j-k} \qquad \ldots (6\text{-}19)$$

Depending on the value we pick for the smoothing constant α, we will get the coefficients in Eq. (6-19). For instance, if $\alpha = 0.1$, we get

$$F_{j+1} = 0.1x_j + 0.09x_{j-1} + 0.081x_{j-2} + 0.0729x_{j-3} + \ldots \qquad \ldots (6\text{-}20)$$

Equation (6-20) shows clearly how gradually decreasing weights are given to the older data. We also observe that the larger the value of α, the less the weight given to the older data (the coefficients decrease more rapidly). That is, a higher value of α will make the forecast more responsive to changes in the trend; a lower value of α will suppress random variations and make the curve smoother. (Note that to compute F_{j+1} we will use our original Eq. (6-18), and not Eq. (6-19). Thus we need store only the last values F_i and x_j and not any of the previous values. Hence the method of exponential smoothing is computationally very attractive.)

To the question what is the 'best' value of α, there is no unique answer. It is a matter of experience and judgement. The problem warrants detailed analysis and trial forecasting with two or three values of α and their comparison with observed data. As a rule of thumb, the following values of α may be considered. Use

$\alpha = 0.1$, if there is no trend,
$\alpha = 0.5$, if there is a slight trend, and
$\alpha = 0.9$, if there is a marked trend.

It is left as an exercise for you to write a computer program which performs forecasting using α from 0.1 to 1.0 in steps of 0.1, given a set of monthly observations over a four-year period. Notice that when $\alpha = 1$, there is no smoothing; it is simply using the last observation to forecast the next.

Adaptive forecasting: Suppose for a given inventory system the demand forecasting was made using a certain value of the smoothing constant α and the forecast was found to be reliable. It does not, however, mean that the same α will continue to give reliable forecasts for all time to come, because the nature of the demand might change. Therefore, there is a need for regular checks to ensure that the value of the smoothing constant being used is the best; and if not α should be altered accordingly. Such a technique is called *adaptive forecasting*. In other words, in adaptive forecasting the forecast error is computed after each observation and the smoothing constant α is altered to minimize this error. Thus the method adapts itself to the demand pattern. Adaptive forecasting is a relatively recent development and has been in wide use only for the past few years.

Time series analysis: The term *time-series* is used for a sequence of data (values of some variable) during successive and equal time periods. Statistical analysis of such a sequence of chronological data is called a time-series analysis. The movements of data in a time series are due to (1) trend, (2) seasonal or periodic variations, (3) cyclical variations, and (4) irregular or random variations. Trend element is the regular movement of series over a long period of time. Seasonal variations are regularly repeating patterns, say, on a yearly basis. The up and down movements over much longer periods are called cyclic variations. The random variations are fluctuations resulting from natural chances.

The purpose of the time series analysis is to identify these four components—using statistical techniques with a view to forecasting the values of the variable in the future.

A time series analysis (of a sequence of observed data) plays a dual role in simulation. It can be used to generate input data (such as demands for an inventory system, riverflow in a reservoir system in Chapter 2) with desired auto-correlation and stochastic distribution to represent future sets of data to the system. Equally important is the use of time series analysis in describing a variety of statistical facts about the output of a simulation (such as the queue lengths in a queueing simulation).

Forecasting through simulation: So far, in this section we have discussed purely *statistical forecasting*. That is, we have confined ourselves to using historical data purely to extract some kind of trend, cyclical, and seasonal variations for predicting the future. This type of forecasting by simply manipulating a time series, has a very serious disadvantage (although it is simple to use and is, therefore, very popular). It does not tell us the reason behind the movement of the data. An entirely different approach to forecasting is through seeking causal relationship. This essentially means that we first identify various determining factors (i.e., independent variables) X_1, X_2, ..., X_p that appear to have determined our variable Y (which we wish to forecast) in the past; then build a model showing how X_1, X_2, ..., X_p produce variable Y.

To illustrate the difference between the two approaches. let us consider the problem of forecasting the flow of water through a river at a certain location. If we have past data on the flow we could analyze the data and predict purely on this basis. Or we could build a model of the river basin relating the rainfalls at various points in the catchment area, existing moisture contents of the soil, extent of vegetation, etc., to the amount of water flowing through the river at that location. Then using the historical data on rainfall, vegetation, soil moisture, etc., we can simulate the model and check if the resultant amount of riverflow matches the historical data on the riverflow during the corresponding period. If not, we revise the model and simulate again. Thus we use historical data to develop, test, and refine the model. Finally, using the forecasts of the determining variables, X_i's (rainfall, moisture, vegetation, etc.), we forecast the variable of our interest, Y. This approach although more complex and time-consuming, allows us to learn from experience and it yields much more reliable forecasts than those obtained by the purely statistical technique of fitting a curve through historical data and extending the curve into the future.

6-7. Remarks and references

Almost every business uses inventory to ensure smooth and efficient running of its operations. The difference between an efficient and a poor inventory policy could save or destroy a firm. It is, therefore, natural that the inventory management problem has been studied very extensively in the literature, and operations research. Although the simple lot size formula, Eq. (6-1), was obtained and used by several individuals, independently—including Ford Harris in 1915 and R. H. Wilson in 1927—the stochastic model of inventory systems was developed only since World War II. In the last 25 years an extensive literature has developed dealing with mathematical analysis of various types of inventory systems. Some of the classical textbooks on mathematical theory of inventory systems are:

> BUCHAN, J., and E. KOENIGSBERG, *Scientific Inventory Management,* Prentice-Hall of India, New Delhi, 1977.
> HADLEY, G. and T. M. WHITIN, *Analysis of Inventory Systems*, Prentice-Hall, Englewood Cliffs, N.J., 1963.
> NADDOR, E., *Inventory Systems*, John Wiley, New York, 1966.
> STARR, M. K., and D. W. MILLER, *Inventory Control: Theory and Practice,* Prentice-Hall of India, New Delhi, 1977.

Mathematical analysis of an inventory system starts getting complicated as soon as the stochastic nature of the demand and of the lead time are introduced. Additional factors, such as interaction amongst different items in a multi-item inventory system, or perishable nature of articles (see Exercise 6-10), or constraints on storage space available, etc., can make an analytic study of an inventory system intractable. In contrast, a computer simulation does not increase that much in complexity when such factors are introduced. For example, the simulation program in Sec. 6-3 or in Sec. 6-4 does not require much greater skill to write than does the program in Sec. 1-3.

An excellent treatment of computer simulation in inventory systems is given in Chapter 5 of

> PRITSKER, A. A. B., and P. J. KIVIAT, *Simulation with GASP II*, Prentice-Hall, Englewood Cliffs, N.J., 1969.

The three illustrative examples of inventory system simulation—two in this chapter and the one in Chapter 1—have been of relatively simple models. Too many specific details of an actual system would have not only consumed more space but have also obscured the essential points of simulating an inventory system. Simulation of more involved inventory systems can be found in numerous papers and articles, such as,

MONTY, G., "Practical Applications of Simulation in the area of Stock Management," *Digital Simulation in Operations Research*, S. H. Hollingdale (Ed.), American Elsevier, New York, 1967.

PACKER, A. H., "Simulation and Adaptive Forecasting as Applied to Inventory Control," *Operations Research*, Vol. XV (July–August 1967), pp. 660–679.

REED, R., and W. E. STANLEY, "Optimizing Control of Hospital Inventories," *Jour. Industrial Engineering*, Vol. XVI, No. 1, January–February 1965.

Simulation of a general multi-item inventory system along with a detailed flowchart is given in

NAYLOR, T. H., *Computer Simulation Experiments with Models of Economic Systems*, John Wiley, New York, 1971, pp. 224–228.

How to search efficiently for an optimal inventory policy (from amongst infinity of them), without having to simulate a very large number of them, is an important problem in its own right. It is discussed in

NADDOR, E., "Optimal and Heuristic Decisions in Single and Multi-item Inventory Systems," *Management Science*, Vol. 21, No. 11, July 1975, pp. 1234–1249.

The ultimate goal of simulation of an inventory system is to decide what policy to use in the future (and not what would have been a good policy in the past). Therefore, forecasting the future demand, based on historical data and other considerations, is an essential ingredient to the study of inventory systems. There are several good books on regression analysis and forecasting based purely on statistical techniques. There are also books dealing with forecasting, particularly in econometrics, business, water resources, etc., based on model building. A good treatment of forecasting without too much of mathematics can be found in

ROBINSON, C., *Business Forecasting : An Economic Approach*, Thomas Nelson and Sons, London, 1971.

6-8.   Exercises

6-1. In deriving Eq. (6-1) the reorder cost r was assumed to be a constant, independent of the number of units ordered. Consider a situation where the administrative cost of placing an order for q units and getting them delivered is $r = r' + aq$, where r' and a are two constants. Show that this situation would also lead to Eq. (6-1).

6-2. A function $f(x)$ attains an absolute minimum at x_0 if the first derivative $\frac{df}{dx} = 0$ and the second derivative $\frac{d^2f}{dx^2} > 0$ at x_0. Verify the latter condition for Eqs. (6-1) and (6-5) by evaluating $\frac{d^2C}{dQ^2}$.

6-3. The simple model used in deriving the lot size formula, Eq. (6-1), assumes that the three parameters (namely, the demand D, reorder cost r, and carrying cost k) are accurately known. In practice, there may be errors in estimating these parameters. Perform sensitivity analysis to show that an x per cent error in any of these parameters causes only $x/2$ per cent error in total cost C, in the vicinity of the EOQ. Also show that an x per cent error in any one of the parameters will result into an x per cent error in the value of economic order quantity.

6-4. Draw a diagram similar to Fig. 6-1 for a production (rather than purchase) environment, showing the gradual rise and fall of inventory. Using this diagram show that formula (6-7) gives the most economical batch quantities in such an environment.

6-5. In Sec. 1-3 (of Chapter 1) an inventory system was simulated assuming the demand to be uniformly distributed. Repeat that simulation experiment assuming the demand to be normally distributed with a mean of 50 units and standard deviation of 10. Compare the two results.

6-6. Change the lead time in the inventory simulation problem in Sec. 1-3 from a constant 3 days to an Erlang distributed delay with the average value $\beta = 3$ days and parameter $m = 2$. Compare the outcome of the two.

6-7. Repeat the simulation experiment performed in Sec. 6-3, under the changed condition that the demand, which follows Poisson distribution, occurs once a day with a mean value of four units. Obtain the service-level vs. the minimum-average stock curve as was done in Fig. 6-6. Compare the two curves.

6-8. (Transients.) Initially an inventory system, like all dynamic systems, will exhibit a transient behaviour for some time before settling down. Simulate the inventory system described in Sec. 1-3 under two very different starting conditions (say, initial stock of 500 units and 0 units), and plot the daily stock on hand vs. time for the first 25 days, to observe the transients. Comment on the curves.

6-9. (Search for optimal policy.) For the inventory system in Sec. 1-3 we considered only five different (P, Q) policies and picked the best out of these. The best of these five is not necessarily the best amongst all possible (P, Q)'s. How will you go about searching for the best? (Hint: Design and run a search on two control variables P and Q to find the optimal policy, using the steepest ascent method.)

6-10. (Perishable inventory.) A perishable product such as fruits, vegetables, ice slabs, and newspapers can be stocked only for a limited time, after which it loses all or most of its value. As an example, consider the following situation: A newsstand can buy a daily newspaper for 20 paise each and sell it for 35. The unsold copies, if any, can be disposed of as waste paper at 5 paise each. The estimated daily demand distribution is as follows:

Demand (No. of copies)	Probability
100	0.05
110	0.10
120	0.20
130	0.35
140	0.25
150	0.05

Write a computer program which simulates alternate policies in order to determine the optimal number of copies the newsstand should procure to maximize the total expected profit.

6-11. Write a computer program to simulate an inventory system which uses a periodic review scheme (T, Z) as shown in Fig. 6-3. The three costs as well as the demand, the lead time, and the initial stock are the same as in the inventory system simulated in Sec. 1-3. Use your program to compare the costs of several (T, Z) policies for a period of 500 days each.

6-12. In Sec. 6-1, we considered only two types of reordering strategies, namely, (P, Q), and (T, Z) schemes. In this problem you are to simulate a mixture of the two, which may be called a (P, Z) policy. Here we review the inventory position only periodically but place a reorder, to bring the inventory position on a level Z, only if the inventory position, at the time of review, is at or below a specified level P. If it is above P we do nothing till the next review time comes.

6-13. Amongst the three reordering schemes—(P, Q), (T, Z) and (P, Z), whose optimal policy do you think should give the lowest cost? Why?

6-14. Write a FORTRAN program to implement a statistical forecasting system, using the exponential smoothing. The smoothing constant α is to be incremented from 0.1 to 1.0 in steps of 0.1. This program reads 24 values of the past data and stores it into an array. To assess the effectiveness of each value of α, forecasting error is to be printed for each forecast.

7

Design and Evaluation of Simulation Experiments

In the last four chapters we have been learning how to produce a computer program for simulating a discrete, stochastic system, such as a queueing system, an inventory system, an activity network, etc. By means of this program we can perform the desired experiment on the system being studied. However, we have a great deal of choice in conducting this experiment. For example, we have a freedom of specifying initial conditions, such as the initial queue length or the initial inventory position. We also have a choice of specifying the run length. For instance, in Chapter 1 we ran the inventory simulation experiment for six months (180 days), but in Chapter 6 a similar experiment was run for 500 days. We also have a choice of conducting a single run of, say, 500 days, or replicating 10 runs of 50 days each; and so forth.

Our objective is to specify these parameters (run lengths, initial conditions, number of replications, etc.) so as to get the maximum useful information about the system's performance while minimizing the computational cost. How it can be achieved is one of the major problems in simulation. At present no unique procedure is available for designing the best simulation experiment. There are only useful aids, which we are going to discuss in this chapter.

7-1. Length of simulation runs

A simulation run is an uninterrupted recording of a system's behaviour under a specified combination of controllable variables. One of the important questions that must be resolved in all simulation experiments involving randomness is how long to run a simulation experiment so that we have a reasonable degree of confidence in the numerical results of the experiment. Before answering this question, let us examine a related but considerably simpler question in classical statistics: Suppose we have a random variable x with mean μ and standard deviation σ. We do not know its probability density function except that it is stationary (i.e., the density function does not vary with time). Suppose we take n independent samples, $x_1, x_2, \ldots, x_n$ and compute the sample mean.

$$\bar{x} = \frac{1}{n} \sum_{i=1}^{n} x_i. \qquad \qquad ...(7\text{-}1)$$

How close is this sample mean $\bar{x}$ to the population mean μ? Clearly, the larger the sample size n the smaller will be the difference between $\bar{x}$ and μ. Asymptotically, as n tends to infinity this difference $(\bar{x} - \mu)$ tends to zero. Furthermore, the *Central Limit Theorem* in statistics tells us that the sample mean $\bar{x}$ is itself a random variable, approximately normally distributed (regardless of the distribution of x) with mean μ and standard deviation $\sigma/\sqrt{n}$, so long as n is sufficiently large (for most distributions of x an $n > 10$ is large enough).

Since the standard deviation of $\bar{x}$ is a measure of its spread (with the same unit as x), we see that, roughly speaking, the accuracy in $\bar{x}$ increases inversely with the square root of n, the number of samples. For a given sample size n, one can compute how close $\bar{x}$ comes to μ with certain probability. Conversely, for a specified tolerance limit (difference between $\bar{x}$ and μ in terms of the number of standard deviations of x) we compute the sample size needed to achieve it.

Example 1: Suppose in a sampling experiment we want that with probability 0.95 our sample mean $\bar{x}$ be within $\sigma/25$ of the true mean μ. That is, we want to choose n so that

$$Pr\{\mu - (\sigma/25) \leqslant \bar{x} \leqslant \mu + (\sigma/25)\} = 0.95.$$

Now, $\bar{x}$ is approximately normally distributed with mean μ and standard deviation $\sigma/\sqrt{n}$. We also know that the fraction of the area under the normal density function curve, as we move $\pm k$ standard deviation from the mean, gives us the probability that a random sample will fall within these limits of the mean. By looking at the table of the areas under a normal density function curve [see Fig. 3-6(a)], we find that for this area to be 95 per cent (i.e., leaving 2.5 per cent under each tail end), we must include 1.96 standard deviations (of $\bar{x}$) on each side of the mean μ. Thus

$$1.96 \times \frac{\sigma}{\sqrt{n}} = \frac{\sigma}{25}$$

or
$$n = (1.96 \times 25)^2 = 2,401.$$

Thus if we take 2,401 independent samples of random variable x and compute the sample mean $\bar{x}$, we can say that 95 per cent probability is that the difference between $\bar{x}$ and the true mean μ will be less than one-twentyfifth of the standard deviation σ.

The general relationship between the parameters in question may be stated as

$$Pr\{\mu - t \leqslant \bar{x} \leqslant \mu + t\} = 1 - \alpha \qquad \qquad ...(7\text{-}2)$$

where t is the tolerance on either side of the mean μ within which we desire our estimate $\bar{x}$ to fall with a probability $1 - \alpha$. Since $\bar{x}$ is approximately normally distributed, its relationship to the standardized normally distributed variable z can be stated as

$$\bar{x} = z \cdot (\text{standard deviation of } \bar{x}) + \mu$$
$$= z \cdot (\sigma/\sqrt{n}) + \mu.$$

Then

$$Pr\{\mu - t \leqslant \bar{x} \leqslant \mu + t\} = Pr\{\mu - t \leqslant z \cdot (\sigma/\sqrt{n}) + \mu \leqslant \mu + t\}$$
$$= Pr\{- t \leqslant z(\sigma/\sqrt{n}) \leqslant t\}$$
$$= Pr\left\{- \frac{t}{\sigma} \sqrt{n} \leqslant z \leqslant \frac{t}{\sigma} \sqrt{n}\right\}. \qquad ...(7\text{-}3)$$

The integral of the standaraized normal density function z from $-\infty$ to a value y is given by

$$\Phi(y) = \int_{-\infty}^{y} \frac{1}{\sqrt{2\pi}} e^{-z^2/2} \, dz = Pr\{z \leqslant y\}.$$

The table of the values of this integral $\Phi(y)$ for various values of y are widely available. Since the normal distribution is symmetric about its mean, and the total area $\Phi(\infty)$ under the curve is 1, it is easy to see that

$$Pr\{- y \leqslant z \leqslant y\} = 2Pr\{z \leqslant y\} - 1. \qquad ...(7\text{-}4)$$

Therefore, in light of Eqs. (7-3) and (7-4), we can rewrite Eq. (7-2) as

$$2Pr\left\{z \leqslant \frac{t}{\sigma} \sqrt{n}\right\} - 1 = 1 - \alpha$$

or

$$Pr\left\{z \leqslant \frac{t}{\sigma} \sqrt{n}\right\} = 1 - \frac{\alpha}{2}. \qquad ...(7\text{-}5)$$

Thus, for a specified value of α, we look into the tables of $\Phi(y)$ and find the corresponding value of y such that $\Phi(y) = 1 - \alpha/2$. Let this value be denoted by $y_{1-\alpha/2}$. This value then is equated to

$$y_{1-\alpha/2} = \frac{t}{\sigma} \sqrt{n}$$

giving us the number of required samples as,

$$n = \frac{(y_{1-\alpha/2})^2 \, \sigma^2}{t^2}. \qquad ...(7\text{-}6)$$

Recall that t is the tolerance limit we are willing to accept; σ^2 is the variance of the parent population, and $y_{1-\alpha/2}$ is the two-tailed standardized normal static for the probability $(1 - \alpha)$. Typically the confidence level $(1 - \alpha)$ might be 90 per cent, for which $y_{1-\alpha/2} = 1.65$; or it might be 95 per cent, for which $y_{1-\alpha/2} = 1.96$; or 99 per cent, for which $y_{1-\alpha/2} = 2.58$.

Example 2: Suppose we have a dairy farm whose daily milk yield varies randomly. We wish to estimate the average value of its daily yield within ± 40 litres of its true average yield with a confidence level of 95 per cent. The standard deviation of the daily yields has been estimated to be 200 litres. For how many days must we measure the daily yield of the dairy farm?

Substituting $t = 40$, $\sigma = 200$, and $y_{1-\alpha/2} = 1.96$ in Eq. (7-6) we get the answer as

$$n = \left(\frac{1.96 \times 200}{40}\right)^2 = 96 \text{ days.}$$

Equation (7-6) is a very commonly used formula for computing the sample size in statistics. In order to use it in determining the sample size we need to know the variance σ^2 (of the distribution being sampled), which in general is not known in advance. It can, however, be estimated as

$$\sigma^2_{\text{est}} = \frac{1}{n-1} \sum_{i=1}^{n} (x_i - \bar{x})^2. \qquad \qquad ...(7\text{-}7)$$

But when the estimation (7-7) is used in place of true population variance σ^2, the normalized random variable

$$z = \frac{\bar{x} - \mu}{\sigma_{\text{est}}} \sqrt{n}$$

is no longer distributed according to the standardized normal distribution; instead it follows a Student-t distribution. However, if n is sufficiently large (> 50) the difference between the two distributions becomes negligible. Fortunately, in most simulation experiments the run length is large enough to satisfy this condition.

Run length of a static stochastic simulation: We can use Eq. (7-6) for determining the run length in a simulation experiment provided the two conditions under which the equation was derived are met, namely: (i) the distribution is stationary, i.e., the simulation has reached a steady state before we start observing $x_1, x_2, \ldots$, and (ii) the samples $x_1, x_2, \ldots$, are not correlated (i.e., are statistically independent). There are some stochastic simulations which are basically static, where time plays no role. For example, the game of craps in Exercise 3-3 and the simulation of a PERT network belong to this category. In both these cases there is no transient state. Apart from the influence of the seed for starting the random number generator, the simulation is essentially in the steady state from the moment the simulation starts. The output consists of statistically independent events, each of which follows the same probability law. For such static simulations Eq. (7-6) can be used for determining the run length. Let us consider an example of a static stochastic simulation to see how the run length is determined using Eq. (7-6).

Example 3: Consider the game of dice (called craps) which you were asked to simulate in Exercise 3-3 of Chapter 3. In that exercise you were simply asked to perform one run of 100 games and print the net winnings of A, the roller of the dice. Suppose the following is the outcome of 100 games (all rolls were made by player A):

No. of times A wins $= 56$

No. of times A loses $= 44$

Hence, the net win of A is Rs. 12 in 100 games, or Re. 0.12 per game.

Is this experimental run long enough for us to make a statement with a certain degree of confidence that the game is expected to favour the player A (who rolls the dice) and that the expected value of his win is Re. 0.12 per game? If not, how long should our run be so that our experimental average of wins per game is accurate within ± 0.005 rupee with a probability of 95 per cent?

Had we known the standard deviation σ we could have used formula (7-6) to find the number of rolls n, because t and α are specified. In the absence of that knowledge, we can use the following procedure of computing upper and lower confidence limits, U and L, respectively, defined as

$$U = \bar{x} + y_{1-\alpha/2} \frac{\sigma_{est}}{\sqrt{n}}$$

$$L = \bar{x} - y_{1-\alpha/2} \frac{\sigma_{est}}{\sqrt{n}} \qquad \qquad ...(7\text{-}8)$$

for a set of n runs, where the estimated standard deviation σ_{est} is given by Eq. (7-7).

In other words, we have defined U and L as an interval about the estimated average $\bar{x}$ such that the interval $(U-L)$ will contain the true mean μ with confidence level $(1 - \alpha)$.

Now we run the simulation for 1,000 games, obtaining numerical values for $\bar{x}$ and σ_{est} from the 1,000 observations [using Eqs. (7-1) and (7-7)] and then computing U and L [using Eq. (7-8)]. If U and L fall within the specified tolerances, i.e., $(U-L) \leqslant 2 \times 0.005$, then we know that the interval defined by L and U will contain the true mean, $(1 - \alpha)$ per cent of the time, and that $\bar{x}$ is the best estimate of the true mean. If L and U do not fall within the specified tolerances we continue the simulation for, say, another 1,000 rolls and obtain a new set of x, σ_{est}, L and U values and check. This process of doubling of sample size is repeated until L and U do fall within specified tolerances, and, once they do, the simulation is terminated. These computations can be programmed in the simulator itself so that the computer will automatically terminate the simulation after the game has been played a sufficient number of times.

Table 7-1 illustrates a summary of these computations as they might appear in a simulation of the craps game:

n	$\bar{x}$	σ_{est}	U	L	$U-L$
1,000	+ .05000	0.99925	+ .11193	− .01193	.12386
2,000	+ .02500	0.99994	+ .06882	− .01882	.08764
4,000	− .00650	1.00010	+ .02449	− .03749	.06198
8,000	− .01620	0.99933	+ .00566	− .03816	.04382
16,000	− .00800	1.00000	+ .00750	− .02350	.03100
32,000	− .00400	1.00001	+ .00652	− .01539	.02191
64,000	− .00528	0.99999	+ .00247	− .01303	.01550
128,000	− .01498	0.99989	− .00951	− .02046	.01096
154,000	− .01578	0.99988	− .01079	− .02077	.00998

Terminate the simulation

Table 7-1: Confidence Interval Computations.

$t = \pm .005, (1 - \alpha) = 0.95.$

An important lesson to be learned from this table is that had we based our conclusion only on the first two thousand samples, we would be led to believe that the game is in the favour of the person who rolls the dice; while in the reality he will lose in the long run.   Thus, inadequate run-lengths in a simulation study can lead to disastrously wrong conclusions.   Another observation to be made is that run lengths in simulation studies could easily go into hundreds of thousands of observations.

The game of craps is not difficult to analyze by elementary probability considerations.   It is left as an exercise for you (Exercise 7-1) to show that the true expected value $\mu = -0.01414$. Comparing the estimated value $\bar{x}$ in the last row of Table 7-1, we find $\mu - \bar{x} = -.01414 + .01578 = 0.00164$ which is well within the tolerance specified.

This procedure, used in Example 3 and shown in Table 7-1, can be modified, so that we converge to the required run length faster.   Instead of increasing n successively till tolerance is met (as done in Table 7-1), we will evaluate the approximate sample size n^* needed, using Eq. (7-6) and σ_{est} for σ, based on an initial run of, say, m observations.   If $m \geqslant n^*$, we have met the accuracy criterion, and therefore the run is terminated. If $m \leqslant n^*$, we collect $(n^* - m)$ more observations, and recompute the sample mean $\bar{x}$ and reestimate the population variance σ_{est}^2, using Eq. (7-7). On substituting the new values of σ_{est} and n^* in Eq. (7-8), we will get the new tolerance interval $U - L$.   If this interval is narrow enough to meet the constraints we stop; otherwise, once again we estimate the sample size and repeat the process. The following flowcart (Fig. 7-1, page 150) describes this iterative procedure pictorially.

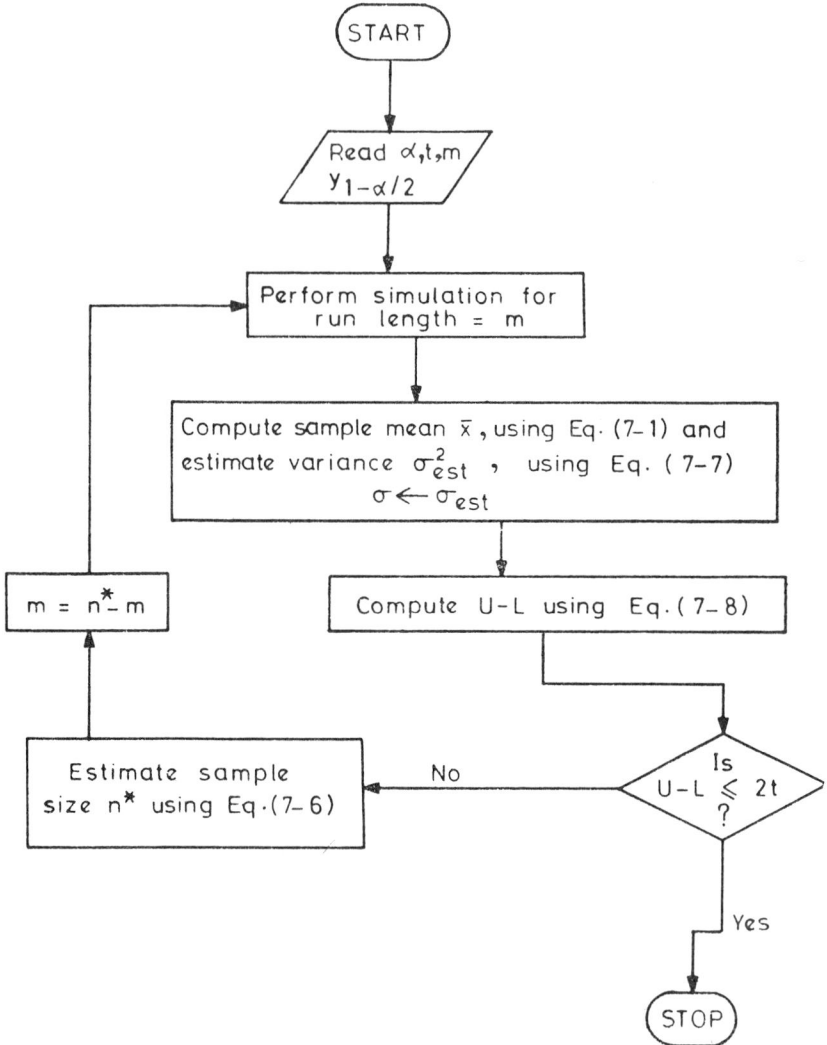

Fig. 7-1:   Achieving specified statistical accuracy.

Run length of a dynamic stochastic simulation: As pointed out earlier, Eq. (7-6) will not be valid for determining sample size if (i) the distribution is not stationary or (ii) if the samples $x_1, x_2, \ldots, x_n$ are correlated. In most dynamic system simulation both of these problems arise. They exhibit very prominent and distinct transient behaviour and their output data are strongly correlated. For example, in queueing systems as well as in inventory systems we will encounter these two problems. Let us first see how the transients can be eliminated.

Elimination of transients: Since the transients are due to initial bias, different initial conditions will produce transients of different lengths and magnitude. There are several methods of removing the effect of transients. The most commonly used approach is to ignore an initial section of the simulation run. The run is started from an empty state and stopped after a certain period (when the system is considered to have settled down to a steady state). The state of the system at that time is left intact. The run is then restarted and statistics gathered from the second start. In practice, one simply wipes out the statistics gathered up to a certain time from the start. To determine this initial 'cut-off' period no simple rules are available. It is often decided by making some pilot runs to see how long the initial bias persists.

Another method of reducing the effect of transients in statistics being gathered is to start the system in an initial state which is close to the steady state. Since the transients are due to the difference between the steady state and the initial state, the smaller the difference, the shorter would be the duration of transients. This method requires some *a priori* knowledge of the system's steady state, and this may not always be available.

A third strategy which may be used for reducing the effect of the initial bias is to ensure that the runs have been made long enough to have made the initial bias negligible.

Autocorrelated observations: The second assumption made in deriving Eq. (7-6) was that the n observations or samples $x_1, x_2, \ldots, x_n$ were statistically independent or uncorrelated. This condition is generally satisfied in static simulation, but for many dynamic simulations it is not. Let us illustrate it with an example of waiting time in a queueing system:

Consider a single-server queueing system with specified arrival and service patterns. We wish to simulate it in order to determine the average waiting time. We can estimate the average waiting time (as we did in Chapter 4) by accumulating the waiting time of n successive customers and dividing it by n. This simple average (in a single run of length n) is given by

$$\overline{w} = \frac{1}{n} \sum_{i=1}^{n} w_i \qquad \ldots(7\text{-}9)$$

where w_i's are the waiting times of the individual customers.

Clearly these waiting times of successive customers are not independent. In a queue, the waiting time of the kth customer depends on the waiting time of the customer ahead of him. If w_k happens to be long, the likelihood of w_{k+1} of being long is also high. A sequence of data that has this property, of one value affecting the subsequent values, is called *serially correlated* or *autocorrelated*. It is not difficult to see that in a queueing system, as the utilization factor increases (i.e., as the average queue length increases) the degree of autocorrelation will increase. We can also say, intuitively speaking, that two successive samples when they are statistically not independent contain less information about the parent population than they would if they were statistically independent. Therefore, we can surmise that to achieve a given level of confidence we would require a larger number of samples (of an autocorrelated sequence) than the one given by Eq. (7-6). Before we can compute the required sample size in such a case, we must first determine the degree to which the data is correlated.

In a sequence of observations $x_1, x_2, \ldots, x_n$ the extent to which values separated by m units affect each other can be measured by

$$r_m = \frac{1}{n-m} \sum_{i=1}^{n-m} (x_i - \bar{x})(x_{i+m} - \bar{x}) \qquad \ldots(7\text{-}10)$$

where x_i is the ith observation and $\bar{x}$ is the mean value of x_i's as given by Eq. (7-1). The quantity r_m is called an *autocovariance coefficient* or *autocorrelation coefficient with lag m*. For the specific case $m = 0$, r_0 is nothing but the estimate σ_{est}^2 of the variance of the distribution from which x_i's are drawn as given in Eq. (7-7).

Using Eq. (7-10) one can compute all of these coefficients $r_1, r_2, \ldots$. In all physical systems as m increases coefficient r_m will decrease, because the effect of one value on another becomes weaker as the distance between two observations becomes longer. Thus after a certain number M, these coefficients may be considered to have become zero, i.e.,

$$r_{M+1} = r_{M+2} = 0.$$

This cut-off point M must be large enough to include coefficients that are significant, but it must be much smaller than n, the sample size. An accepted rule of thumb is to keep $M < n/10$, if each of these r_m's is significantly different from zero. (Selecting an exact value of M involves a decision that can be made on the basis of a few trial runs.)

The effect of all nonzero autocorrelation coefficients, are included in the following expression for the estimate of the variance of $\bar{x}$:

$$\sigma_{\bar{x}}^2 = \frac{\sigma^2}{n} \left\{ 1 + 2 \sum_{k=1}^{M} \left(1 - \frac{k}{M+1} \right) r_k \right\}. \qquad \ldots(7\text{-}11)$$

If the sequence is free from any autocorrelation (i.e., the successive data are independent), only the first term in Eq. (7-11) remains, and σ^2/n gives the variance of the sample mean $\bar{x}$, as it should. The second term is the contribution of the autocorrelation. The presence of positive autocorrelation implies greater statistical variability in $\bar{x}$ as compared to the case when the sequence is uncorrelated. Thus to get the same variance we would have to increase n, the number of observations.

Armed with formula (7-11), we can now handle the case when the samples are not statistically independent. To evaluate the run length we substitute the expression

$$\frac{\sigma^2}{n} \left\{ 1 + 2 \sum_{k=1}^{M} \left(1 - \frac{k}{M+1} \right) r_k \right\}$$

in place of σ^2/n and get the following expression for the run length n for the autocorrelated case:

$$n = \frac{(y_{1-\alpha/2})^2 \sigma^2 \left[1 + 2 \sum_{k=1}^{M} \left(1 - \frac{k}{M+1} \right) r_k \right]}{t^2} \qquad ...(7\text{-}12)$$

where the autocorrelation coefficients r_k's are given by Eq. (7-10).   Using formula (7-12), instead of (7-6), we can determine the sample size needed in an autocorrelated case.

Example 4:   A sequence of 500 observations were made, and were found to be serially correlated.   The autocorrelation coefficients were estimated using Eq. (7-10), as $r_1 = 0.33$, $r_2 = 0.25$, and $r_3 = 0.15$.   Others were not significantly different from zero.   The mean (of the 500 samples) was found to be 20.5 and the variance as 1020.0.   Calculate the minimum sample size to assume that the estimate lies within ± 2 units of the true mean with confidence level of $(1 - \alpha) = 0.95$.

Using formula (7-12) we get

$$n = \frac{(1.96)^2 . (1020)}{(2)^2} \left\{ 1 + 2 \left[\left(1 - \frac{1}{4} \right) (0.33) \right. \right.$$
$$\left. \left. + \left(1 - \frac{2}{4} \right) (0.25) + \left(1 - \frac{3}{4} \right) (0.15) \right] \right\}$$
$$= 979.61 (1.82) \simeq 1783$$

Thus the existence of autocorrelation made our sample size 82 per cent larger.

The only difficulty one may encounter in using this approach is the amount of computation time required in evaluating autocorrelation coefficients.   There is another method, which does explicitly evaluate the corrected value of the variance (due to autocorrelation) and thus is not as time consuming.   The method, known as *blocking* or *batching method,* is used very commonly to handle correlated data.   It can be described as follows:

Blocking method: The n observations x_1, x_2, ..., x_n are grouped into b consecutive blocks, each of length $p = n/b$.   Then let the block averages be denoted by

$$v_1 = \frac{x_1 + x_2 + \ldots + x_p}{p}$$

$$v_2 = \frac{x_{p+1} + x_{p+2} + \ldots + x_{2p}}{p}$$

$$\ldots\ldots\ldots\ldots\ldots\ldots\ldots\ldots\ldots\ldots\ldots\ldots\ldots\ldots$$
$$\ldots\ldots\ldots\ldots\ldots\ldots\ldots\ldots\ldots\ldots\ldots\ldots\ldots\ldots$$
$$\ldots\ldots\ldots\ldots\ldots\ldots\ldots\ldots\ldots\ldots\ldots\ldots$$

$$v_b = \frac{x_{p(b-1)+1} + x_{p(b-1)+2} + \ldots + x_n}{p}$$

The block size p is chosen large enough so that v_i's are independent of each other. At the same time p should not be so large as to make b so small (for a given $pb = n$) that the distribution of $\bar{x}$ does not approximate normal.

Now regard these $v_1, v_2, \ldots, v_b$ as samples and compute the mean and the variance of the blocked output as follows:

$$\bar{v} = \frac{1}{b} \sum_{i=1}^{b} v_i = \frac{1}{bp} \sum_{i=1}^{n} x_i = \frac{1}{n} \sum x_i = \bar{x}$$

and the variance of the block mean $\bar{v}$ is given by

$$\sigma_{\bar{v}}^2 = \frac{\sigma_v^2}{b}.$$

Observe that $\bar{v}$, the mean of the block means v_i is exactly the same as the mean $\bar{x}$ of all the measurements. However, division of x_i's into blocks with the assumption that the block means are independent, together with the application of the Central Limit Theorem, allows us to use the simple formula for estimating the variance of the blocked mean. This allows us to compute a confidence interval.

Since in the blocking method we are taking one long run and breaking it into b blocks of size p each, we are in effect repeating an experiment of length p a total of b times, such that the final state of one run becomes the initial state of the next. This arrangement is better than starting all b runs from the same (arbitrary) initial state, because the state at the end of a run is likely to be more representative than an arbitrary initial state. However, this identification of the initial state of one run with the final state of the previous run, will introduce correlation between the means of successive runs v_i's. This correlation can be reduced to negligible values if the block length p is sufficiently large. The actual value of block length p can be determined by performing a few test runs to determine correlation between successive v_i's.

A number of studies have been performed to compare the effectiveness of the preceding two methods of dealing with a correlated data sequence. For the general use, no clear evidence has emerged in favour of one method over the other. It is found that the first method (since we are not throwing away any information by grouping the data together) requires fewer samples than the blocking method for obtaining the same confidence level. However, the computer time needed for estimating the autocorrelation coefficients may become so large as to overwhelm the gain resulting from the fewer observations. Intuitively, it is evident that the ratio of the computational time for computing one sample point x_i to the time for computing an autocorrelation coefficient will decide which way the balance tilts. Since this ratio depends on the system being simulated (and on the computer being used) no general verdict can be given which holds for all simulations.

7-2. Variance reduction techniques

Most simulation experiments are conducted for obtaining some important characteristic of a population, such as the average waiting time per customer in a queue. For that purpose we make n observations, $x_1, x_2, \ldots, x_n$ and obtain the mean $\bar{x}$. How close the sample mean $\bar{x}$ is to the population mean μ, is indicated by the standard deviation $\sigma_{\bar{x}}$ (of the sample mean $\bar{x}$). The larger the sample size n, the closer will $\bar{x}$ be to μ. This phenomenon is called *stochastic convergence*. The difficulty with stochastic convergence is that it is slow. In the previous section we made quantitative study of the influence of the number of observations, n, on the accuracy of $\bar{x}$, under different conditions. We saw that whether samples were statistically independent or autocorrelated, whether we used a single long run of length n, or b replications of n/b observations each, the standard deviation of the sample mean could always be expressed as

$$\sigma_{\bar{x}} = \frac{1}{n} \quad (a \text{ factor independent of } n)$$

Therefore, to reduce the standard deviation by a factor F we have to make F^2 as many observations.

In many applications, particularly in the presence of autocorrelation, one often finds that far too many observations are needed to obtain a reasonable accuracy in estimating the mean according to formulas (7-6) or (7-12). To get around the difficulty a number of techniques have been developed for reducing the variance without increasing the sample size. The following are some of the better-known variance-reduction techniques.

(i) **Antithetic sampling:** Suppose we have made two simulation runs —each of length $n/2$—in order to estimate the mean value of some random variable of our interest (assuming n to be an even number). Let the values of the observations in the two runs be

$$y_1, y_2, \ldots, y_{n/2}$$

and

$$z_1, z_2, \ldots, z_{n/2}.$$

The averages of these two replications are

$$\bar{y} = \frac{2}{n} \sum_{i=1}^{n/2} y_i$$

$$\bar{z} = \frac{2}{n} \sum_{i=1}^{n/2} z_i$$

and their variances are

$$\sigma_{\bar{y}}^2 = \sigma_{\bar{z}}^2 = \frac{2\sigma^2}{n}$$

where σ^2 is the variance of the parent population. The grand mean of the two replications is

$$\bar{x} = \frac{1}{n} \sum_{i=1}^{n/2} (y_i + z_i) = \frac{\bar{y} + \bar{z}}{2};$$

i.e., the average of the two averages, as expected. The variance of this grand mean $\bar{x}$ is

$$\sigma_{\bar{x}}^2 = \frac{1}{n} \sum_{i=1}^{n/2} [(y_i - \bar{y})^2 + (z_i - \bar{z})^2],$$

which turns out to be

$$\sigma_{\bar{x}}^2 = \frac{\sigma_{\bar{y}}^2 + \sigma_{\bar{z}}^2}{4} + \tfrac{1}{2} \text{Cov}(\bar{y}, \bar{z}), \qquad \ldots(7\text{-}13)$$

where $\text{Cov}(u, v)$ denotes the covariance of random variables u and v. If the two replications are independent the covariance term will be zero, and the variance estimate will then be identical to the one obtained by making a single run of the length n. If, however, we introduce a *negative correlation* between each of the $n/2$ pairs of observations (i.e., when the value y_i tends to be high, the value z_i will tend to be low, and vice versa), the second term in Eq. (7-13) will be negative, and the variance of the mean of the $n/2$ pairs of observations

$$\frac{y_1 + z_1}{2}, \frac{y_2 + z_2}{2}, \ldots, \frac{y_{n/2} + z_{n/2}}{2}$$

will be less than the variance of the mean of one continuous run of n observations. This method of purposely introducing a negative correlation between pairs of observations, for obtaining a more statistically reliable answer, is called *antithetic sampling*.

The most commonly used procedure for generating negatively correlated pairs of samples is to perform two identical simulation runs but using different sets of uniformly distributed random numbers (between 0 and 1). If in the first run the random numbers used are $u_1, u_2, \ldots, u_{n/2}$, then in the second run they are made to be $(1 - u_1), (1 - u_2), \ldots, (1 - u_{n/2})$. Thus if u_i is greater than the average value, $(1 - u_i)$ will be less, and vice versa. Thus these two sets of random numbers are negatively correlated. Therefore, the corresponding outputs y_i, z_i will also tend to be negatively correlated. Although the two sets of numbers undergo a variety of transformations during the simulation, it is expected that the outcome after the transformation will retain some negative correlation.

It is left as an exercise to employ the foregoing antithetic sampling method to the simulation of a PERT network. Instead of making a single run of, say, length 1,000 (as was done in Chapter 5), one would perform the simulation in 500 pairs, so that the duration of an activity is first obtained based on a random number u_j and in the second of the pair the duration for the same activity is based on $(1 - u_j)$.

Although this method of using random numbers in pairs u_i and $(1-u_i)$ is the most common procedure of implementing antithetic sampling, there are other methods that have been tried and found successful in specific simulations.   For example, in a single-server queue, we know that roughly speaking, the time a customer spends in the system is negatively correlated to its interarrival time because the longer the time the kth customer takes in arriving after the arrival of $(k-1)$th customer the shorter would be the waiting time of the kth customer.   On the other hand, the service time and the time a customer spends in the system are positively correlated.   Thus, interarrival times and the service times have opposite effects on the time a customer spends in the system (as well as on idle time, queue length, etc.). We can, therefore, reduce the variance if we perform the queueing simulation twice, under identical starting conditions, as follows: Use the random number sequence that generates the interarrival times on the first replication to generate the service times on the second, and use the random number sequence that generates the service times on the first replication to generate the interarrival times on the second.

The antithetic sampling has been found to be a useful technique in practice.   Its only requirement is that we must find some way of introducing a negative correlation between two sets of inputs, which is usually not a difficult task.   In general, however, it is not easy to determine how much of the negative correlation between the paired inputs finds its way into the corresponding outputs, to realise a reduction in variance.   A major advantage of antithetic sampling is that this technique can be added to any existing computer simulation program with only minor changes.

(ii) **Correlated sampling:**   This method is almost opposite to the antithetic sampling technique, and is useful when we are interested in estimating the differences in average characteristics of two alternate designs or strategies.   Suppose $\bar{A}$ and $\bar{B}$ are samples which estimate, say, the average waiting time per customer using two different queue disciplines.   We are interested in estimating the difference between the two performances.   If completely random samplings were used to obtain $\bar{A}$ and $\bar{B}$, then the difference is given by

$$\bar{D} = \bar{A} - \bar{B}$$

and the confidence we have in this value of the difference is determined by its variance, which is

$$\sigma^2_{\bar{D}} = \sigma^2_{\bar{A}} + \sigma^2_{\bar{B}}$$

if A and B were statistically independent.   But if the same set of random numbers are used to generate the stochastic variates in the two experiments, $\bar{A}$ and $\bar{B}$ are likely to be positively correlated.   In that case variance of the difference could be much smaller because

$$\sigma^2_{\bar{D}} = \sigma^2_{\bar{A}} + \sigma^2_{\bar{B}} - 2 \operatorname{Cov}(A, B)$$

Thus we can reduce the variance at no increase in computer running time.

(iii) **Importance sampling:** The idea of importance sampling is to use a sampling procedure which deliberately distorts the original distribution so that a larger proportion of samples is drawn from the interval of importance. Then an appropriate weighting function is used to multiply the sampled data which makes correction for the distortion introduced.

For example, suppose the Indian Railways wishes to estimate the average educational level of passengers travelling in its air-conditioned first class. It is known that there is a great deal of variation in the educational level of women passengers, varying all the way from 0 years of schooling to 16 years. For men, on the other hand, the variation is much smaller. Most of them have at least a bachelor's degree and go up to a Ph.D. (14 years to 19 years).

Suppose 80 per cent of the (adult) passengers are men and 20 per cent women, and we wish to take a sample of 20 passengers. If simple random sampling were employed, it would consist of approximately 16 men and 4 women. However, it is intuitively clear that since there is a wider variation in women's educational level, variance in their case is much greater, and hence the average will be less meaningful if a small sample is used. It would, therefore, be better to sample, say, 12 women and only 8 men. Such a sample would give a better estimate of the average. We must, however, apply appropriate weights to obtain the correct overall average.

As another example let us consider an inventory system, in which the unit backorder cost is much higher than the unit holding cost (it was 10 times in Example 2 of Chapter 6). For an optimal choice of P and Q the average backorder cost will be a significant part of the total average cost, but the backorders will occur infrequently. Under these circumstances a reliable estimate of the average daily cost $\bar{C}$ requires us to choose the run length n large enough so that a sufficient number of backorder situations occur, to obtain an accurate estimate of the average backorder cost. This run length would be wastefully large for estimating the average carrying cost and the average reorder cost. It is, therefore, worth while to search for an importance sampling scheme that allows us to include a larger number of backorder situations than their natural occurrences.

In general, the most difficult part of using the importance sampling is the determination of the appropriate distortion to be applied to the given distribution.

(iv) **Control variates:** When simulating a complex system one often finds that a simplified version of the system can be handled analytically and the value of the parameter can be calculated, corresponding to the parameter of interest in the simulation. For example, suppose we wish to simulate a multi-server queueing system with a complicated priority scheme, and the parameter of our interest is the mean queue length. We look for a simplified model and find that the first-come-first-served, single-server queueing system is mathematically tractable. The average queue length is given by Eq. (4-15) if the interarrival and the service times follow the negative exponential distribution.

Next we simulate the simpler model using a sequence of random numbers $u_1, u_2, \ldots, u_n$. Let $\overline{X}$ be the estimate of the parameter of interest (say, the mean queue length) obtained through simulation. Let $\overline{X}'$ be the value of the same parameter obtained analytically. The difference

$$E = \overline{X} - \overline{X}'$$

gives us the error due to sampling when the sequence of random numbers $u_1, u_2, \ldots, u_n$. This error E may also be used as an estimate of the sampling error in the more complex simulation, provided we use the same sequence of random numbers $u_1, u_2, \ldots, u_n$.

Therefore, as the last step, we simulate the given complex system using the random number sequence, $u_1, u_2, \ldots, u_n$, and obtain the value of the parameter corresponding to $\overline{X}$. Let this value be $\overline{Y}$. Now we correct this observed value $\overline{Y}$ by subtracting the estimated sampling error E from it. Thus the estimated value of the parameter (say, the mean queue length) obtained is

$$\overline{Z} = \overline{Y} - E = \overline{Y} - \overline{X} + \overline{X}'$$

The variance $\sigma_{\overline{z}}^2$ of this new estimate will be smaller than the variance of $\overline{Y}$ because $\overline{X}$ and $\overline{Y}$ have strong positive correlation since they both use the same sequence of random numbers as input.

This technique of using a control variate, which clearly affects the response in both systems (complex and simple) to introduce a positive correlation between their responses is easy to apply. It does not require any replication or tampering with the sampling mechanism.

(v) **Stratified sampling:** Another method of reducing variance without having to increase the number of sample points, is to break the parent population into classes (of strata) such that there is a minimum variation within each class. Then we take an appropriately small number of samples (only one sample is needed if variance is zero) from each strata. These samples are then combined to obtain an overall estimate of the mean. Clearly such sampling would be more efficient than a simple random sampling.

There are various ways of stratifying the population. The most effective would be to classify it such that the variance is the same for each class. But this would require greater knowledge of the population being sampled than is usually available. We must also know how many samples to take from the ith strata.

Such stratified sampling has been used by statisticians for a long time in order to get more information out of a specified number of samples. In a typical simulation situation, however, an appropriate stratification does not come by easily.

(vi) **Russian Roulette and splitting:** Suppose we wish to determine the probability of getting number 3 as the sum of two dice, by rolling one die at a time. Instead of making two rolls and then observing their sum, we can roll one die and proceed with the second only after observing the outcome of the first roll. If the first roll produces number other than 1 or 2, we do not need to toss the second die. We mark this trial as failure, and go to the next trial. This approach makes it unnecessary to toss the second die 4 out of 6 times, without affecting the accuracy of our estimate.

In general, this technique is used by classifying experiments with partial results at each stage as 'interesting' or 'uninteresting' and then proceeding further with only the interesting one. This method can be extremely effective in variance reduction, if good definitions of interesting and uninteresting are available at each stage of the experiment. Although this basic approach has been used for a long time in sequential sampling schemes by quality control engineers, it is not easily applicable to a typical simulation experiment.

To summarize, since simulation is an expensive technique and the stochatsic convergence is slow, the computational cost often increases heavily with degree of accuracy wanted. For this reason we are led to seek methods, other than increasing sample size, to reduce random error. These methods, of reducing the variance of the observed mean, can be very effective if we have intimate knowledge of the system under study. In using a variance reduction technique we are not getting something (added precision) for nothing. We are using additional information we have about the system to obtain greater precision. Not all variance reduction methods are suited for all occasions. In fact, an indiscriminate use of variance reduction techniques could worsen rather than improve the precision.

7-3. Experimental layout

So far in this chapter we have been concerned with the problem of specifying how a simulation experiment is to be conducted under a given set of operating conditions (i.e., for a given set of values for the controllable variables). We did not pay attention to the problem of picking the operating conditions themselves. We assumed that they were given to us. In this section we will discuss the problem of selection of operating conditions.

An independent design variable in an experiment is called a *factor* and a dependent variable is called a *response*. For example, in the inventory simulation problem we have seven *factors* (or design variables). These are the three costs, k, r, and b; the reorder point and quantity P, Q; and finally the two probability density functions for demand and lead time. The total inventory cost C is a response. In simulating the inventory problems in Chapter 1 as well as in Chapter 6 we were to find the value of the cost C for a specified set of factors. If our purpose of simulating an inventory system is merely to compare costs under a number of specified operating conditions then what was done in Chapter 6 was adequate. However, if our purpose is to detect and estimate the functional relationship,

$$C = f(k, r, b, P, Q, \text{demand, lead time})$$

that exists between the response C and the seven factors, then our task is not yet over.

The number of different choices we have for a factor are called its *levels*. If there are k different factors involved in an experiment and each has L different levels then the total number of different input combinations or design points (also called *treatments*) is

$$L^k.$$

If we conduct identical experiments with all these L^k design points, we are using the so-called *full factorial design*.

A full-factorial design will often turn out to be very expensive in terms of the computer time.   For example, in an inventory problem, suppose there are only two levels for each of the seven factors.   Then we have $2^7 = 128$ different treatments.   If for each of these 128 experiments we used a run length of 180 days (six months) and 30 replications for each run we would have $128 \times 180 \times 30$ different runs.   If each run uses 15 seconds of computer time, we would require 16 hours of computer time to conduct the full factorial experiment.

Each of the seven factors has an effect on the response (which is the total inventory cost C).   This is determined by comparing the response of the two (L, in general) treatments where all other factors except one were varied.   Next we determine the effect of two factors together, and so on.

Fractional factorial design: Often a full factorial design can be too costly to undertake, in which case one investigates the model with less than the full factorial design.   A question then arises regarding the effect that this reduction in treatment combination has on our ability to detect and estimate the functional relationships between the factors and the response. One systematic method of partial layout is called a *fractional factorial design*.

A great deal of classical literature exists on design of experiments, as part of statistics.   These concepts and statistical tools were developed for experiments in agriculture and industry.   Their use is not particularly prevalent in design of simulation experiments, because they assume the existence of a steady state and independent output data on which to base statistical tests—conditions frequently not met in simulation experiments.

Search for optimal design points: A common purpose of many simulation studies is to determine the combination of input parameters that produce a minimum or a maximum in the output.   For example, the ultimate purpose of simulating an inventory system is, usually, to find that policy (P, Q) which gives the minimum total inventory cost C, where costs k, r, b

and the demand and lead time distributions are specified. There are various search methods available in optimization theory (e.g., steepest ascent method) that tell how to search for an optimum point on a *response surface* which would lead us to the desired point with a minimum computational effort.

7-4. Validation

How do we know that the model we have used is an accurate representation of the system being simulated? This is an all-important question and must be answered satisfactorily before a simulation study can be made use of. Without a valid model we have nothing. In fact, without establishing the validity of the model, if we accept the (erroneous) simulation results the consequences may be disastrous.

What is a valid model? Since no simulation model will duplicate the given system in every detail it is not an appropriate question to ask if a simulator is a 'true' model of a real system. We should only ask if the model is a 'reasonable' approximation of the real system. The acceptable levels of reasonableness and approximation will vary from system to system and simulation to simulation. There is no universally acceptable criteria for accepting a simulation model as a valid representation. There are only guidelines that aid in establishing confidence in the model.

The validation efforts can be grouped into two parts: validation of the abstract model itself and validation of its implementation. The first part consists of examining all assumptions which transform the real-world system into the conceptual model. A great deal of judgement and an intimate knowledge of the real system are involved in this step. The validation of the abstract model is often highly subjective. Testing the validity of an implementation is a more objective and easier task. It consists of checking the logic, the flowchart, and the computer program to ensure that the model has been correctly implemented.

The easiest method of validating an implementation is the use of sample problems. The sample inputs should be chosen such that the corresponding output can be obtained analytically (or historically). For example, in Exercise 1-3, to validate the implementation of the pure-pursuit model we used the analytic expression for the pursuer's path when the target flies in a straight line. If the simulated path of the pursuer closely matches the analytically obtained path then we can conclude that the flowchart in Fig. 1-2 and the corresponding program are valid. Likewise, in Exercise 4-5 we used specific input distribution to validate the flowchart and computer program which implemented a single-server queue model. Similar sample problems can be generated for other simulation models using simple artificial inputs, for which the output can be analyzed. This method is useful and reasonable for validation in many cases. There are, of course, cases when this method may not exercise the simulation adequately, or output may not be predictable analytically even for very simple inputs.

Validating existing systems: When the simulated system exists in real life, then the most obvious and the best approach is to use the real world inputs to the model and compare its output with that of the real system. This process of validation is straightforward enough in principle but may present some difficulties when carried out.   Firstly, it may not always be easy to obtain input and output data from a real-life system without disturbing it.   Secondly, even if we could get actual input output of an existing model it would not generally be for very long periods.   Since the data are usually probabilistic, we know from earlier sections in the chapter, that for small lengths of simulation runs the variability of the model output would be large.   Therefore designing tests that work with small samples is difficult.   What usually is done is to simulate the model several times (replicate) with different sequences of random numbers and obtain the range of variation amongst these.   Then, if the model is valid, the real output should lie somewhere in the middle of the range of model output.   The third problem is to establish that the model output and the real-system outputs are 'practically' from the same population.

If the outputs to be compared are sample means (e.g., average queue length, waiting time, idle time), one could use any of a number of statistical tests (called 'goodness of fit' tests) available to measure the discrepancy between the two outputs (i.e., model output and the real-system output). One such test is the chi-square test, which has already been described in Chapter 3.   Others are Kolmogorov-Smirnov test, Cramer-von Mises test, and Moments test.   One could also use *hypothesis testing* to determine if there is any significant difference between, say, the averages of the independent set of observations.   One illustration of test of means is given in Exercise 7-7.

In most simulation experiments the output that is obtained is a time series (such as the queue lengths at various times, or stock level at different times), which are autocorrelated.   How to compare two autocorrelated time series and test them for equivalence?   Sepectral analysis is one of the methods that has been suggested in the literature.

Validating first-time model: If a model is intended to describe a proposed or hypothetical system (which does not exist at present or did not exist in the past), then the task of validation is even more difficult.   There are no historical data available to compare its performance with.   Since hypothetical systems are, by their very nature, based upon assumptions, it is the validity of these assumptions the simulation model is dependent on.   A number of guidelines for testing validity of such system have been found useful.   These are—

1.   **Subsystem validity:**   A model itself may not have any existing system to compare it with, but it may consist of known subsystems each of hose validity can be tested separately.

2. **Internal validity:** One tends to reject a model if it has a high degree of internal variability. A stochastic system with high variance due to its internal processes will obscure changes in the output due to input changes. The test can be performed by replicating a simulation run with several different random number sequences and then computing the variance of the outputs. If the variance is too high we reject the model.

3. **Sensitivity analysis:** Sensitivity analysis consists of systematically varying the values of parameters or the input variables one at a time (while keeping all others constant) over some range of interest and observing the effect upon the model's response. Sensitivity analysis will tell to which parameters the system is more sensitive. The parameter to which the system response is relatively insensitive, we need not pay very close attention to. The knowledge how far the assumed parameter values could be from the true one without significantly affecting the response helps building our confidence in the model.

4. **Face validity:** If the model goes against the common sense and logic, it should be rejected (even if it behaves like the real system). If those with experience and insight into similar systems do not judge the model as reasonable, it has to be rejected.

These and other validation tests do not completely validate a model. While failure to pass a validation test would result in rejection of a model, passing these tests does not guarantee that the model is valid. It only builds up our confidence in the model.

Ideally errors of modelling should be separated from the errors in its implementation (programming errors, etc.) by first validating the abstract mathematical model before writing a simulator for it. In practice, however, it is rarely possible to check the validity of the mathematical model without examining its computer version. This is because of the mathematical intractability of a model, which was the reason for simulating it in the first place.

Although validation is often messy, expensive and time consuming, involves subjectiveness and judgement, and is rarely conclusive, it must always be attempted. However inconclusive, it does provide a check against grosser errors and gives us confidence to use the simulation results for decision making.

7-5. Summary and conclusions

The considerations in developing and using computer simulation models will naturally depend on the system being studied and on the scope of the study. The way a simulation experiment proceeds will vary from system to system. However, there are certain basic steps which can be identified as common to all digital simulations which may be summarized as follows:

1. Problem definition and planning of the study.
2. Model building—including identification of those aspects of system

performance that are of interest to us and data collection for determining values of the system parameters.

3. Flowcharting—to show the logical steps to be performed by the computer in simulating the mathematical model obtained in Step 2 above.

4. Choice of a programming language. There are usually two options available at this point. The first option is to use a high-level general-purpose language such as FORTRAN, (or ALGOL, PL/1, BASIC, etc.) as we have done throughout this book. The second option is to use a special-purpose simulation language, such as, GPSS, (or SIMSCRIPT, SIMULA, etc.). Both of these approaches are extensively used in simulation studies. Use of a simulation language can save time and drudgery for the programmer if the system being simulated is very complex. On the negative side, he would have to learn a new language and the program written in a special purpose language would usually eat up more computer time and memory.

5. Program writing. While converting the flowchart into a running program (in the language chosen in Step 4) special attention should be paid to modularization. The simulator should consist of a number of natural and simple modules (subprograms) which can be tested independently and allow changes in the model conveniently. Intermediate print statements should also be included for diagnosis in validating the debugging stages. These statements may be removed before running the validated program. The format of the final output should be designed for easy interpretation.

6. Validation of the model.

7. Design of experiments—including removal of unwanted transients, determination of run lengths, initial conditions, and number of replications.

8. Execution of simulation run, analysis and interpretation of results.

Some of these steps have to be performed iteratively till acceptable results are obtained.

7-6. Remarks and references

The problems associated with the designing of simulation experiments have been classified into two types by Conway in

CONWAY, R. W., "Some Tactical Problems in Digital Simulation," *Management Science*, Vol. 10, No. 1, October 1963, pp. 47–61.

The types are (a) *strategic planning problems*, and (b) *tactical problems*. The strategic planning is concerned with how to lay out a set of simulation experiments so that the desired information is obtained. The tactical planning involves the conducting of each experiment most efficiently. It includes the decisions on run length, number of replications, starting conditions, use of variance reduction techniques, etc. A good treatment on strategic and tactical designs can be found in Chapters 4 and 5 of

> SHANNON, R. E., *Systems Simulation : the Art and Science*, Prentice-Hall, Englewood Cliffs, N.J., 1975.

Amongst other textbooks that emphasize statistical design of simulation experiments are

> MIRHAM, G. A., *Simulation : Statistical Foundations and Methodology*, Academic Press, New York, 1972.
> KLEIJNEN, J. P., *Statistical Techniques in Simulation*, Marcel Dekker, 1974.

A good survey of application of experimental design techniques to simulation is given in

> BURDICK, D. S., and T.H. NAYLOR, "Design of Computer Simulation Experiments for Industrial Systems," *Comm. ACM*, Vol. 9, No. 5, May 1966, pp. 329–339.

An updating of this paper with particular application to laying out of simulation experiments for inventory systems can be found in

> HUNTER, J. S., and T. H. NAYLOR, "Experimental Design for Computer Simulation Experiments," *Management Sci.*, Vol. 16, No. 7, March 1970, pp. 422–434.

A good treatment on estimation of a simulation run length is given in

> FISHMAN, G. S., "Estimating Sample Size in Computing Simulation Experiments," *Management Sci.*, Vol. 18, No. 1, September 1971, pp. 21–38.

and on variance reduction techniques is given in

> FISHMAN, G. S., "Variance Reduction in Simulation Studies," *Jour. Stati. Comput. Simulation*, Vol. 1, 1972, pp. 173–182.

Various methods of conducting an efficient search for optimal values of the response in simulation experiments is discussed in textbooks by G. A. Mirham; R. E. Shannon; and J. P. Emshoff and R. L. Sisson, cited earlier.

Some papers suggested on the topic of validation are:

> NAYLOR, T. H., and J. M. Finger, "Verification of Computer Simulation Models," *Management Sci.*, Vol. 14, No. 2, Oct. 1967, pp. 92–101.
> VAN HORN, R. L., "Validation of Simulation Results," *Management Sci.*, Vol. 17, No. 5, January 1971.
> AIGNER, D. J., "A Note on Verification of Computer Simulation Models," *Management Sci.*, Vol. 18, No. 11, July 1972, pp. 615–619.

7-7. Exercises

7-1. Show analytically that in a game of craps, as stated in Exercise 3-3, the probability that the player rolling the dice wins is 488/990. Thus in the long run out of every 990 games played he wins 488 games and loses 502, which means a net loss of 14 games out of every 990. Hence the expected value of the win per game is $-14/990 = -0.01414$.

7-2. In this exercise you are to apply the principle of antithetic sampling to reduce variance in simulating a PERT network.   Simulate the network given in Fig. 5-8, in 500 pairs as follows: Obtain the duration of a given activity first by using random numbers u_i and u_i' (in the Box-Muller formula).   For the second of the pair use numbers $(1 - u_i)$ and $(1 - u_i')$ to generate the duration of that particular activity.   Rewrite the program given in Sec. 5-6 to incorporate this feature.   Compare the result of a single run simulation of length 1000 with that of a paired run simulation of length 500 pairs.

7-3.   Formula (7-6) for determining the sample size was derived under the assumption that the sample mean $\bar{x}$ has the normal distribution. In some simulation experiments this assumption may be questionable.   In that case, Chebyshev's inequality could be used, which says that in a set of n independent measurements $y_1, y_2, \ldots, y_n$ at least $(1 - 1/k^2)$ fraction will be within k standard deviations of the population mean μ.   In other words

$$Pr\{|y - \mu| > k\,\sigma_y\} \leqslant \frac{1}{k^2}$$

Applying this to sample $\bar{x}$, we get

$$Pr\left\{|\bar{x} - \mu| > k\,\frac{\sigma_x}{\sqrt{n}}\right\} \leqslant \frac{1}{k^2}$$

Use this inequality to calculate the sample size n required to determine the sample mean $\bar{x}$ within $\mu \pm k\sigma_x$ at $\alpha = 0.05$, for several values of k from 0.05 to 0.5.   Compare these within the values of n obtained using Eq. (7-6).   Show that at $\alpha = .05$ level we have to take about 5.3 times as many samples (which is the price we pay for not being able to assume a normal distribution for $\bar{x}$).

7-4.   In many simulation studies, the output is in the form of a proportion of successes.   For example, in simulation of a military weapon we are interested in its 'kill probability' (fraction of targets destroyed).   Show that in cases where the outcome is of go-no go type, the number of samples n needed to determine an estimate of the proportion of success within a fraction f with confidence interval $(1 - \alpha)$ is

$$n = \left(\frac{y_{1-\alpha/2}}{2f}\right)^2$$

where $y_{1-\alpha/2}$ is the two-tailed standardized normal static for the probability $(1 - \alpha)$.

7-5.   In Sec. 7-1 we were concerned with the precision of the observed mean $\bar{x}$.   Sometime we are concerned with the precision of the estimated variance also.   Derive a formula similar to Eq. (7-6) to determine the number of observations n needed to estimate variance q within $\pm p$ percentage with a probability $(1 - \alpha)$.   Show that it can be approximated with

$$n = 1 + \frac{2\,(y_{1-\alpha/2})^2}{(p/100)^2}.$$

7-6.   Given the following output sequence of 40 numbers x_i's compute
(a) the sample mean, (b) the variance autocorrelation coefficients with lag
1, 2, and 3 using Eq. (7-10).

9.1,	8.9,	10.3,	9.9,	9.0,	10.2,	11.0,	11 3,	9.8,	10.3,
10.8,	10.6,	9.3,	9.9,	10.4,	9.4,	9.8,	9.7,	9.5,	10.6,
10.8,	10.8,	10.7,	10.0,	10.6,	9.6,	9.4,	9 5,	10.4,	10.2,
9.8,	10.0,	9.9,	9.4,	9.1,	8.8,	10.0,	10.7,	10.3,	11.1

7-7.   Partition the sequence in Exercise 7-6 into 8 blocks of length
5 each.   Compute the mean and the variance of the blocked data.

7-8.   Run the simulator for the inventory system whose flowchart and
FORTRAN program are given in Sec. 6-4 for the policy $P = 120$ and $Q = 80$
and starting stock $= 0$.   Get the daily stock as the output and plot it for
first 100 days to show the transients.   Repeat the experiment with starting
stock $= 100$ units.

7-9.   Using the simulator of Sec. 6-4, attempt a systematic search for
an optimal inventory policy.

7-10.   Suppose $\{x_1, x_2, \ldots, x_N\}$ and $\{y_1, y_2, \ldots, y_M\}$ are independent samples from two approximately normal populations having means μ_1 and μ_2
(unknown) and the same variance σ^2 (also unknown).   Let $\bar{x}$ and $\bar{y}$ denote
the two sample means.   Clearly, the random variables $\bar{x}$ and $\bar{y}$ have means
μ_1 and μ_2 and variance σ^2/N and σ^2/M, respectively. The random variable
$(\bar{x} - \bar{y})$ has mean $(\mu_1 - \mu_2)$ and variance $(\sigma^2/N + \sigma^2/M)$.

(a)   Show that the variable

$$t = \frac{(\bar{x} - \bar{y}) - (\mu_1 - \mu_2)}{s\sqrt{1/N + 1/M}}$$

has the Student-t distribution with $(N + M - 2)$ degrees of freedom,
where s^2 is the estimate of the variance, given by

$$s^2 = \frac{\sum_i (x_i - \bar{x})^2 + \sum_j (y_i - \bar{y})^2}{N + M - 2}.$$

(b)   Suppose the following are two sets of samples:

x :   79,   84,   120,   108,   114,   103,   122,   120
y :   54,   99,   91,   103,   90,   113,   108,   87,   100,   80

Calculate $\bar{x}$, $\bar{y}$, s^2; and test the hypothesis that the two means are
equal, i.e., $(\mu_1 - \mu_2) = 0$.

8

Simulation Languages

As we saw in previous chapters, computer simulation is essentially an experimental technique, used for studying a wide variety of systems. The purpose of the experiment is to observe the behaviour of a given system (actually a specific model of the system) within a given environment which would eventually provide a basis for understanding the system and making decisions. The abstract model of the system being simulated takes the form of a computer program, and the system behaviour is given by the output, as the program runs.

Throughout this book we have been using FORTRAN for this purpose, because it is the best known and most readily available computer language. (We could have used ALGOL, PL/I, COBOL, or any of the other general-purpose languages, if we had desired to do so.)

You might have observed that even a moderately complex simulation model (such as a 2-server queue in Sec. 4-3 or an activity network in Sec. 5-5) can become difficult to program, to debug, and to modify. A programmer who has to perform simulation frequently would be better off learning a higher-level special-purpose language, which facilitates simulation programming. The extra effort he invests in learning such a simulation language would be made up by the ease and increased speed with which he can now write a simulation program.

Besides being a programming aid, a simulation language often serves another very useful purpose. It provides a conceptual framework in which the system analyst can work while building a model of the system. The language imposes a certain amount of precise thinking on the system analyst and forces him to seek answers to numerous useful and appropriate questions. A simulation language also provides a terminology for describing a complex dynamic system.

Unfortunately, there is a bewildering variety of simulation languages. Of scores of simulation languages that have been designed, implemented, and used, there is no single language which can be termed as the "best," "most useful," or "universally" available. Most of these languages are suited for a narrow class of applications. If we were simulating a military system we might pick MILITRAN; but for simulating a world dynamics model we would perhaps use DYNAMO; for simulating a sampled-data system we might use BLODIB; but for simulating a job-shop scheduling, GPSS would be preferred.

In addition to the nature of a system being simulated, the availability of the hardware and the software also dictates the choice of a language. If we have only a minicomputer at our disposal, we would not consider implementing a "large" language such as SIMSCRIPT II.5 for our simulation experiments. Availability of a simulation language is an obvious but very important consideration in choosing a language. All languages are not available on all computer systems.

In this chapter we will present an overview of simulation languages without describing any one specific language in all its details. The details can be found in various manuals.

8-1. Continuous and discrete simulation languages

As discussed earlier, simulation is divided into two categories: discrete and continuous. Accordingly, most of the simulation languages also fall into one of the two classes. Continuous simulation languages are designed for simulating continuous models and discrete simulation languages for discrete models—models that change their states abruptly at discrete points in time. More recently, a few languages have been designed which are suitable for both discrete as well as continuous models. Such a language, called a *combined simulation language,* is written particularly for system-models in which some of the variables change continuously and other variables change discretely. These continuous and discrete variables, of course, interact with each other. For example, the number of passengers in a lift change discretely whereas the lift's distance from the ground floor or its speed varies continuously. GASP IV is perhaps the best known example of a combined simulation language. Other examples are GSL-A (*Gene*ralized *S*imulation *L*anguage), CLASS (*C*omposite *L*anguage *A*pproach for *S*ystem *S*imulation), and PROSE (*Pro*blem Level Programming System).

8-2. Continuous simulation languages

Before the digital computers came into widespread use, analog computers were being used for simulating continuous dynamic systems. The system being simulated was generally an engineering system, described by differential equations, for which analytic solutions were hard to obtain. The system was represented by means of a block diagram (such as the one shown in Fig. 2-5 of Chapter 2), which was then simulated on the analog computer by suitably patching together corresponding blocks available on the analog computer. As soon as the digital computer arrived, some of its advantages (such as greater accuracy, freedom from scaling) over the analog computer became obvious. Therefore, special program packages (canned programs) were implemented on digital computers to make a digital computer appear like an analog computer.

These so-called *digital analog simulators* (program packages) were meant either to replace an analog computer or check the results of an analog simulation on a digital computer. Such a simulation language (that makes a digital computer emulate an analog computer) is called a *block-structured continuous system simulation language*. It requires the user to prepare an analog-computer-type block diagram and then input this diagram. Later, more versatile *expression-based simulation languages* were developed.

8-3. Block-structured continuous simulation languages

As pointed out in the last section, block-structured continuous simulation languages were the first to be devised. They were designed to simulate only those systems that could be represented as analog block diagrams, and thus their application area is restricted. The first such digital analog simulator was designed by R. G. Selfridge in 1955 and implemented on the IBM 701 computer. It used Simpson's rule for integration. Selfridge's simulator was followed by a host of similar (block-oriented) languages, in the late 1950's and the early 1960's. The better-known amongst these were DEPI (1958, on DATATRON 204 Computer, using the fourth-order Runge-Kutta method for integration); DEPI-4 rewritten DEPI for the IBM 704 computer, in 1959); DYSAC (in 1961, on the CDC 1604 computer, fourth-order Runge-Kutta); DAS (in 1962, on the IBM 7090 computer, using Euler's formula for integration) and MIDAS (in 1963, using variable-step fifth-order predictor-corrector method for integration). MIDAS became an outstanding success. Initially it was an interpreter. In 1966 a compiler version was also written. It is available on many computers including the IBM 1620, 7040, and 7090 families, and UNIVAC 1107 and 1108.

By the mid-1960's the use of the digital computer for simulation of continuous systems was well-established and so were the block-oriented simulation languages. The development of new languages has, of course, continued. We will now briefly describe a block-oriented continuous simulation language and illustrate its use with an example:

A block-structured language requires the user to first prepare a block diagram to represent the system to be simulated (just as he would do to simulate it on an analog computer). Then he must provide "patching" instructions, which specify how these blocks are to be connected together.

A typical block-oriented language (such as the IBM 1130 CSMP) provides a number of standard functional blocks (implemented in the form of subroutines). These include the common simulation elements such as integrators (I), multipliers (X), summers ($+$), as well as more specialized functional elements, such as limiter (L), unit delay (U), hyteresis or dead space (D), and zero-order hold (Z). In addition to these fixed functional blocks, the language generally also provides a few elements for which the user himself can define the functional relationship. For example, the IBM 1130 CSMP provides 25 different types of specified blocks and five blocks which the user can specify by supplying appropriate subroutines. As an example, Fig. 8-1 shows the diagrams for two of the blocks in the IBM 1130 CSMP.

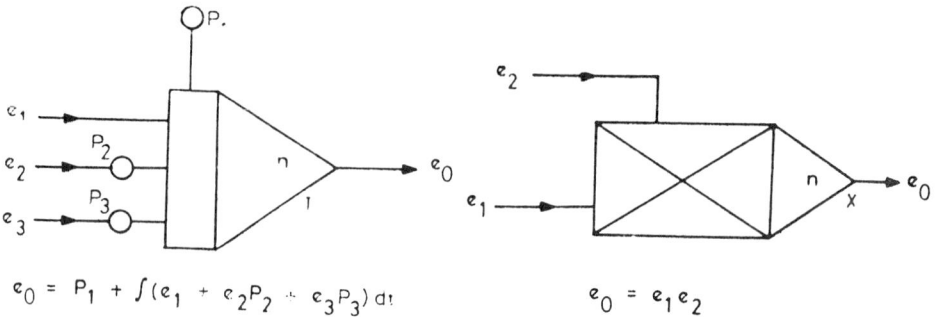

$$e_0 = P_1 + \int (e_1 + e_2 P_2 + e_3 P_3)\, dt \qquad\qquad e_0 = e_1 e_2$$

Fig. 8-1:   Integrator (I) and Multiplier (X) blocks (n represents the block number).

Typically these blocks in the language may have zero, one, two, or three inputs, depending on the type of the block. For example, in Fig. 8-1, the integrator has three inputs and the multiplier has two. A constant block, on the other hand, has no input at all. The output of each block is a single-valued scalar function of the independent variable (time), its inputs and parameters. Each of the elements (or the blocks) is identified by its type denoted by a specific symbol in the language (such as I, X, $/$, $+$, etc.) and by its block number n—which is an arbitrary positive integer used for referring to a block whenever necessary.

In order to simulate the given continuous system we first represent it by means of a block diagram (just like the one we would prepare if we were to solve the problem on an analog computer). This block is then put into a computer program (in the block-oriented language under discussion) by means of three types of statements: (1) *Configuration statements* are the set of patching instructions which define the interconnections between the blocks. (2) *Parameter statements* associate the numerical values with the block elements to specify the exact functional operations of the blocks. (3) *Function generation statements* define the input/output of the Function Generator elements (if any have been used).

As an example, let us consider the classical problem of a *host-parasite* system. There is a host population H (i.e., food for parasites) which reproduces at a known constant rate $\left(\dfrac{dH}{dt} = K_1 H\right)$ if there were no parasites to devour it. The parasite population P decreases (die off) at a known rate $\left(\dfrac{dP}{dt} = -K_2 P\right)$ if there is no host population to live on. A decrease in the number of hosts and an increase in the number of parasites occurs as functions of the number of "encounters" between hosts and parasites. The system is thus described by a pair of first-order, non-linear differential equations:

$$\frac{dH}{dt} = K_1 H - K_3 HP \qquad \qquad ...(8\text{-}1)$$

$$\frac{dP}{dt} = - K_2 P + K_4 HP \qquad \qquad ...(8\text{-}2)$$

Suppose the values of the four constants are as follows:

$K_1 = 0.05$/hour   (increase of 5% per hour)
$K_2 = 0.10$/hour   (decrease of 10% per hour)
$K_3 = 0.0002$/parasite hour
$K_4 = 0.0002$/host hour

That is, one host is devoured and one parasite is born every 5,000 hours as a result of the number of "encounters," which is proportional to the product of hosts and parasites.

We are given the initial populations $H(0)$ and $P(0)$ (say, 1,000 and 500, respectively), and wish to determine the two populations as functions of time.

The system is represented by means of a block diagram shown in Fig. 8-2. (Block numbers 4, 19, and 26 were assigned arbitrarily.)

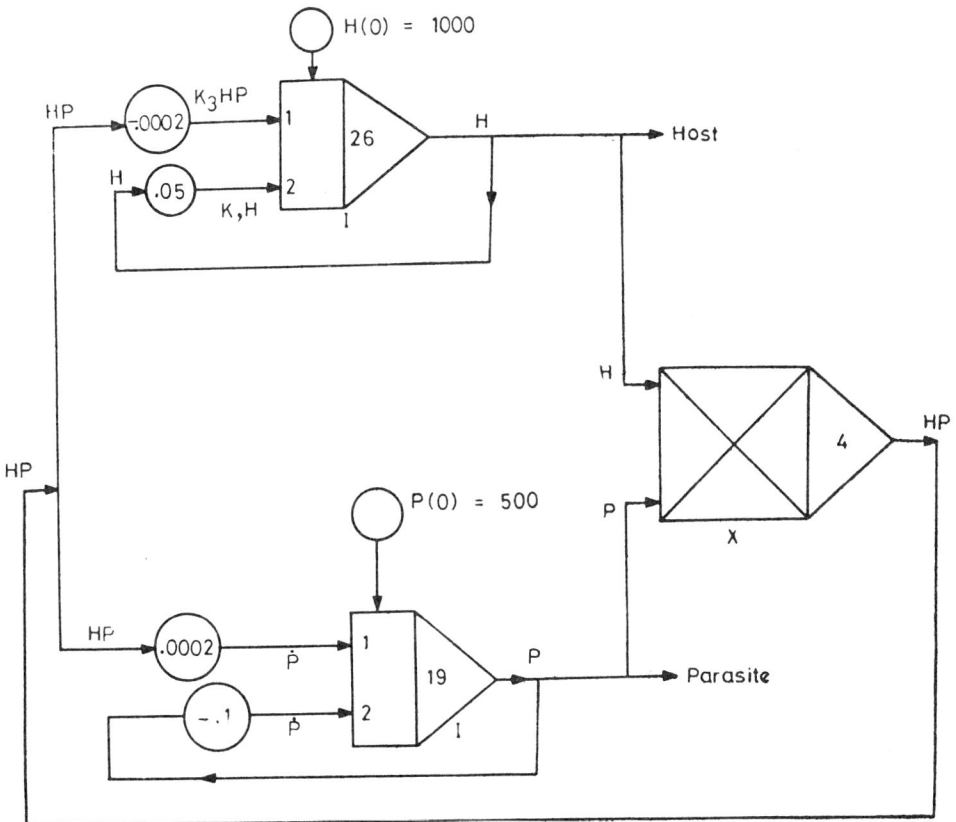

Fig. 8-2:   Block diagram for the Host-Parasite System.

In order to feed this block diagram to the computer, the programmer must supply a set of patching instructions to the computer. A commonly used method would be to type in or punch cards as follows:

CONFIGURATION SPECIFICATION

BLOCK NUMBER	BLOCK TYPE	INPUT 1	INPUT 2	INPUT 3
26	I	7	26	0
19	I	7	19	0
7	X	26	19	0

which means that integrater block 26 has its input terminal 1 connected to the output of block 7, and its input terminal 2 connected to the output of block 26 itself. And so on.

The intitial conditions and the parameters of the integraters might be typed in the following form:

INITIAL CONDITIONS AND PARAMETERS

BLOCK	IC	PAR 1	PAR 2
26	1000.0	−.0002	.05
19	500.0	.0002	−.1

Finally, we must specify the integration interval, duration of the simulation run, what variables we wish to be displayed, and how these are to be outputted (e.g., on a printer, a plotter, or a CRT screen).

The foregoing discussion was intended to give you a glimpse into the fundamental nature of block-oriented continuous system simulation languages. Many details have of necessity been left out. These can be found in the manuals for the specific language provided by the manufacturer. It is left as an exercise for you to complete the study of this Host-Parasite problem using the block-oriented continuous system simulation language available with your computer centre.

The most significant advantage of a block-oriented language is its remarkable simplicity and naturalness with which a continuous dynamic system can be simulated. The above example illustrates how easy it is to program using this type of language. A novice can learn to use such a language in an hour or two. With an interactive block-oriented language a small inexpensive digital computer system can be made to appear like an analog/hybrid computer with the added advantage of much greater accuracy and freedom from scaling. The main disadvantage of a block-oriented language is relative inflexibility. The system being simulated has first to be represented by means of a block diagram. Consequently a block-oriented language is popular amongst those who naturally use "analog type" block diagrams to represent the system they are studying, often without explicitly writing model equations. For instance, control engineers usually specify systems in terms of a number of simple blocks, each of which becomes a single simulation block. Another example of a convenient and at the same time powerful block-oriented simulation language is described below:

MOBSSL-UAF: (*Merritt* and Millers *Own Block Structured Simulation Language—Unpronounceable Acronym For*) is an interactive augmented block-structured simulation language for continuous systems. As in the case of other block-structured languages (such as MIDAS, PACTOLUS, 1130 CSMP), it is an extremely simple language to learn, and one need not have any prior programming knowledge or experience. MOBSSL is a descendant of the IBM 1130 CSMP, but it has overcome some of the rigidity of the latter by incorporating additional features, such as, disk I/O blocks; a gradient processor; a variable constant; a storage block; a large selection of trigonometric functions; and digital-to-analog and analog-to-digital blocks for hybrid computation. MOBSSL-UAF was developed at the University of Southern California in 1969 and implemented on a number of mid-sized computers including PDP-11/40, IBM 360/44 as well as on CDC 3600, IBM S/370.

8-4. Expression-based languages

A purely block-oriented continuous system simulation language is severely limited because of its small specialized vocabulary. It does not allow any FORTRAN-type statements. Therefore no relationship or equation in the system can be expressed directly. The system must first be represented in an analog-like block diagram. Thus the block-oriented languages are suited for those who "think analog," and mode their system by a block diagram and not for those who model their system as a set of equations. Around 1965, after the outstanding success of MIDAS (which was a purely block-oriented language), this limitation was realized, and a successor of MIDAS called MIMIC was written for the IBM 7090 family of computers. In MIMIC one could write FORTRAN-like statements also (along with representing the block diagrams). Such a feature eliminates the necessity of drawing a block diagram. Differential, algebraic and logical equations (representing the model of the system being simulated) can then be written directly as statements or expressions in the language.

As an example, let us again consider the host-parasite system discussed in Sec. 8-3 and represented by Eqs. (8-1) and (8-2). The system may be simulated using the following set of statements in an expression-based continuous system simulation language called BEDSOCS:

```
10   LET K1 = 0.05
20   LET K2 = 0.10      }  (constants)
30   LET K3 = 0.0002
40   LET K4 = 0.0002
```

```
 50   LET H  = 1000          ⎫  (initial conditions)
 60   LET P  = 500           ⎭
100   DYNAMIC
150   EQUATIONS
160   DER  H = K1*H — K3*H*P      ⎫
170   DER  P = — K2*P + K4*H*P    ⎬  (equations)
180   DISPLAY  H/100, P/100       ⎭
200   EQUEND
300   DYNEND
```

Continuous system simulation languages such as BEDSOCS (*Bradford EDucational Simulation language fOr Continuous System*) are called *expression-based* or *statement-based* continuous system simulation languages. Expression-based languages do not need to follow block-structures of the analog patchboards but directly implement the differential equations of the model. A large number of expression-based languages have been designed and implemented—some popular, others obscure. We will first discuss some of the important common characteristics of these languages and then give a brief survey of some better known members in this class:

(a) **Methods of integration:** In most expression-based languages several different routines are available for the user to choose from. They include both fixed step-size routines and variable integration step-size routines. For example, in S/360 CSMP five fixed-size routines are available: fixed Runge-Kutta, Simpson's, trapezoidal, rectangular, and second-order Adams. Two variable step-size routines are also available: fifth-order Milne predicter-correcter and fourth-order Runge-Kutta. The integration step Δt is automatically varied during the problem execution to satisfy the user-specified error criterion. If none of these seven methods satisfy the S/360 CSMP requirement, he could use a dummy integration routine named CENTRL and specify any other method of integration he wishes.

In contrast to S/360 CSMP, some of the smaller languages have only one subroutine for integration. For example, BEDSOCS uses the 4th order variable-step Runge-Kutta-Merson method of integration. MIMIC and GASP-PL/I also have a single integration subroutine based on a version of the fourth-order variable-step Runge-Kutta method. DYNAMO uses Euler's method of integration.

(b) **Automatic Sequencing of Statements:** As every programmer knows, an assignment statement in a program would be invalid if all the variables appearing on the right hand side had not already been defined (or evaluated) by earlier statements. Likewise, it is necessary to ensure in a simulation program (as in any other program) that the statements appear in a correct sequence. However, in writing a simulation program for a large complex system, this task (of ensuring a correct sequence of statements) may be too much of a burden on the programmers. Therefore, most of the expression-based simulation languages have a built-in facility which automatically sorts the input statements into a proper calculational order. Thus the user is free to input the statements in any arbitrary order, and not be burdened with putting them in a correct sequence.

(c) **Intermediate Language:** Most of the expression-based languages are designed to be extensions of some well-known, existing high-level language. For example, BEDSOCS is an extension of BASIC. Similarly, DSL/90 and S/360 CSMP are extensions of FORTRAN. Thus the capability of FORTRAN is available to the user of the S/360 CSMP. Expressions in S/360 CSMP can be intermixed with FORTRAN statements. The standard FORTRAN library of functions such as cosine, tangent, absolute value are available to the programmer. A preprocessor first translates all the non-FORTRAN statements (of S/360 CSMP) into FORTRAN. These statements along with the FORTRAN statements (which were intermixed with the S/360 CSMP statements) constitute a single program, which then gets compiled by the FORTRAN compiler and run.

The advantages of having an intermediate language are obvious—the power, flexibility, ease of implementation. The price one pays for this facility is increased preprocessing time, as the language first has to be translated into the intermediate language and then into the machine language before being executed. For example, a simulation program written in MIMIC (a language where the compiler translates simulation programs directly into machine language without going through an intermediate language) takes much less translation time than the same program written in DSL/90 (or S/360 CSMP). Another disadvantage of using an intermediate language is that the programmer has also to become proficient at the intermediate language in order to use the simulation language effectively.

(d) **Prepackaged Input Output:** In an expression-based continuous system simulation language the input is usually of free-form. The user does not have to format it. Similarly, the output is also displayed (printed or plotted) in a fixed format by means of a built-in output package. One has only to specify the variables to be displayed and the increments of the independent variable (time). For instance, in our example of the BEDSOCS program for host-parasite problem we simply asked that the host-population, H, and the parasite population, P, be displayed on the CRT screen against time, with a vertical scale of 100 creatures per unit height of the screen, with a single statement DISPLAY H/100, P/100. This prepackaging of input/output relieves the programmer from the task of formatting them.

(e) **Macro Facilities:** An important feature available in many of the expression-based languages is the powerful function-defining capability called *macro*. It allows the user to build larger functional blocks from the basic functions available in the language, and thereby, to identify, a subsection of a simulation block diagram or the corresponding subset of structure statements. Once defined, macro functions may be used any number of times, as if they were operators of the language.

As an illustration, we will show how this facility is used in S/360 CSMP, with the help of the following example.

Suppose we wish to simulate a control system that involves several transfer functions with differing parameter values, but all having the general form:

$$\frac{Z(s)}{X(s)} = \frac{s^2 + as + b}{s^2 + cs + d},$$

where s is the Laplace operator.

A simple technique for modeling such transfer functions is to define a new variable Y such that

$$\frac{Y(s)}{X(s)} = \frac{1}{s^2 + cs + d},$$

where the numerator is unity but the same denominator is used. Then, solving for the highest-order derivative of Y, one obtains

$$s^2 Y = X - cs\,Y - d\,Y.$$

Note that this is equivalent to the time domain statement

$$\ddot{Y}(t) = X(t) - c\,\dot{Y}(t) - d\,Y(t)$$

which is readily modeled by the S/360 CSMP statement

$$S\,2\,Y = X - C * SY - D * Y.$$

Then by two successive integrations we obtain $Y(t)$. Since

$$Z(s) = s^2\,Y + as\,Y + b\,Y,$$

we finally obtain $Z(t)$ by combining terms with the following S/360 CSMP statement

$$Z = S\,2\,Y + A * SY + B * Y.$$

The user may define a macro to represent this general functional relationship, assigning it some unique name, say, FILTER. The S/360 CSMP statements to define this new macro might be as follows:

$$\text{MACRO } Z = \text{FILTER } (A, B, C, D, X)$$
$$S\,2\,Y = X - C * SY - D * Y$$
$$SY = \text{INTGRL} (0.0, S\,2\,Y)$$
$$Y = \text{INTGRL} (0.0, SY)$$
$$Z = S\,2\,Y + A * SY + B * Y$$
$$\text{ENDMAC}$$

Such macro definition cards will be placed at the beginning of the S/360 CSMP deck before any structure statements in the initialization or dynamic segments. As shown above, the last card of a macro definition in S/360

CSMP must consist of just the word ENDMAC. There are some other simple rules that have to be observed in defining and u ing the macro facility.

(f) **Optional Block-Oriented Representation:** Many of the expression-based languages incorporate the facilities of a block-oriented language also. This accommodates both type of users—those who model their system as a set of equations and those who model their system as a set of interconnected blocks. Most of the popular expression-based languages, such as S/360 CSMP, CSSL, DSL, have this facility.

There are many other features which distinguish these languages. For example, BEDSOCS incorporates only *first order* derivative equations, but many languages can accept higher order equations written directly. For instance, in such a language

$$\frac{d^3x}{dt^3} = y$$

could be written directly as

$$DER\,3\,(X) = Y$$

and would not have to be converted into three equations such as

$$DER\,(X) = Z\,1$$
$$DER\,(Z\,1) = Z\,2$$
$$DER\,(Z\,2) = Y.$$

It is neither possible in this limited space, nor desirable to give a complete description of any specific expression-based simulation language. Such descriptions can be found in various manuals supplied by the manufacturers. We will merely highlight some features of a few of the better-known languages in this class:

DSL: DSL (*Digital Simulation Language*) is a classic and a very well-known continuous system simulation language. This language, which was developed by IBM, first in 1964 as DSL/90 for its 7090/7094 computers, has gone through many revisions, modifications, and implementations for different computers. Some of these are DSL/40 (for the IBM 7040); DSL/44 (for the IBM 360/44); DSL/1130 (for the IBM 1130); DSL/1800 (for the IBM 1800); and DSL/360 (for the IBM System 360). It has also been implemented on IBM's System 3 and System 7. System/360 CSMP is an implementation of DSL to some of the IBM 360 computers. DSL is an extension of FORTRAN.

S/360 CSMP: S/360 CSMP (*Continuous System Modeling Program*) language can handle either expressions or block-oriented descriptions. As mentioned earlier, it is a preprocessor with FORTRAN as an intermediate language, i.e., it accepts a simulation model description and run-time instructions and produces a FORTRAN program which can be compiled and executed. The user's original program can contain FORTRAN statements and use FORTRAN subroutines. Capabilities of this language include seven integration methods, over 50 simulation functions, and macros, and excellent diagnostics and debugging aids. Input/output formats are rich and include various tabular and plot arrangements. It is not a difficult language to learn, but it is computationally expensive.

CSSL: CSSL (*Continuous Systems Simulation Language*) was defined in 1967, in accordance with the recommendations made by a Simulation Software Committee formed by Simulation Councils, Inc. The Committee has combined desirable features of a simulation language, related to: application areas, programming skills and digital computers. The language has a powerful capability to be extended in order to satisfy users requirements. As other good languages it does have error control and debugging facilities. Integration can be done with the use of several available numerical methods.

Numerous versions of CSSL have been implemented. For example, CSSL III on CDC 6400 and XDS Sigma 7; CSSL IV on IBM 360/370, UNIVAC 1108/1110, DEC 10, and CDC 6600/7600. A version of CSSL, called RSSL, has also been implemented on CDC 7600. Languages called HYTRAN and SL-1 are also versions of CSSL.

DARE: DARE (*Differential Analyzer REplacement*) is a series of continuous system simulation languages for batch and on-line use. One version, DARE P(*Portable*), has been developed by the University of Arizona. DARE P has been implemented on IBM S/360, CDC 6000 series, and DEC 10 machines. Except for a small set of machine dependent routines, the system is coded entirely in FORTRAN. The program is modular, and it uses system independent FORTRAN-based methods for writing and manipulating solution files. Users can add new integration algorithms or special library of subroutines. FORTRAN can be used to control logic of the simulation studies and define special functions. Problem equations are entered in a form resembling mathematical notations, and the associated procedural language is FORTRAN. Input data are provided by format-free data cards. Outputs can be generated on a line-printer, or a CalComp plotter can be used. The following integration methods are incorporated: Runge-Kutta Merson, fourth-order Runge-Kutta, third-order Runge-Kutta, two-point Runge-Kutta, Adam's two-point predictor, simple Euler one-point predictor, and two methods (Pope's and Gear's) for solving systems of stiff differential equations. The language can be used interactively using PDP-9 computers. Other versions of DARE run on the PDP-11 series computers, including one version which runs on the PDP-11V03 (LSI-11 microcomputer).

DYNAMO: DYNAMO (available on IBM 360, 370, 7090, B 5500, UNIVAC 1107, 1108) is the most widely used simulation language amongst economists and social scientists. It was developed in the late 1950's by J. W. Forrester and his *industrial dynamics* group at MIT. It uses first-order difference equations to approximate the modeled continuous process. The dynamic systems are described in terms of levels and rate equations and continuous variables. The level variables (commodities, money, population, etc.) characterize the state of the system at any particular time. They accumulate the flows described by the rate equations and variables. These equations and variables define how quickly the levels are changing. Using these two types of equations and variables it is possible to model many systems that can be classified as feedback systems. The DYNAMO compiler accepts the model written in the form of level, rate and auxiliary equations using special postscript notation. The compiler functions are: (a) error control; (b) sequencing equations according to the structural concepts of system dynamics; (c) compilation of the program defining the model; and (d) execution of the program and generation of output in a tabular or graphical form. The language has many computational facilities in the form of special statistical and mathematical functions. One of the significant weaknesses of the language is a very primitive and inaccurate integration scheme (Euler's method). In spite of this deficiency DYNAMO has been extensively used to model and solve numerous information feedback systems. It has great appeal to social scientists because of its conceptual simplicity and ease of use.

Like many other simulation languages DYNAMO has evolved and improved over the years. The latest version DYNAMO III extends the capabilities of DYNAMO II by the addition of arrays.

MIMIC: As mentioned early in this section, MIMIC was one of the first expression-based continuous system simulation languages, developed originally in 1965 for the IBM 7090 family of computers. It still remains a popular language for solving engineering problems and is regarded as an alternative language to DYNAMO. This language has very rigid coding requirements, and has only one integration subroutine, which uses fourth-order Runge-Kutta variable-step method. A MIMIC program is directly translated into a machine-language program (without going through an intermediate language, such as FORTRAN), and it has only limited diagnostics. Therefore MIMIC is an inexpensive language to use in terms of the preprocessing time. It has been implemented on the UNICAC 1107, 1108, and CDC 6000 series of computers amongst numerous others.

8-5. Discrete-system simulation languages

Although many small as well as large programs for simulating discrete systems have been and are being written in general-purpose languages, such as FORTRAN, languages designed specially for simulating discrete systems are becoming increasingly popular. These languages offer many convenient facilities such as automatic generation of streams of pseudo-random numbers for any desired statistical distribution; automatic data collection; their statistical analysis and report generation; good diagnostics; automatic handling of queues; etc.   In addition a good simulation language also provides the model builder with a view of the world that makes model building easier.   It gives him a vocabulary for describing dynamic systems and powerful concepts for expressing the relevant aspects of system behavior.   Thus a simulation language can be of help even at the model-building stage.   There are three major problems with using such languages: (i) The programmer has to learn a new language, which he may not be motivated to do, if he practices simulation only on rare occasions or simulates small systems.   (ii) Discrete-system simulation languages are highly problem-oriented.   A language very natural and convenient for simulating one class of discrete systems may not be so natural for another class of systems. (iii) The language a programmer is familiar with and is natural to his class of problems may not be available in his computing centre.   However, with steadily increasing power of computing centres and declining cost of hardware, it is becoming quite common for centres to have a repertoire of several simulation languages to suit different urers.   This, along with improved language-design techniques, better documentation and training methods, is bound to make simulation languages more popular.

Every discrete-system simulation language must provide the concepts and statements for (a) representing the state of a system at a single point in time (static modeling); (b) moving a system from state to state (dynamic modeling); and (c) performing relevant chores, such as, random number generation, data analyses, and report generation.   Items in the third category are handled in a similar way in most languages and usually do not cause any problem when the programmer moves from one language to another.

It is items (a) and (b) which have been treated differently in different languages.   From this point of view discrete-system simulation languages can be classified into three main categories:

(1) event-oriented languages,
(2) activity-oriented languages, and
(3) process-oriented languages (including transaction-flow type).

(1) **Event-oriented languages:**   In an event-oriented language each event is represented by an instantaneous occurrence in simulated time and must be scheduled to occur (in advance) when a proper set of conditions exists.   The state of the system changes at the occurrence of an event. The languages in this category are used to model processes that are characterized by a large number of entities.   The two well-known representatives of this group of languages are SIMSCRIPT and GASP (to be discussed shortly).

(2) **Activity-oriented languages:**   In an activity-oriented language the discrete occurrences are not scheduled in advance.   They are created by a program which contains descriptions of conditions under which any activity can take place.   These conditions are scanned before each simula-

tion time advance and if all necessary conditions are met, the proper actions are taken. According to this concept, the activity-oriented languages have two major components: a test component and an action component. An activity-oriented language should be considered for use if the model has the following characteristics: (i) the model uses a next event or variable-time increment type of timing, (ii) the process simulated is highly interactive but involves a fixed number of entities with events happening irregularly, and (iii) event occurrence is controlled by cyclic scanning activity programs. Two examples of languages in this class are CSL (on IBM 7090/94, 1620; Honeywell 400/1400, 200/2200 machines) and MILITRAN (on IBM 7090/94 machines).

(3) **Process-oriented languages:** A key feature of a process orientation is that of a single process routine, composed of a number of segments describing a sequence of activities. Each segment behaves as an independently controlled program. On receiving control, only the statements composing the segment are executed, and then control is returned. Thus the model is defined as a series of occurrences (called processes), and the explicit interaction between the processes is brought about by the process routine. Some of the languages belonging to this class are: SIMULA (to be described shortly); ASPOL (CDC 6000 series); SIMUFOR (IBM 360/370) and SIMPL/I and SOL (UNIVAC 1107, 1108).

Transaction-flow oriented language: Trnsaction-flow oriented languages form a subcategory of process-oriented languages except that the flow of activities passes through specially defined blocks. The system model is represented by a flow-chart consisting of the language blocks. The program creates transactions, executes them in the blocks and moves them along the flow-chart. Writing a program is reduced to specifying a flow-chart representation. Unlike the statement-based languages discussed under (1), (2), and (3) above, these languages are flow-chart oriented. They are easy to use at the expense of a loss of flexibility. The best known language in this class is GPSS (to be discussed shortly).

It must be emphasized here that the classification of discrete system simulation languages is never absolute. There are languages which may fall in more than one category. Moreover, there are several other ways of classifying these languages: whether they are interpretive systems or compiler-based; whether they are extensions of an existing general-purpose language or are built from scratch; whether they are block-oriented or statement-oriented; and what classes of problems they are suited for. We will now give a very brief description of three of the most popular discrete-system simulation languages, namely, SIMSCRIPT, GPSS, and SIMULA.

8-6.   SIMSCRIPT

SIMSCRIPT was developed at the RAND Corporation in the early 1960's and was first released in 1962. It grew out of earlier work in developing programming packages at RAND Corporation. It has undergone many revisions and improvements, including the development of SIM-SCRIPT I.5. A completely new version SIMSCRIPT II was released by the RAND Corporation in 1968. The latest version is SIMSCRIPT II.5, which was released in 1972. The following description of SIMSCRIPT II holds for SIMSCRIPT II.5 also. The language is very FORTRAN-like in appearance; in fact initially it was implemented with FORTRAN as an intermediate language. SIMSCRIPT II (or II.5) can be viewed as a general programming language with extra features for discrete-event simulation. Because of this general power and its FORTRAN base, SIMSCRIPT has been a widely implemented and used discrete-simulation language. It has been implemented on IBM 7090, 7094, 360, 370 series; CDC 3600, 3800, 6000, and 7000 series; Philco 210, 211, and 212; UNIVAC 490, 1107, and 1108; Honeywell 600, 6000; GE 625, 635; RCA 70, 45, 50 computers, and perhaps on others.

SIMSCRIPT II can be learned and used at different levels of sophis-tication. Level 1 of SIMSCRIPT II is comparable to a very simple algo-rithmic language such as BASIC. An inexperienced user would appreciate such features as : format-free data and ease of programming, simplified output options and automatic mode conversion. Consider, for example, the following simple statements in SIMSCRIPT II.5 (or II):

```
READ X, Y AND N
PRINT 1 LINE WITH X, Y, X/Y, N**2 AS FOLLOWS
X = **.*, Y = **.*, X/Y = **.**, N SQUARED = ****
```

The first statement reads the values of three variables called X, Y, and N from punched cards. The second statement evaluates X, Y, X/Y and N^2 and displays their values.

The next level can be described as a FORTRAN-plus language. Addi-tional capabilities can be found primarily in the area of data structures. The language allows construction of piecemeal arrays (e.g., two-dimen-sional arrays with a different number of elements in each row) and complex tree structures. Every program consists of a main program and subrou-tines. The latter are recursive. Input-output capabilities include those of FORTRAN, but an extensive report generator is available.

Level 3 of SIMSCRIPT II provides ALGOL-like (or PL/I-like) state-ments. The first three levels view SIMSCRIPT II as an algebraic pro-cedural language.

Level 4 gives SIMSCRIPT II a power to define and manipulate *entities*, *attributes* and *sets*. An entity is a program element similar to a subscripted variable. When an entity is created it can be interpreted as a generic defi-nition for a class of entities. Individual entities have values, called attri-butes, which define a particular state of the entity. Attributes are named, not numbered. For example, we may define EMPLOYEE to be an entity and AGE, SALARY as attributes of EMPLOYEE. Each EMPLOYEE has his own AGE and SALARY attributes. Entities can be of two types: *permanent* (specified for all time of program execution) and *temporary* (specified dynamically as the program proceeds). *Temporary entities* are physically created and destroyed through special statements. *Permanent entities* have their attributes stored as arrays. Entities may be declared as temporary or permanent in the PREAMBLE of a SIMSCRIPT II program.

Both temporary and permanent entities can belong to sets and own sets. SIMSCRIPT uses pointers to chain together entities that are members of *sets*. Commands are available to manipulate these sets, for instance: create an entity, file in set, remove an entity from a set, search a set, etc. There are also special commands to establish different set disciplines, such as: first-in, first-out or last-in, first-out, or sorting the elements of the set according to some attribute values.

The primary task of Level 5 is keeping track of dynamics of the model. It has a provision for describing system dynamics, for controlling system dynamics for modelling statistical phenomena, and for model debugging and analysis. As mentioned earlier, the time-dependent behavior of the system is modeled by events, which are changes of state taking place instantaneously at discrete points in simulated time, initiated by the execution of an event routine. Simulated time is controlled by the timing routine, which schedules events by means of an events set or "calendar" containing event notices. The events calendar is a queue with elements "ranked low" by time of occurrence, i.e., the sooner an event is to occur, the closer to the front of the queue it is placed. An event notice is a temporary entity that has attributes, such as, the event time and the type of event to occur. It is created and placed in the events set according to its scheduled time of occurrence. Each activity in SIMSCRIPT II is represented by two events which specify its start and finish.

SIMSCRIPT II requires a model to be specified only in terms of separate events, and scheduling an event means filing an "event notice" in the "events set." Events can be generated and scheduled both (1) internally and (2) externally (triggered by event data cards). In the first case, we write a statement to cause an internal event by another event, for example, the following statement

SCHEDULE A DEPARTURE AT TIME . V + 8.5

schedules an event called DEPARTURE to occur at the current simulated time, given by the variable TIME . V, plus 8.5 time units. In the second case, event data cards (which are read in chronological order, and contain the name of events, the time at which they occur, and other optional data) schedule events. The scheduling of events is usually accomplished by computing a delay time by use of statistical sampling subroutines. SIM-

SCRIPT II provides eleven functions for generating pseudo-random samples from the following statistical distributions: Uniform, normal, Poisson, exponential, beta, Erlang, lognormal, binomial, gamma, Weibull, and uniformly distributed integers.

The language also provides for collecting statistical information from a simulation run. Two statements, ACCUMULATE and TALLY, are used in the PREAMBLE to instruct the compiler to generate automatic data collection and analysis statements at appropriate places in the program. A FORTRAN subroutine can be invoked from a SIMSCRIPT II program. The language has some capabilities to detect programming errors by the compiler as well as by the runtime system.

8-7. GPSS (*General Purpose Simulation System*)

GPSS, one of the earliest discrete simulation languages, was developed by Geoffrey Gordon and presented in two papers in 1961 and 1962. The first release of this language was implemented on the IBM 704, 709, and 7090 computers. Since then improved and more powerful versions have been developed and implemented, including GPSS II, GPSS III (1965), GPSS/360 (1967), GPSS/360's second version, and GPSS V. The latest version, GPSS V, is a superset of all other implementations of GPSS; a program written in GPSS/360 will run under GPSS V. Through all these versions of this language the fundamental concept of block-diagram structure has been retained.

GPSS was designed specially for analysts who were not necessarily computer programmers. It is particularly suited for modeling traffic and queueing systems.

A GPSS programmer does not write a program in the same sense as a SIMSCRIPT programmer does. Instead, he constructs a *block diagram*—a network of interconnected blocks, each performing a special simulation-oriented function. GPSS V provides a set of 48 different (types of) blocks to choose from—each of which can be used repeatedly. Each block has a name, and a specific task to perform.

Moving through the system of blocks are entities called transactions. Examples of transactions are: customers, messages, machine parts, vehicles, etc. Typical blocks are: (i) GENERATE, creates transactions; (ii) QUEUE, creates a queue of transactions and maintains certain queueing statistics; (iii) TABULATE, tabulates the time it took the transaction to reach that point from the time it entered the simulated system; (iv) TERMINATE, destroys transactions and removes them from the system.

The sequence of events taking place in the simulated systems is realized by the movement of transactions from block to block. There can be many different transactions in the block diagram, but each of them at any given instant of time is located at some block. A block can contain and act upon one or many transactions simultaneously. Usually transactions are temporary entities that are generated, moved between blocks and removed by the GPSS program. Some transactions are permanent and remain present in the simulation system throughout the entire period of the simulation run. Blocks that can handle only one item at a time are called the *facilities*. An example of a facility is a machine or a person. A related transaction may be a job that has to be performed by the machine or the person. A *storage* represents another block type that can be used by one or more transactions simultaneously. Examples of storages are groups of machines or a warehouse.

GPSS handles the advancement of time by a block called ADVANCE. When a transaction enters this block, an action time is computed and added to the current time to produce a block departure time. When the time reaches the departure time the transaction will be moved, if possible, to the next block in the chart. Transactions might possess certain attributes which can be used to make logical decisions within a block. The GPSS program has also a capability to collect statistical data about the simulated process, e.g., the current number of transactions in a storage or the length of a queue.

Simple mathematical calculations can be carried out with the use of variable statements. Unlike in SIMSCRIPT, there are no elementary mathematical functions in GPSS, such as the trigonometric or logarithmic functions. GPSS can, however, generate a number of basic random variates.

Program's output is produced in a standard form without any specific request from the user. It is also possible to create the output report in some other form specified by the user. Written tabular reports as well as graphs can be generated. Programming errors are detected during the compile as well as the run time. Minor potential errors are communicated to the user by the system-generated warning messages.

Because of its flowchart orientation, GPSS can perhaps be learned more quickly than any other discrete simulation language. A GPSS program is usually much shorter than the same program coded in other discrete simulation languages. It is best suited for systems which can be described in terms of spatial flow (of dynamic elements such as people, cars, telephone calls, orders, etc.) through a fixed-block diagram. But it is difficult to use when the model does not lend itself to being described in terms of transactions flowing through a network of blocks. Thus simplicity and compactness in GPSS (as compared to SIMSCRIPT) has been achieved at the price of flexibility. GPSS is not as general a discrete simulation language as SIMSCRIPT is.

8-8. SIMULA (*SIMU*lation *LA*nguage)

SIMULA 67 is a true extension (i.e., a superset) of ALGOL 60, and is therefore a general-purpose programming language, despite its name. It was originally implemented on the UNIVAC 1107 in early 1965; and has since been implemented on many other computers, including Burroughs B5500; CDC 3000 and 6000 series; and IBM 360 and 370 series. The language was designed to provide simulation facilities without losing advantage of a powerful general-purpose language. Just as GPSS and SIMSCRIPT are the two most popular discrete simulation languages in the U.S.A., SIMULA appears to be most popular in Europe. The instructions have the form of ALGOL statements, and therefore it is necessary that the user has some knowledge of ALGOL.

The basic idea behind SIMULA is to add to ALGOL the concept of a collection of programs, called *processes,* conceptually operating in parallel. The qualitative description of a process has a static part—a sequence of attribute declarations, and a dynamic part—a sequence of statements, called an "operation rule," describing the dynamic behaviour of the process. The processes perform their operations in groups called *active phases.* A process carries data and executes action. The operation rule specifies the actions to be taken. The operation rule consists of events taking place at one instant of simulated time. There is also a mechanism that activates and deactivates events belonging to the process. In a simulation study we may deal with several processes that have the same data structure and operation rule but differ in the values of attributes related to the data structure. Such a group of alike processes is called the *process class.*

In a SIMULA program, the definition of a process class is accomplished in a *block* (an extension of ALGOL block), which is SIMULA's fundamental way for program decomposition. A block is an independent, self-contained part of the program. The data structure is defined as a part of the block head, and the statements of the block define the operation rule. We may look at a block as being a formal description of an aggregated data structure and the actions defined by the block statements. When a block is executed, a *block instance* is generated. SIMULA is capable of generating several instances of a given block which may interact or exist at the same time. The need to manipulate block instances and relate block instances to each other makes it necessary to give names to the individual block instances and structure them. SIMULA does it by an extensive list-processing capability, built into the language.

In the broad repertoire of SIMULA statements there are special simulation oriented statements that can postpone actions, render the process inactive, etc. SIMULA's program is a set of blocks that organize the total execution as a sequence of active phases related to different block instances.

SIMULA 67 provides 10 random number procedures for drawing samples from different probability distributions, including uniform, exponential, normal, Poisson, and Erlang. Although there is no automatic collection of statistics in SIMULA 67 (as is provided in GPSS, for instance), a procedure "accum" is available to accumulate the simulated time integral of any variable desired. Usually the SIMULA programmer will define any required statistical algorithm in the base language, ALGOL 60.

8-9.   Factors in selection of a discrete system simulation language

Assuming that a decision has been made not to use a general-purpose language, such as FORTRAN, what simulation language should we use for simulating a discrete system? As we have seen in the preceding sections, the three discrete simulation languages (and many others) represent different approaches to event scheduling. They are based on distinct key concepts and offer various facilities to aid in the process of formulating, programming and running the simulation model. Clearly, the proper choice of a simulation language is heavily problem dependent. In spite of this model-language interrelationship, it is possible to suggest some general criteria that should be satisfied by a good discrete simulation language. These criteria may also serve as a basis for comparing the existing languages. We will first list criteria for evaluating simulation languages and then use them to compare the three leading languages: SIMSCRIPT, SIMULA, and GPSS. The criteria can be grouped under the following four headings.

(i) **Language generality and programming power:** The language should be able to handle a wide area of applications. This implies that it should offer strong algorithmic capabilities, as well as, special simulation-oriented features. Among them are: numerical computing, simulation concepts for system description; capability to handle sets, lists, and queues; random variates generation; performance data collection; and flexible data displaying. Although the general applicability of a language is desirable, sometimes there are good reasons for developing and using very specialized and limited simulation languages as long as the user can fit his problem into the scope of the language. Such limited languages may often offer a substantial efficiency.

(ii) **Ease of use:** Ease of use includes the natural translation of the system under study to a corresponding computer program (model closeness), reduction in debugging effort, convenient documentation and flexible design of experiments. One of the benefits of model-closeness is a high degree of readability, ease of modifications and reduced need for documentation. The reduction of debugging effort is related to the language definition as well as the quality of implementation. In general we would like to see that most of the programming errors are detected in the compilation phase and those discovered by the runtime system trigger meaningful diagnostic messages. Good debugging facilities are very important in a simulation language implementation because of the extensive use of list processing and other dynamic data structures.

The design of experiments should be flexible in the sense of combining many computer runs to one run and convenient reporting of numerical results. Language simplicity is another desirable feature. Here one has to strike a good balance between the richness of the language concepts and the relative ease of learning and using these concepts. Ease of language use is also facilitated by free format for input and default output formats that handle a wide class of problem needs.

(iii) **Machine efficiency:** Usually the cost of developing a simulation model and coding it forms a major part of the simulation cost. Nevertheless, run-time efficiency becomes important in those cases where a large number of multiple runs are required or the simulation program is used over an extended period of time. Machine efficiency is to a large extent a property of the quality of compiler implementation, which in turn depends on the language structure and content. The two usual measures of machine efficiency are: execution time and memory requirement. These are important both during the preprocessing and the run-time.

(iv) **Availability:** This is a very practical aspect of any computer language. The language must be available and supported on the most important type of computers in order to be useful. It is also very desirable that the language is machine-independent, i.e., the preprocessors implemented for different machines should be compatible so that the source programs can be transported from machine to machine without significant modifications.

It is difficult to provide an unbiased comparison of available languages. One reason is that individuals have unequal experience with different implementations, another is the subjective documentation provided by the language or computer manufacturers.

In view of the four criteria outlined above the following salient features—both good and bad—of the three major languages discussed in Secs. 8-6 through 8-8 may be useful in making a selection.

SIMSCRIPT

    (a) machine-independent general-purpose simulation language;
    (b) algorithmic capabilities comparable to those of ALGOL or PL/I;
    (c) simulation concepts are relatively few and very general;
    (d) data collection facilities are excellent;
    (e) input-output facilities are good;
    (f) security (error detection) is poor;
    (g) flexibility for experimental design is good;
    (h) machine efficiency is high; and
    (i) harder to learn than GPSS.

GPSS
  (a) restricted to simple queueing problems;
  (b) poor computational facilities;
  (c) inflexible input-output;
  (d) no language extension possible;
  (e) easy to learn and use;
  (f) good debugging facilities; and
  (g) machine efficiency is often poor since GPSS is an interpretative system.

SIMULA
  (a) algorithmic capabilities comparable to ALGOL;
  (b) collecting statistical data over the system behavior quite adequate but inferior to SIMSCRIPT;
  (c) input-output facilities comparable to SIMSCRIPT;
  (d) language extension possibilities allow us to construct special problem-oriented languages;
  (e) SIMULA is a complex language, but once mastered it is easy to use;
  (f) very good debugging features;
  (g) good program readability and structuring;
  (h) possibilities for experimental design comparable to SIMSCRIPT; and
  (i) machine efficiency of SIMULA 67 compiler appears to be on the average at least as good as that of a corresponding SIMSCRIPT compiler.

In addition to these three, there are a number of other discrete simulation languages that are used quite frequently. One of them is GASP (*General Activity Simulation Program*), which was developed and implemented at U.S. Steel Corporation in the early 1960's by P. J. Kiviat. An improved version GASP II was developed by P. J. Kiviat and A. A. B. Pritsker at Arizona State University in the mid and late 1960's. A completely revised and extended version called GASP IV can handle both discrete and continuous system simulation. GASP IV was developed and implemented by A. A. B. Pritsker and his group at Purdue University in the early 1970's. GASP II has been implemented on a number of different machines, including the IBM 1130, GE 225, 415, and CDC 3400. GASP consists of a large collection of FORTRAN subroutines, which serve as high-level programming statements. To use GASP II and GASP IV one must be well-versed in FORTRAN programming. GASP IV extended to PL/I is called GASP-PL/I, which is also a combined-system simulation language.

Another discrete language that must be mentioned is CSL (Control and Simulation Language). It is a FORTRAN-based language developed by

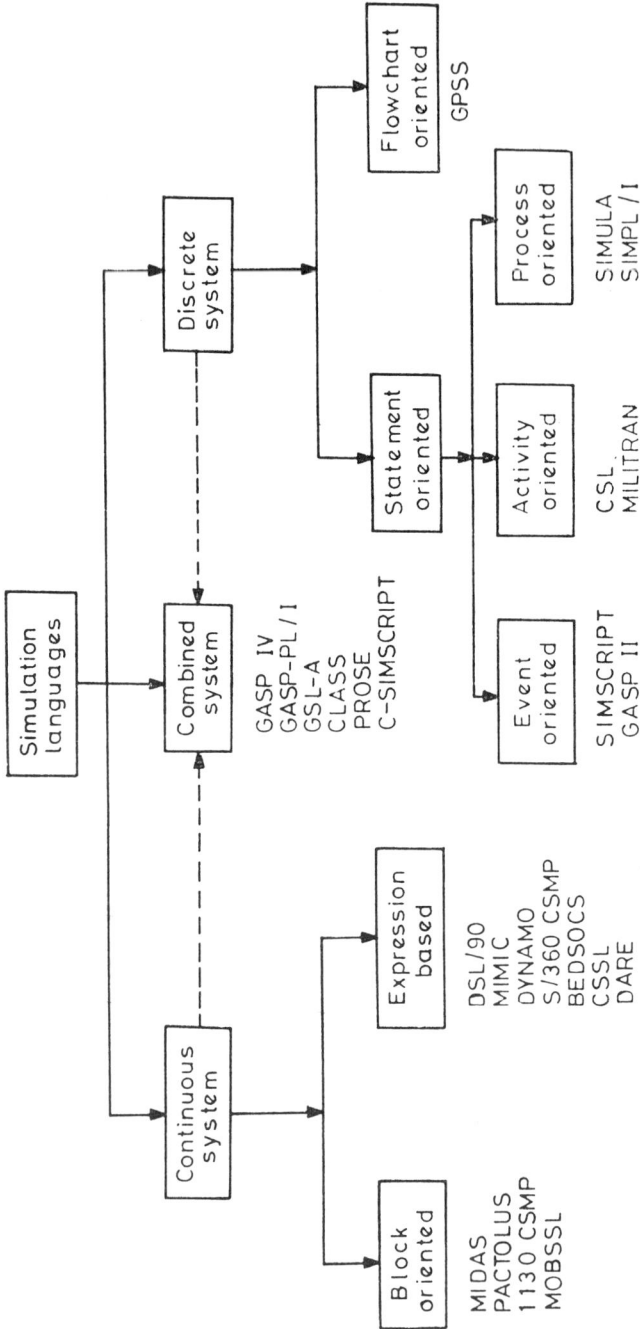

Fig. 8-3: Classification of simulation languages.

John Buxton in 1961-62 and later extended by Alan Clementson. It has been implemented and, like SIMULA 67, is in wide use in Europe. It is supported by IBM, U.K. CSL may be classified as an activity-oriented language.

A third language that deserved mentioning is SIMPL/I. It is a relatively new simulation language based on PL/I, introduced by IBM in June 1972. It has been implemented on IBM System/360. It is an extension of PL/I with facilities for discrete simulation, including list-processing commands.

Finally, we will mention SOL, a self-contained ALGOL-like early language which embodies many of the features of GPSS in a much more readable and elegant form. Arithmetic facilities are good, although inferior to ALGOL. A compiler translates into an intermediate language, which is executed by interpretation.

The chart in Fig. 8-3 gives the summary of the classification of simulation languages.

8-10. Remarks and References

The topic of simulation languages is vast, and even an entire volume is not adequate to cover the subject in sufficient details, let alone a single chapter. On each of the dozen or so major languages that have been discussed in this chapter, there is at least one book. Every language has two aspects—the basic concepts behind it and the implementation details (which must be mastered before one can make an effective use of the language). This chapter provides little help on the latter aspect; only a careful reading of the latest manual on the language and painstaking practice can do this. We have described only the basic concepts.

One of the earliest comprehensive surveys of continuous system simulation languages was compiled and presented in 1965 in

CLANCY, J. J. and M.S. FINEBERG, 'Digital Simulation Languages: A Critique and a Guide,' *Proc. Fall Joint Computer Conf.,* Vol. 27, Part I, 1965, pp. 23–36.

This survey includes 31 simulation languages. Another review paper on continuous simulation languages of that period is

BRENNAN, R. D. and R. N. LINEBARGER, 'A Survey of Digital Simulation: Digital Analog Simulator Programs,' *Simulation,* Vol. 3, No. 6, Dec. 1964, pp. 22–36.

The Simulation Software Committee of the Simulation Councils, Inc., which was formed in May 1965, for proposing a standard language for continuous system simulation, published the following classic paper in December 1967:

'The SCi Continuous System Simulation Language (CSSL)', *Simulation,* Vol. 9, No. 6, Dec. 1967, pp. 281–303.

This report surveyed the state of the art and proposed a standard continuous system simulation language, which would combine the simplicity of a block-oriented language and yet provide all the power and flexibility of an expression-based language. CSSL, the ideal language proposed in this paper, has served as a communication language for the past ten years amongst simulation programmers. It has also been implemented widely in different versions, and has had a profound effect on other continuous system simulation languages that have been developed since. The starting point of CSSL was an already-successful language MIMIC. The design of CSSL was heavily influenced by DSL/90, FORTRAN, and ALGOL.

Some of the more recent surveys of continuous simulation languages can be found in

NILSEN, R. N. and W. J. KARPLUS, 'Continuous System Simulation Languages: A State-of-the-Art Survey,' *Proc. International Assoc. for Analog Computation,* No. 1, Jan. 1974, pp. 17–25.

This paper provides an excellent review and comparisons of many expression-based continuous simulation languages available commercially as of 1973, including MIMIC, DYNAMO, CSMP/CSMP III, CSSL-III, SL-1, and PROSE.

An excellent and recent treatment of a DSL language can be found in

SHAH, M. J., *Engineering Simulation Using Small Scientific Computers,* Prentice-Hall, Englewood Cliffs, New Jersey, 1976.

BEDSOCS is described in the textbook by Ord-Smith and Stephenson, which was referred to in Sec. 2-8. Likewise, MIMIC is described well in Y. Chu's textbook also referred to in Sec. 2-8. A more recent view on certain aspects of MIMIC can be found in

PETERSON, N. D., 'MIMIC, An Alternative Programming Language for Industrial Dynamics,' *Socio-Econ. Plan Sci.,* Vol. 6, Pergamon Press, Oxford, U.K., 1972.

For DYNAMO the following manual is recommended:

PUGH, A. L,, *Dynamo III User's Manual,* Pugh-Roberts Associates, 5 Lee Street, Cambridge, MA, Oct., 1974.

For DARE the following two articles are good references:

AUS, H. M. and G. A. KORN, 'The Future of On-Line Continuous-System Simulation,' *Proc. AFIPS/FJCC,* Vol. 39, 1971.

and

LUCAS, J. J. and J. V. WAIT, 'DARE P—A Portable CSSL-type Simulation Language,' *Simulation,* Vol. 24, No. 1, Jan., 1975.

For CSMP the following two IBM manuals are suggested— first one for the 1130 CSMP (block-oriented) and the second one for the S/360 CSMP (expression-oriented).

Introduction to 1130 Continuous System Modeling, Program II, GH20-0848,

and

Continuous System Modeling Program III (CSMP III) Program Reference Manual, SH19-7001,

both published by IBM Data Processing Division, White Plains, N.Y., 10604. A reference for MOBSSL is

MERRITT, M. J. and D. S. Miller, 'MOBSSL—Augmented Block Structured Continuous System Simulation Language for Digital and Hybrid Computers,' *Proc. AFIPS/FJCC,* Vol. 35, 1969.

A good survey of the development of discrete simulation languages in the late 1950's and 1960's is given in

TOCHER, K. D., 'A Review of Simulation Languages,' *Operations Research Quarterly,* Vol. 16, No. 2, 1965, pp. 189–218.

KIVIAT, P. J., 'Development of Discrete Digital Simulation Languages,' *Simulation,* Vol. 8, Feb. 1967, pp. 65–70.

KRASNOW, H. S., 'Simulation Languages,' in *The Design of Computer Simulation Experiments,* (ed. T. H. Naylor), Duke University Press, Durham, N.C., 1969, pp. 320–346.

TOCHER, K. D., 'Simulation Languages,' in *Progress in Operations Research,* Vol. 3, (ed. J. S. Aronofsky), John Wiley, New York, 1979, pp. 72–113.

An excellent in-depth comparison of five well-known discrete languages, from the viewpoint of a language designer and implementer (and not just the user) can be found in

DAHL, O. J., 'Discrete Event Simulation Languages,' in *Programming Languages* (ed. F. Genuys), Academic Press, New York, 1968, pp. 349–395.

This paper first discusses the underlying features and requirements of a discrete-event simulation language and then shows how these different features were implemented in GPSS, SIMSCRIPT, SIMULA, SOL, and CSL.

Some of the more recent reviews of discrete simulation languages can be found in

FISHMAN, G. S., *Concepts and Methods in Discrete Event Digital Simulation,* John Wiley, New York, 1973.

KLEIN, H., 'A Second Survey of User's Views of Discrete Simulation Languages,' *Simulation,* Vol. 17, No. 2, 1971.

ROBINSON, L. F., 'How GASP, SIMULA, and DYNAMO View a Problem,' in *Progress in Simulation* (ed. I. M. Kay and J. McLeod), Gordon and Breach, New York, 1972, pp. 167–214.

KAY, I. M., 'An Over-the-Shoulder Look at Discrete Digital Simulation Languages,' *Proc. AFIPS/SJCC,* Vol. 40, 1972, pp. 791–798.

BOBILLIER, P. A., B. C. KAHAN, and A. R. PROBST, 'Summary of Current Simulation Languages,' Appendix E in *Simulation with GPSS and GPSS V,* Prentice-Hall, Englewood Cliffs, N.J., 1976, pp. 465-482.

The last reference compares GPSS V, SIMULA 67, SIMSCRIPT II, and SIMPL/I. In the paper by Kay all significant discrete languages are classified into three groups—the GASP-type languages, the GPSS-type languages, and the SIMSCRIPT-type languages. The paper also gives a very exhaustive list of problem areas where discrete system simulation has been applied.

Although many surveys and reviews of different simulation languages have been published from the viewpoint of the facilities available, ease of programming and areas of their applicabilities, the studies regarding the speeds of executions of different languages on a typical problem are few. The following are two such studies:

TOGNETTI, K. P. and C. BRETT, "SIMSCRIPT II and SIMULA 67—A Comparison,' *The Australian Computer Journal,* Vol. 4, No. 2, 1972.

VIRJO, A., *A Comparative Study of Some Discrete Event Simulation Languages,* Finnish State Computing Centre, Helsinki, Finland, 1972.

The latter paper reports the results of testing of different versions of GPSS, SIMSCRIPT, and SIMULA on IBM and UNIVAC machines using three different problems—a queueing system N-machine workshop, a telephone system, and a PERT network. Similarly, Tognetti and Brett have compared the performance of SIMSCRIPT II (on IBM 360/50) and SIMULA 67 (on CDC 3300). Both these studies have concluded that on the whole the performance of SIMULA 67 was the best.

The following are the recommended sources for various discrete simulation languages discussed in the text:

GORDON, G., *The Application of GPSS V to Discrete System Simulation,* Prentice-Hall, Englewood Cliffs, N.J., 1975.

DAHL, O. J., B. MYHRHAUG, and K. NYGAARD, *SIMULA begin,* Auerbach, Philadelphia, 1973.

KIVIAT, P. J., R. VILLANUEVA, and H. M. MARKOWITZ, *SIMSCRIPT II.5 Programming Language,* CAC, Inc., Los Angeles, Calif., 1973.

SIMPL/I (Simulation Language Based on PL/I), Program Reference Manual, SH19-5060, IBM Data Processing Division, White Plains, N.Y.

PRITSKER, A. A. B., *The GASP IV Simulation Language,* John Wiley & Sons, New York, 1974.

PRITSKER, A. A. B., and R. E. YOUNG, *Simulation with GASP-PL/I,* John Wiley & Sons, New York, 1975.

The last two books have excellent treatment of a combined system (both continuous and discrete) simulation—one using GASP IV and the other with GASP-PL/I. An earlier book by Pritsker and Kiviat on GASP II (for discrete systems only) has already been referred to in Sec. 4-5. A good example of how a simulation language can help at the system modeling stage is shown in

PRITSKER, A. A. B., 'GASP IV Can Broaden Your Modeling Perspective,' *Simuletter.* Vol. 5, No. 4, July 1974.

A partial roster of well-supported simulation languages in the USA as of 1974-75 is given in

SAMMET, J. E., 'Roster of Programming Languages for 1974-75,' *Comm. ACM*, Vol. 19, No. 2, Dec. 1976, pp. 655–699.

A brief but recent review and classification of (discrete, continuous and combined) simulation languages can be found in

SHANNON, R. E., 'Introduction to Simulation Languages,' *Proc. Winter Simulation Conference,* Dec. 5–7, 1977, pp. 15–20.

The silver-jubilee issue of *Simulation* (Vol. 29, No. 5, November 1977) is recommended for some views (of well known people in the field) on the past, present, and future of system simulation.

Index